PLAYS TWO

Robert Bolt

PLAYS TWO

THE THWARTING OF BARON BOLLIGREW
VIVAT! VIVAT REGINA!
STATE OF REVOLUTION

OBERON BOOKS
LONDON

The Thwarting of Baron Bolligrew first published in 1966 , *Vivat! Vivat Regina!* first published in 1971, *State of Revolution* first published in 1977, all by Samuel French Ltd.

First published in this collection in 2001 by Oberon Books Ltd. (incorporating Absolute Classics)
521 Caledonian Road, London N7 9RH
Tel: 020 7607 3637 / Fax: 020 7607 3629
e-mail: oberon.books@btinternet.com

A catalogue record for this book is available from the British Library.

ISBN: 1 84002 158 6

Cover illustration: Andrzej Klimowski
Cover typography: Jeff Willis

Printed in Great Britain by Antony Rowe Ltd, Reading.

Contents

5

THE THWARTING OF
BARON BOLLIGREW

Characters

STORYTELLER

THE DUKE

HIS KNIGHTS

SIR DIGBY VAYNE-TRUMPINGTON

SIR GRACELESS STRONGBODY

SIR PERCIVAL SMOOTHELY-SMOOTHE

SIR OBLONG FITZ OBLONG

JUNIPER

CAPTAIN

JASPER, 15th BARON BOLLIGREW

SQUIRE BLACKHEART

PEASANTS

MEN-AT-ARMS

LORD MAYOR

OBIDIAH
a peasant

MAGPIE

A SECRETARY

DR MOLOCH

MAZEPPA

THE DRAGON

A CORPORAL

A COOK

DRUMMER AND CYMBALIST

The Thwarting of Baron Bolligrew was first performed at the Aldwych Theatre, on 11 December 1965, with the following cast:

STORYTELLER, Michael Jayston
DUKE, John Nettleton
TRUMPINGTON/PEASANT, Andrew Lodge
STRONGBODY/MAN-AT-ARMS, Oliver Maguire
SMOOTHE, Philip Brack
OBLONG, John Normington
JUNIPER/PEASANT, Peter Mair
CAPTAIN/BADGER, Terence Rigby
BOLLIGREW, Leo McKern
BLACKHEART, Nicholas Selby
PEASANTS, Malcolm McDowell, Ian Collier,
                        Andrew Jack, James Sport
MAN-AT-ARMS, Edward Clayton
LORD MAYOR, Peter Harrison
OBIDIAH, Davyd Harries
MAGPIE, Richard Moore
DR MOLOCH, Ken Wynne
MAZEPPA/PEASANT, Iain Blair
DRAGON, Robert Bolt
JONES/PEASANT, Colin Bell
COOK/DASHWOOD, Terence Sewards

Director, Trevor Nunn
Set Designer, Elizabeth Duffield
Lighting Designer, David Read
Costume Designer, Ann Curtis
Composer, Guy Woolfenden

The action of the play takes place on a bare stage.

ACT ONE

The curtain rises on a stage which is dark except for a single spot down centre, in which stands the STORYTELLER. He wears something unique, to set him apart.

STORYTELLER: A long time ago – in the days when dragons were still common – there lived a Duke. And whenever news was brought in of a dragon ravaging some part of the country the Duke sent one of his Knights away in shining armour to deal with it. After a few weeks the Knight would return with the tip of the dragon's tail to prove that he had killed it. Dragons are excessively vain, and when the tips of their tails are cut off they die, of mulligrubs. The return of the Knights would be announced like this:

> *(A fanfare sounds. The lights come up, revealing a stage bare of scenery except for drapes and a cyclorama. At a round table sit the DUKE and the KNIGHTS. The DUKE is an elderly, well-fed aristocrat, well-meaning and indolent. He wears civilian garb, fairy-tale period. The KNIGHTS wear armour, except for JUNIPER, who wears less magnificent civvies than the DUKE. They wear surcoats bearing the Royal Strawberry. The seat on the DUKE's left is vacant, and other empty ones are to be seen round the table.)*

> *(Moving to one side and announcing.)* Sir Digby Vayne-Trumpington!

> *(TRUMPINGTON enters.)*

DUKE: Ah, there you are, Trumpington. Glad to have you back. Got the tip of the dragon's tail?

> *(TRUMPINGTON places the bright blue tail-tip on the table. The DUKE inspects it.)*

Not very big, is it?

TRUMPINGTON: It was not a large dragon, Your Grace, no; but singularly vicious.

FIRST KNIGHT: They can be tricky, those little blue beggars.

> *(There is a murmur of agreement.)*

DUKE: Not complaining, Trumpington. We can't all be St
    Georges, can we?
    (*While TRUMPINGTON sits, there is a fanfare.*)
STORYTELLER: Sir Graceless Strongbody!
    (*There is a pause all looking off expectantly.*)
DUKE: (*Indulgently.*) Likes to make an entrance,
    Strongbody... (*The pause continues. Less indulgently.*)
    Call him again.
STORYTELLER: Sir Grace...!
    (*STRONGBODY enters dragging a huge green tail. Murmurs
    of appreciation and then polite clapping come from the
    KNIGHTS.*)
DUKE: I must *say*, Graceless! I think we'll have this stuffed,
    gentlemen. How d'you do it?
STRONGBODY: (*Gruffly.*) Oh, usual methods, ye know.
DUKE: Aha – 'Deeds not Words', the old Strongbody
    motto.
    (*There is another fanfare.*)
STORYTELLER: Sir Percival Smoothely-Smoothe!
    (*SMOOTHE enters.*)
DUKE: Good show, Smoothe; back on time as usual. Find
    your dragon?
    (*SMOOTHE puts down two red tail-tips.*)
    Good Lord, *two* dragons!
SMOOTHE: No, Your Grace, one dragon with two tails.
DUKE: Well I never saw such a thing in my life. Gave you
    a bit of trouble I dare say?
SMOOTHE: (*Sitting.*) Not really, Your Grace. It seemed to
    be confused.
DUKE: Ah, modest, modest. I like that, Smoothe, like it.
    Well now, who's missing? (*Looking at the vacant seat to his
    left.*) Oh, Oblong. Not like him to be late. Well we'll just
    wait for Oblong, gentlemen, and then I have a little
    announcement to make, yes...
    (*There is another fanfare.*)
STORYTELLER: Sir Oblong fitz Oblong!
    (*SIR OBLONG FITZ OBLONG enters sadly. He is short,
    plump, with a pink innocent face topped by a tonsure of*

white hair. He is pedantic and almost priggy, and wears silver armour.)

DUKE: There you are, Oblong; mission accomplished?

OBLONG: Yes, Your Grace.

DUKE: Got the tail?

OBLONG: Yes, Your Grace.

DUKE: *(Kindly.)* Well perk up, man. Whatever's the matter?

OBLONG: *(Producing a tail.)* It was a very small dragon. Your Grace. Small and, er, pink. I don't think it can have been fully grown. It meant no harm I'm sure. *(He regards the small pink tail on table, then takes a handkerchief from the sleeve of his armour and blows his nose.)*

DUKE: Now Oblong, we all know how you feel about animals, and I'm sure respect you for it. *(He looks round.)* *(There is a murmur of confirmation from the KNIGHTS.)* But – Duty First, eh?

OBLONG: *(Bracing.)* Yes, Your Grace. *(He sits left of DUKE.)*

DUKE: That's it. *(Patting OBLONG's shoulder as he sits.)* Never knew an Oblong hold back in the face of duty. *(Briskly.)* Now, Juniper my dear chap, read the next item on the agenda will you?

JUNIPER: Er, 'Activities for the coming Season', Your Grace.

DUKE: Exactly! *(Rising.)* Gentlemen, a happy announcement: There *are* no activities for the coming season. These *(The tails on the table.)* were the last dragons in the Dukedom. Thanks to your untiring efforts over the years our peasantry may now reap their harvests – and pay their taxes – without interference. Our townsfolk can make their profits – and pay their taxes freely. And in short, there isn't a blessed thing for us to do.
(The KNIGHTS rise and congratulate one another noisily shaking hands, patting backs, etc. The hubbub dies and they all sit.)

OBLONG: How perfectly splendid, Your Grace.

DUKE: Isn't it, isn't it?

OBLONG: Now we can move on somewhere else.

DUKE: *(Faintly.)* Er, 'move on', Oblong?

OBLONG: Yes, Your Grace.

DUKE: Whatever for?

OBLONG: (*Mildly puzzled.*) To succour the poor and needy, Your Grace. Up North, for instance – dragons, barons, goblins. Having a very thin time of it up North, the poor and needy.

DUKE: But my dear fellow – the climate!

OBLONG: Well, South, then, Your Grace.

SMOOTHE: (*Gently.*) May I say something, Your Grace?

DUKE: Smoothe! Yes! Please, please.

SMOOTHE: Well gentlemen, we've put this district into some sort of shape – and it's not been easy as you know. It seems to me we've earned a breather.

DUKE. Earned a breather. Well said, Smoothe. Late lie-in in the morning. Bit of jousting in the afternoon perhaps. Substantial supper; jolly good game of musical bumps and off to bed. (*Appealing all round.*) Where's the harm in that?

(*A murmur of considered agreement.*)

I'll put it to the vote. Democratic procedure – Can't say fairer than that, Oblong. All those in favour of the programme just outlined, please say 'Aye'.

ALL: (*Except OBLONG.*) Aye!

DUKE: Thank you. All those in favour of moving on, to wild, wet, baron and dragon infested areas, please say 'Aye'.

OBLONG: Er, Aye.

DUKE: (*Cheerfully.*) Well there it is, old man. You're outvoted.

OBLONG: (*Diffident.*) Under the terms of our Charter, Your Grace, I *think* a vote on this subject has to be unanimous. Nobody must disagree.

DUKE: (*Weakly.*) That right?

JUNIPER: (*Looking at the Charter on the table.*) I'm just looking... Yes, here it is, Your Grace, Clause Seven. (*He passes the Charter to the DUKE.*)

DUKE: Well... (*Petulantly.*) Very ill-judged Clause, I would say. Now what?

JUNIPER: If we can't agree, Your Grace, we must refer the matter to the Royal Court.

STRONGBODY: (*Gloomily.*) And we know what they'll say…

OBLONG: I'm sorry to be the fly in the ointment, gentlemen, but – to succour the poor and needy – dash it all gentlemen, it's our Knightly Vow!

(*At this, ALL look uncomfortably at the table. The small pink tail twitches slowly in the silence. ALL look. OBLONG is distressed.*)

Oh dear; Your Grace, would you mind…

DUKE: (*Testy.*) Yes, yes, take it away if it upsets you: take them *all* away.

(*OBLONG rises and picks up the tails.*)

OBLONG: (*Muttering; embarrassed.*) 'Scuse me, gentlemen – I – (*He moves to go, then turns. Apologetically.*) – er – oh dear…

(*OBLONG exits with the tails, watched by ALL.*)

JUNIPER: Well, there goes the late lie-in.

STRONGBODY: And the joustin'.

TRUMPINGTON: And the musical bumps.

JUNIPER: And the substantial suppers.

FIRST KNIGHT: (*Uneasy.*) Got a point there, you know, about the Knightly Vow.

DUKE: Yes, yes; capital creature; heart of gold; but…

SMOOTHE: But inclined to be dogmatic, Your Grace.

DUKE: Exactly.

SMOOTHE: I think I see a possible solution.

(*ALL raise their heads and look to SMOOTHE.*)

Supposing Oblong were to leave us. On a mission. A mission to – say – the Bolligrew Islands.

DUKE: The Bolligrew Islands!

FIRST KNIGHT: I say, that's a bit steep.

TRUMPINGTON: D'you think he'd go?

JUNIPER: It's worth trying. Your Grace might have him appointed a Royal Knight Errant.

DUKE: And then when he'd gone we could put the matter to the vote again and – er…

JUNIPER: And nobody would disagree!

DUKE: Unanimous vote, as required by our Charter!

SMOOTHE: Exactly, Your Grace.

DUKE: (*Solemnly.*) There's no doubt, gentlemen, the
Bolligrew Islands *need* a Knight Errant.

JUNIPER: Unquestionably.

DUKE: And Oblong is the obvious choice.

FIRST KNIGHT: That's true.

DUKE: I dare say he'll be very happy there.
(*SMOOTHE coughs warningly. OBLONG enters.*)
Oblong my dear chap, what would you say to the idea of
a mission to the Bolligrew Islands?

OBLONG: I should say it was a very *good* idea, Your Grace!
When do we start?

DUKE: Well, we were thinking of a – more of a – one man
mission, you know.

OBLONG: Oh. Me?

DUKE: Yes. Smoothe here suggested you.

OBLONG: (*Sharply.*) Very good of you, Smoothe. I'm not
going.

DUKE: 'Not', Oblong?

OBLONG: No! The Bolligrew Islands! That's where Baron
Bolligrew lives – the one that pulled down the church!

DUKE: (*Shocked.*) Did he really? I didn't know that.

OBLONG: Well he did. And there's that dragon in the
Bolligrew Islands too.

SMOOTHE: A very *poor* specimen, I believe.

OBLONG: It isn't. It's one of those black ones with red
eyes.

FIRST KNIGHT: (*Uncomfortably.*) It's a bit steep, you know.

SMOOTHE: Quite right, quite right. We ought not to
persuade Sir Oblong.
(*OBLONG moves to his chair but is stopped by SMOOTHE's
next words.*)
It is a pity, though. I understand that Baron Bolligrew
hunts.

OBLONG: (*Sharply.*) Hunts?

SMOOTHE: (*Looking up in mock surprise.*) Er, hunts, yes.

OBLONG: (*Suspiciously.*) What does he hunt?

SMOOTHE: (*Looking to the DUKE.*) Pretty well anything, they say.

DUKE: Foxes.

SMOOTHE: (*Nodding.*) Foxes, bears –

TRUMPINGTON. Deer –

JUNIPER: Badgers –

OBLONG: Oh the villain!

SMOOTHE: (*Offhand.*) Hares, of course – little, trembling hares...

OBLONG: It – really it makes one's blood boil!

SMOOTHE: Your Grace, if Sir Oblong *were* going on this mission I expect His Majesty would make him a Royal Knight Errant, don't you?

DUKE: Couldn't refuse. And then you could wear the purple robe, you know, with the Royal Coat of Arms and so on. I think Oblong would look well in purple, don't you, Juniper?

OBLONG: (*Taken with it.*) Really? I must say – hares and badgers you say?

SMOOTHE: Oh anything.

OBLONG: The perfect brute! Your Grace, I'll go.

DUKE: Excellent conclusion to a good morning's work, gentlemen. How about a little refreshment?

STORYTELLER: Lemonade and ice-cream on the South Terrace!

DUKE: Meeting adjourned!

(*The DUKE and KNIGHTS exit, rolling the table with them. The lights go out, except for the single spot centre as the STORYTELLER moves below it.*)

STORYTELLER: So Sir Oblong was appointed a Royal Knight Errant and at length –

(*A brown paper parcel is thrown on from wings and caught by the STORYTELLER.*)

– a parcel from the King's Court arrived at the Duke's Castle – (*He opens the parcel.*) – containing Sir Oblong's purple robe.

(*OBLONG enters into the spot, and is assisted into the robe by the STORYTELLER.*)

Sir Oblong put it on and he found a berth on a ship –
(*The CAPTAIN enters carrying a 'mast and sail'.*)
– which was making the short but dangerous passage to
the Bolligrew Islands.
(*The CAPTAIN and OBLONG traverse the stage, there is a
lightning flash and a thunderclap, in cover of which the
STORYTELLER exits.*
The lights come up.)

OBLONG: These are the Bolligrew Islands are they,
Captain?

CAPTAIN: Yus. 'Orrible aren't they? See the ruin up there?
That's the church Baron Bolligrew pulled down some
years back.

OBLONG: He's a difficult man to get on with, I believe.

CAPTAIN: 'Orrible. That's not the worst of it neither.

OBLONG: No?

CAPTAIN: No. See that 'illside; all black and smoky like?

OBLONG: Oh yes.

CAPTAIN: Dragon.

OBLONG: I beg your pardon?

CAPTAIN: Dragon done it. Breathin' fire like. 'Orrible.

OBLONG: Doesn't Baron Bolligrew do anything about it?

CAPTAIN: Not 'im. 'Untin's all 'e cares about. 'Untin' and
grindin' the faces of the poor. Reg'lar terror. You thinkin'
of settlin' 'ere?

OBLONG: Er, well I was, yes…

CAPTAIN: Wouldn't live 'ere for a million pounds myself.
'Ere we are 'owever. If you'll just stand on one side, sir.
Ava-a-a-ast! Bel-a-a-ay! (*He pulls a cord, the sail furls.*)
There you are sir, now you can go ashore and…
(*There is a crash of a shotgun offstage.*)
Look out! 'Ere 'e is.
(*JASPER, 15th BARON BOLLIGREW enters, carrying a
twelve-bore shotgun. He is small but burly, with a red face
and black whiskers; choleric and selfish but with the fascination
of childish greed. He is anachronistically dressed in a loud
check jacket, bowler hat, breeches, gaiters. He walks deliberately
to the others. Accompanying him is SQUIRE BLACKHEART,*

huge and stupid. He wears black armour topped by enormous
black plumes. He moons stolidly throughout the interview,
chewing his moustache.)

BOLLIGREW: Missed 'im. You Captain Asquith of the ship
Winkle?

CAPTAIN: Yes, my lord.

BOLLIGREW: You brought me a new whip?

CAPTAIN: Yes, me lord.

BOLLIGREW: New spurs?

CAPTAIN: Yes, me lord.

BOLLIGREW: New boots?

CAPTAIN: Boots, me lord?

BOLLIGREW: Yes, boots. Me new ridin' boots.

CAPTAIN: They didn't say nothin' about no boots, me lord.

BOLLIGREW: Ho, didn't they?

CAPTAIN: No, me lord.

BOLLIGREW: Well you go back and get 'em.

CAPTAIN: (*Glancing fearfully back at the 'voyage' just made.*)
But me lord...

BOLLIGREW: Don't argue with *me*, Asquith. Just turn your
ship round and get me boots.

CAPTAIN: Yes, me lord.
(*The CAPTAIN hoists sail and exits to more thunder and*
lightning, watched by ALL.)

BOLLIGREW: Insolent beggar! Who might you be?

OBLONG: Oblong fitz Oblong.

BOLLIGREW: Gentleman?

OBLONG: Yes?

BOLLIGREW: Me friend, Squire Blackheart.

BLACKHEART: 'D'you do?

OBLONG: How...

BOLLIGREW: Knight Errant, eh?

OBLONG: Yes. (*Modestly.*) A recent appointment.

BOLLIGREW: Knight Errant, Blackheart.
(*BLACKHEART grunts and nods gloomily.*)

BOLLIGREW: D'you hunt?

OBLONG: Well, as a matter of...

BOLLIGREW: I do.

OBLONG: Yes, I hear you're a keen sportsman, Baron.

BOLLIGREW: Keen sportsman. Right. (*Lugging out an enormous gold watch.*) See that? 'Presented to the Master of Bolligrew Hounds' – that's me, of course 'as a mark of admiration and gratitude, by the Chairman of the Hunt Committee'. Handsome timepiece, eh?

OBLONG: Lovely. Who is the Chairman of the Hunt Committee?

BOLLIGREW: I am. Solid gold that watch. Had to evict three or four entire families to pay for it, didn't we, Blackheart?

BLACKHEART: Mm.

BOLLIGREW: Blackheart does all the evictin' work round here. (*Replacing the watch.*) Well. Give you a day tomorrow if you like. We're after a badger.

OBLONG: Baron Bolligrew, I do not hunt!

(*There is a short silence.*)

BOLLIGREW: Doesn't hunt, Blackheart.

(*BLACKHEART grunts and nods gloomily.*)

BOLLIGREW: (*To OBLONG.*) Afraid of horses, very likely.

OBLONG: (*Stiffly.*) Some of my best friends are horses...

BOLLIGREW: Feller's potty, Blackheart.

BLACKHEART: Hey!

BOLLIGREW: What?

BLACKHEART: Magpie.

(*BOLLIGREW raises his gun. ALL follow a flight of an unseen bird above, then OBLONG 'accidentally' steps backwards onto BOLLIGREW's foot. BOLLIGREW roars and the gun roars. BOLLIGREW hops, furious, watched apprehensively by OBLONG. BLACKHEART, oblivious, continues to watch the flight of the bird, off.*)

BOLLIGREW: (*Eyeing OBLONG narrowly.*) Did you do that on purpose? He did that on purpose, Blackheart.

BLACKHEART: (*Lowering his gaze to BOLLIGREW.*) What?

BOLLIGREW: He trod on my toe. (*Still eyeing OBLONG narrowly.*) Now, look here, Oblong, if you don't 'unt, what've you come for?

OBLONG: (*Searching his armour for the paper.*) I have my instructions somewhere. (*Putting on his spectacles.*) It's all pretty run-of-the-mill stuff. (*Clearing his throat.*) Item: rebuild Bolligrew Island Church. Item: Restore justice to Bolligrew Island Magistrates Court. Item: Suppress Bolligrew Island Dragon.

(*BOLLIGREW listens with mounting indignation but now laughs.*)

BOLLIGREW: Suppress...? Feller's goin' to suppress the dragon, Blackheart!

(*BLACKHEART grins, the grin broadens, he breaks into guffaws.*)

And – and – restore justice to – to the Magistrates Court!

(*BOLLIGREW and BLACKHEART hold on to each other, helpless.*)

(*To OBLONG, wiping his eyes.*) Here, here – you like to see the Court in session?

OBLONG: At the earliest opportunity, Baron.

BOLLIGREW: Nothing easier. (*He takes a whistle from his pocket and blows.*)

(*The RAGGED PEASANTRY enter. They are barefoot, and dressed in ragged clothes of sacking. Two MEN-AT-ARMS follow, with a bench which they put down. They wear conventional medieval costume, surcoats bearing the golden toad of the BOLLIGREWS. Last comes the LORD MAYOR. He is a timid man, wearing slightly less ragged peasant costume, with shoes, and topped by a waistcoat and his Chain of Office.*)

Ready, Blackheart old man?

BLACKHEART: Ready when you are, my dear feller.

(*BLACKHEART and BOLLIGREW sit.*)

There you are, Oblong. Court's in session.

(*OBLONG sits.*)

BOLLIGREW: What the blazes do you think you're doing?

OBLONG: I am taking my seat on the Bench, Baron.

BOLLIGREW: And who the blazes gave you a seat on the Bench?

OBLONG: My Royal Commission gives me a seat on the Bench, Baron.

BOLLIGREW: Oh. (*Recovering.*) Well that's all right. We don't mind, do we, Blackheart?

BLACKHEART: Don't we?

BOLLIGREW: No. Loyal subjects of His Majesty, Blackheart and me, Oblong – hope you'll notice that. Right – First Case!

(*The MEN-AT-ARMS seize a diminutive PEASANT.*)

FIRST MAN-AT-ARMS: First case!

PEASANT: (*Fearfully.*) Here, my lord.

SECOND MAN-AT-ARMS: First case present, my lord!

BOLLIGREW: What's the charge?

FIRST MAN-AT-ARMS: On the last day of last month, my lord, at about tea-time, prisoner was seen to prevent a horse from eating a double row of runner beans in 'is garden.

BOLLIGREW: Oh. But look here, why *should* he let horses eat his runner beans?

FIRST MAN-AT-ARMS: (*Slightly shocked.*) 'Twas your horse, my lord.

BOLLIGREW: Was it! Guilty!

OBLONG: *Not* guilty!

BOLLIGREW: Squire Blackheart, what do you think?

BLACKHEART: Guilty. Definitely.

BOLLIGREW: That's two to one. Seven days bread and water and – let's see, prisoner aren't you the one with the strawberry bed?

PEASANT: I 'ave got a few strawberry plants, my lord, yes...

BOLLIGREW: Good – and a fine of three baskets of strawberries. You can deliver them to the Castle – back door, mind – after you've served your sentence. Next case.

MAN-AT-ARMS: Here, my lord.

BOLLIGREW: You?

MAN-AT-ARMS: Yes, my lord.

BOLLIGREW: But that's one of your men, isn't it Blackheart?

BLACKHEART: (*Affixing a monocle.*) It is. It's my Second Huntsman.

BOLLIGREW: Who's had the blazin' impudence to charge this man?

LORD MAYOR: (*Timidly determined.*) Er, me, my lord.

BOLLIGREW: You Lord Mayor? Well I can only say that I'm surprised.

LORD MAYOR: My lord, if you feel that my bringing the case is in any way disrespectful, of course...

BOLLIGREW: (*Holding up a solemn hand.*) This is a Court of Law. Case is brought now, Lord Mayor, and must just go forward for an impartial hearing. So let's hear whatever cock-and-bull story you've cooked up.

LORD MAYOR: Well, yesterday morning, my lord, I was in my sweet-shop when I saw this fellow coming along the High Street with a number of dogs.

BLACKHEART: Hounds, Lord Mayor. We call 'em hounds.

LORD MAYOR: Hounds. Thank you. (*He clears his throat, then continues to BOLLIGREW.*) He came into my shop, took down a jar of best quality humbugs and gave them to these hounds...!

BLACKHEART: (*His brow clearing.*) Oh that's all right, Lord Mayor! Wouldn't do 'em any harm. Hounds like humbugs. Often noticed it myself.

LORD MAYOR: (*Querulous.*) Very well, Squire; if you can afford to give your hounds best quality humbugs at fourpence a quarter, very well. But my point is this – do you think your man paid for them? He did not. (*Shrill.*) He never does!

BOLLIGREW: (*Weakly.*) Blackheart, I don't think I can be followin'. Is he suggestin' that your man should *pay* for his humbugs?

BLACKHEART: That your point, Lord Mayor?

LORD MAYOR: It is, Squire, yes.

BLACKHEART: Seems to be a deuced ugly spirit about, old man.

BOLLIGREW: Well I – I'm dumbfounded, Blackheart, I leave it to you.

BLACKHEART: Case dismissed.

BOLLIGREW: Yes? Very well, then. Lord Mayor, I personally take the gravest possible view of this incident. But in the light of my colleague's recommendation to mercy and your hitherto excellent record, I will dismiss you with a caution. Next case!

OBLONG: But this is scandalous!

BOLLIGREW: (*Nodding; humbly.*) You're probably right, Oblong. I tell you frankly, I'm too soft-hearted to be a good Magistrate. (*Jovially.*) Ah – it's you, Bobblenob. Brought me money?

OBIDIAH: No, my lord. (*He kneels.*) Mercy...

OBLONG: Will somebody please tell me the circumstances of this case?

BOLLIGREW: Ah yes. The circumstances my dear chap are as follows. About ten months ago this man, Obidiah Bobblenob, wilfully and maliciously chucked half a brick through one of my greenhouses...

OBIDIAH: No my lord! Beg pardon my lord, but I didn't, really I didn't!

BOLLIGREW: You see the sort of chap he is, Oblong; thoroughly hardened character; refuses to admit it even now. Without the slightest provocation he pitches a brick through my greenhouse. And what did I do? I fined 'im a pound. One miserable pound. I think you'll agree I was lenient.

OBLONG: How do you make your living, Obidiah?

OBIDIAH: I'm an egg-painter by trade, sir. I sells 'ard-boiled eggs in the market, with designs and funny faces painted on them in different colours.

BOLLIGREW: And a very profitable line it is, as I expect you know!

OBLONG: Then did you pay your fine?

OBIDIAH: No sir, I couldn't!

OBLONG: Why not?

BOLLIGREW: It's a funny thing is that. It seems he had his eggs all ready for market, and the night before some hooligan broke into his cottage and smashed 'em up. That's right, isn't it, Bobblenob?

OBIDIAH: (*Whispers.*) Yes, my lord.

BOLLIGREW: Mm. So you see, Oblong, when the next Court came round he couldn't pay. However, I wasn't disposed to be hard on him – the Bobblenobs have lived on the estate for generations. Pretty little house Bobblenob lives in – got a pond in the garden, hasn't it, Bobblenob?

OBIDIAH: Yes, my lord.

BOLLIGREW: Yes. (*Briskly.*) So all I did was to add another pound to the fine, and leave it at that. (*He smiles complacently at OBLONG, as one expecting approval.*)

OBLONG: So then he owed you *two* pounds.

BOLLIGREW: (*Calculating.*) Er, one and one – two. Yes exactly two pounds.

OBLONG: And then what?

BOLLIGREW: Well, Oblong, it's an extraordinary thing but the same thing happened again.

OBLONG: So he couldn't pay the fine again.

BOLLIGREW: Exactly –

OBLONG: So you added another pound –

BOLLIGREW: Making three.

OBLONG: And then it happened again.

BOLLIGREW: You're right, my dear chap; it did!

OBLONG: And it's gone on happening ever since.

BOLLIGREW: My dear Oblong, what a brain you must have!

OBLONG: And who is the mysterious 'hooligan' who breaks in and smashes Obidiah's eggs every day before market day, so that he can't pay his fine on Court day?

BOLLIGREW: I've no idea. Have you Bobblenob?

OBIDIAH: (*After a fractional hesitation.*) No my Lord.

BOLLIGREW: Well now: It's nine so far so today makes it ten. Nice round number. Ten pounds next Court, Bobblenob. Let's see, there's a market tomorrow morning, isn't there? We'll have a special Court for you that afternoon. And see what you can do at the market, there's a good chap.

OBIDIAH: (*Whispers.*) Yes, my lord.

BOLLIGREW: That's it. I'm relying on you, Bobblenob to save me from a painful duty. (*He digs BLACKHEART in the ribs and laughs.*)

(*BLACKHEART stares at him woodenly. BOLLIGREW
stops laughing, turns to OBLONG, sighs.*)
I'm wasted on Blackheart, I really am. Well – Last Case?
MAN-AT-ARMS: *Last* case, my Lord!
BOLLIGREW: Court will rise.
(*BOLLIGREW and BLACKHEART rise, then OBLONG.*)
And you can all clear off.
(*ALL except BLACKHEART, BOLLIGREW and OBLONG
exit hurriedly, the MEN-AT-ARMS taking the bench.
BOLLIGREW takes a cigar from his pocket and lights it.*)
(*Insolently.*) Got the picture?
OBLONG: I have indeed.
BOLLIGREW: (*Nodding sympathetically.*) There's nothing *you*
can do here, Oblong. Go back where you came from, eh?
OBLONG: Baron, Squire – I wish you good-day. (*He turns
to go.*)
BOLLIGREW: Oblong!
(*OBLONG turns. BOLLIGREW approaches, pointing at him,
warningly.*)
I've a short way with Knights Errant.
OBLONG: Well, I've a fairly short way with Barons. Good-day.
(*OBLONG exits. BOLLIGREW looks after him thoughtfully.
He turns and looks at BLACKHEART. BLACKHEART is
mindlessly gazing over the audience, sucking one end of his
moustache. BOLLIGREW approaches him.*)
BOLLIGREW: Blackheart. (*Handing him a cigar.*) Have a
cigar.
BLACKHEART: Mm? Oh, thanks. (*He takes the cigar.*)
BOLLIGREW: (*Lighting his cigar.*) We shall have trouble
with that feller, Blackheart.
BLACKHEART: Little fat feller just now?
BOLLIGREW: That's the one. He, er –
(*He takes BLACKHEART by the elbow; they patrol
downstage, smoking cigars.*)
He fancies himself as a bit of a fighter for one thing.
BLACKHEART: (*Interested.*) Oh?
BOLLIGREW: Mm. Didn't you notice how he kept lookin'
at you?

BLACKHEART: No?

BOLLIGREW: Oh.

BLACKHEART: (*Anxiously.*) How was he lookin' at me?

BOLLIGREW: Well you know, like he thought you were a big bag of wind.

BLACKHEART: What?

BOLLIGREW: Mm, you know – like he thought you were a big feller but not much good in a scrap.

BLACKHEART: He didn't!

BOLLIGREW: He did. I wondered how you could put up with it. 'How does Blackheart put up with it,' that's what I kept wonderin'. I mean it's not the thing, is it, for a gentleman to put up with that?

BLACKHEART: (*Going.*) I'll flatten 'im!

BOLLIGREW: Er – Blackheart.

(*BLACKHEART turns. BOLLIGREW beckons him back.*) There *is* a complication.

BLACKHEART: Oh?

BOLLIGREW: Mm. This feller's a Royal Knight Errant, ye see. Got the purple mantle.

BLACKHEART: I'm not afraid of...

BOLLIGREW: No, no, no – of course you're not. But – we could have trouble from the mainland you see. I mean, we don't want a Royal Commission, do we? I mean, we don's want the Islands *swarming* with Knights Errant, poking their long noses into every blazin' thing, do we?

BLACKHEART: (*Sobered.*) Goo' Lor' no. Better leave 'im alone, eh?

BOLLIGREW: Mmm – don't know about that. You *are* a gentleman.

BLACKHEART: (*Laughing.*) Well, I should hope so!

BOLLIGREW: Yes. Well then, you're entitled to satisfaction. But, just make sure you do it in the proper form.

BLACKHEART: Right. (*He glances off uneasily, then draws close to BOLLIGREW.*) What *is* the proper form?

BOLLIGREW: Oh. Well. First, you must throw down the gauntlet.

BLACKHEART: (*Gazing at it.*) Me gauntlet.

BOLLIGREW: That's it. Chuck it down. That's a challenge.
Then if he picks is up...
BLACKHEART: Yes?
BOLLIGREW: You can clobber him.
BLACKHEART: Right.
BOLLIGREW: If he *don't* pick it up...
BLACKHEART: Yes?
BOLLIGREW: Then insult him. And if he *still* won't fight...
BLACKHEART: Yes?
BOLLIGREW: Then you can't touch him.
BLACKHEART: Well what's the good of that?
BOLLIGREW: Ah. You see, old man, you must do it in
front of witnesses. This feller, ye see, has set himself up
as the Champion of the poor and needy. And if 'e won't
fight after *that*...
BLACKHEART: Yes?
BOLLIGREW: Well then, his sweaty friends will see what
sort of Champion they've got! Won't they?
BLACKHEART: (*With a grunt.*) Yes, but look 'ere, where's
me satisfaction?
BOLLIGREW: That, Blackheart, would satisfy any
gentleman that ever breathed.
BLACKHEART: Oh. Right. Let's have it again. That's
gauntlet, insult, sweaty...?
BOLLIGREW: (*Looking at him dubiously.*) Tell you what.
Come up to the castle and I'll jot it down for you.
BLACKHEART: Oh. Right.
(*BLACKHEART and BOLLIGREW move to exit, as the
STORYTELLER enters, meeting them. He is struggling on
with the church ruins.*)
BOLLIGREW: Evening.
STORYTELLER: Good evening, Baron.
BOLLIGREW: What you got there then?
STORYTELLER: The ruins of Bolligrew Church, Baron. We
shall need them for the next scene.
BOLLIGREW: Church ruins, Blackheart. Thought they
looked familiar.
STORYTELLER: (*Pausing; breathless.*) I wonder if the Squire
would...?

BLACKHEART: My good man, I'm not a bally labourer.

BOLLIGREW: Quite right. You got any heavin' and liftin' to do, find a bally peasant!

(*BLACKHEART and BOLLIGREW exit.*)

STORYTELLER: (*Calling off.*) Sir Oblong!

(*OBLONG enters.*)

I wonder if you'd…

OBLONG: Of course.

(*They lug the ruins into place.*)

Church ruins, eh?

STORYTELLER: Yes, we need them for the next scene.

OBLONG: Mm, pretty. Must have been a pretty little place – I shall enjoy the first part of my mission. (*Anxiously.*) However, I shall need assistance…

STORYTELLER: The poor and needy?

OBLONG: Excellent.

(*The STORYTELLER addresses the audience.*)

STORYTELLER: The poor and needy of the Island, when they heard that he had come to be their champion, flocked in upon the gallant Knight from every side!

(*The PEASANTS and LORD MAYOR enter, OBLONG addresses them. The STORYTELLER exits.*)

OBLONG: Poor and needy, Lord Mayor. I have been sent here by the Duke to help you. Will you help me?

(*Dubious agreement from the PEASANTS.*)

FIRST PEASANT: (*Together.*) Don't see why not…

SECOND PEASANT: (*Together.*) Give it a go…

THIRD PEASANT: (*Together.*) 'pends what kind of 'elp 'e wants.

OBLONG: In the first place I want information. Tell me something about Squire Blackheart. (*He notes down their replies.*)

FIRST PEASANT: 'e's a 'ard case is the Squire, sir.

SECOND PEASANT: You know that black armour of his, sir?

OBLONG: Yes?

SECOND PEASANT: Never takes it off, sir.

THIRD PEASANT: 'E sleeps in it.

OBLONG: (*Noting it all down and nodding gravely.*) One of
   those, is he? Now what about the Dragon?
   (*On the word 'Dragon' the PEASANTS scatter: stop: return.*)
FIRST PEASANT: 'Ere. Don't you go near Dragon, now.
SECOND PEASANT: Gobble you up like a raspberry, 'e
   will.
THIRD PEASANT: Baron 'isself is afeared of Dragon.
OBLONG: My understanding was that the Baron has some
   sort of arrangement with the Dragon.
FOURTH PEASANT: So 'e 'as, sir. Baron 'as this side of
   the Island for grindin' the faces of the poor, and Dragon
   'as that side of the Island for ravagin'. That's the
   agreement. But I reckon the Baron be afeared of 'e all the
   same...
OBLONG: Matters here are worse than I had realised. (*He
   flips shut his notebook.*) Now my first task is to rebuild this
   church. May I count on your assistance?
FIRST PEASANT: Baron isn't goin' to like that, sir.
SECOND PEASANT: 'E doan' 'old wi' churches, sir.
THIRD PEASANT: I mean, 'e pulled it down; stands to
   reason 'e doan' want it buildin' up again.
OBLONG: If we are to consult the likes and dislikes of the
   Baron at every turn, we shall accomplish very little.
   (*There is an awkward silence.*)
   Remember – you will be under the protection of the
   Duke.
FIFTH PEASANT: Meanin' no disrespect sir, but Duke's a
   long way away. We ain't never seen Duke in the Islands, sir.
OBLONG: That is a just observation... (*He considers, mounts
   the ruin, and addresses them, Crispin's Day fashion.*) There
   was a time when the peasants of this island were a
   byword for their fearlessness and sturdy independence!
   In time of Peace they followed the plough with straight
   backs and heads high!
   (*The PEASANTS unconsciously straighten their backs.*)
   In time of War –
   (*The PEASANTS unconsciously fall into martial postures.*)
   – they pressed as though by instinct even to the thickest
   of the fray, hard after the great banner of the Bolligrew,

the Golden Toad, and were a terror to the very cream of foreign chivalry!

PEASANTS: (*Carried away.*) Hurrah!

OBLONG: These were your fathers! Are you their sons?

PEASANTS: Yes!

OBLONG: Then do we build the church?

PEASANTS: We do!

OBLONG: Then (*Pointing dramatically.*) building materials!

PEASANTS: Building materials!

(*The PEASANTS rush off enthusiastically.*)

LORD MAYOR: A wonderful gift for words you have.

OBLONG: Oh it's all part of our training you know, where do *you* stand on this business.

LORD MAYOR: You understand, Sir Oblong, I'm – er – delicately situated.

OBLONG: I do see that.

LORD MAYOR: If there's anything I can do in proper form…

OBLONG: I understand.

LORD MAYOR: But I can hardly take part in, well, a popular uprising.

OBLONG: You're delicately situated.

LORD MAYOR: Thank you. Er – (*He edges closer to OBLONG.*) – between ourselves, you've put your finger on the nub of the matter with this fellow Blackheart. Between ourselves – (*Glancing about.*) – not really out of the top drawer.

OBLONG: No?

LORD MAYOR: No. For all his moustaches. His father – (*He glances around again.*) – his father was an underfootman in the late Lord Bolligrew's time.

OBLONG: Really?

LORD MAYOR: I remember him. I went to school with Squire Blackheart so-called. An inveterate bully, Sir Oblong, and backward in his lessons, very backward… (*The LORD MAYOR breaks off as the noise of the PEASANTS approaches. The PEASANTS enter bearing sections of the church: one with a wheelbarrow, one with a stepladder.*)

FIRST PEASANT: (*Breathlessly.*) There you are, sir!

SECOND PEASANT: Building materials!

OBLONG: Splendid! (*He inspects the contents of the wheelbarrow.*) Mortar and trowel. Splendid, splendid. (*He takes the handles of the barrow.*) Now then. For your manhood and your ancient liberties. Forward!
(*OBLONG steps out rhetorically with the barrow, followed by the PEASANTS, but stops instantly as BLACKHEART enters. The STORYTELLER enters separately at the same moment, and watches soberly.*)
Good evening, Squire.

BLACKHEART: Tchah!
(*BLACKHEART advances deliberately, the PEASANTS shrinking back, and hurls down his gauntlet.*)

OBLONG: You've dropped your glove.

BLACKHEART: I've thrown down me gauntlet. Any gentleman'd know that.

OBLONG: You want me to fight a duel with you, Squire?

BLACKHEART: Right.

OBLONG: Well, I'm not going to.

BLACKHEART: Then – (*An effort of memory.*) – I'm goin' to insult you!

OBLONG: Well please be quick; I have a lot to do and the light's going.

BLACKHEART: (*Studying a grubby scrap of paper.*) Oblong, you're a – a, mm… (*He has difficulty in reading.*)
(*OBLONG peers at the paper.*)

OBLONG: Varlet.

BLACKHEART: Right! A varlet! And a, mm…

OBLONG: Knave.

BLACKHEART: That's it! Knave and varlet! You – you're not a gentleman! Thought of that meself.

OBLONG: The subject seems to obsess you, Squire.

BLACKHEART: (*Amazed.*) Well, if you won't fight *now*…

OBLONG: No.
(*BLACKHEART, nonplussed, consults the paper, then his brow clears.*)

BLACKHEART: Well then, your sweaty friends can see what kind of Champion they've *got*! (*To the FIFTH PEASANT.*) You.

FIFTH PEASANT: (*Approaching; humbly.*) Yes, Squire?

BLACKHEART: Pick up me glove.

FIFTH PEASANT: Yes, Squire. (*He does so.*)

(*Behind OBLONG, the PEASANTS lay down the sections of the church.*)

BLACKHEART: (*To OBLONG; going.*) And a very good evening to *you* Fatty!

(*BLACKHEART exits. The PEASANTS start to leave in the opposite direction.*)

OBLONG: (*Watching BLACKHEART off.*) What a deplorable exhibition! Well now – (*Turning to find the PEASANTS going.*) What's the matter? Stop!

(*All the PEASANTS exit except the FIFTH.*)

My good friend…

FIFTH PEASANT: (*Following the others.*) Sorry, sir. But if you'm afeared to tackle Squire, we'm afeared to 'elp you. And that's the top and bottom of it, sir.

(*The FIFTH PEASANT exits.*)

OBLONG: (*To the LORD MAYOR.*) I'm not afraid of the Squire!

LORD MAYOR: No, no. Of course not.

OBLONG: But duelling is utterly against my principles.

LORD MAYOR: I agree with you, Sir Oblong, I agree with you. (*But he is backing towards the exit.*)

OBLONG: Well, the two of us must just do what we can, eh? (*Attempting to lift a large segment of the church.*) Would you…?

LORD MAYOR: The fact is, sir, I ought to be getting back to the shop, I'm sorry, Sir Oblong, really I am…

(*The LORD MAYOR exits.*)

OBLONG: Dash it! (*Defiantly.*) Yes – I am not often intemperate in my language but *dash* it! What shall I do now?

STORYTELLER: I'm afraid I can't tell you.

OBLONG: But you're the Storyteller aren't you?

STORYTELLER: I am the Storyteller, yes.

OBLONG: Well what happens next in the story?

STORYTELLER: What happens next, Sir Oblong, is that you are left on your own.

(*The STORYTELLER exits.*)

OBLONG: Well that's very inconvenient! (*He appeals to the audience.*) What shall I do? Perhaps I ought to have fought that fellow Blackheart after all? What do you think? (*He continues to ad lib till the audience response is strong.*) Might do him good to learn a lesson, eh? In my younger days I was national Broadsword Champion you know, and – and Area Champion three years running! (*Growing excited.*) After all, he challenged me, didn't he? Perhaps I ought to find the fellow now? Do a little challenging myself? Ha! (*Drawing his sword.*) Have at thee for a foul catiff! Take that – and that – anthatanthatanthat! (*When the response is at its maximum, he pulls himself up.*) No. No. (*He sheathes his sword.*) Certainly not. I have been sent here to set a good example. You ought to be ashamed of yourselves. Duelling is *wrong...* I must manage somehow by myself. (*Attempting to lift a segment of the church.*) No. Now let's see – no. You know at this point in the story I do think they might send *somebody* to help me.
(*MAGPIE enters, unseen by OBLONG. He is excitable and amoral, and wears a lifelike costume of pied feathers.*)
However! Keep trying – no.

VOICE: (*From the audience.*) Behind you!

OBLONG: What? Try a smaller piece? Right. Now, then... No. I really don't see how I'm going to manage, you know. How about this bit...? (*And so on, till the audience response is strong. Then he turns, and sees MAGPIE.*)

OBLONG: Oh. Good Evening.

MAGPIE: You talk.

OBLONG: Certainly.

MAGPIE: Most human beings only twitter.

OBLONG: Most human beings would say most birds only twitter.

MAGPIE: Eh?

OBLONG: Mmm. As a matter of fact, all human beings talk, among themselves.
(*The lights start to dim.*)

MAGPIE: Don't believe it.

OBLONG: Well that's rather narrow minded of you. It takes all sorts to make a world you know.

MAGPIE: My name's Mike Magpie. Your name's Oblong. You saved my life this morning.

OBLONG: Oh, was that you?

MAGPIE: Awk.

OBLONG: He might have missed, you know.

MAGPIE: Not 'im. You saved my life an' you can count on me.

OBLONG: For what?

MAGPIE: Anything! I'm a pretty smart character.

OBLONG: Are you now?

MAGPIE: Oh yes. Brilliant bird – always have been.

OBLONG: Well the immediate task is to rebuild this church.

MAGPIE: Oh! Like, lugging stones about?

OBLONG: Yes?

MAGPIE: Like – work?

OBLONG: Yes, Michael, work.

MAGPIE: Well look 'ere, Obby, work's not in my line. Anythin' in the thieving line now, or the telling lies line, or the leading up the garden path line…

OBLONG: Did you say 'thieving'?

MAGPIE: Yes. You know – pinching things.

OBLONG: (*Quietly.*) What things?

MAGPIE: Shiny things. They're in my nest. 'D'you like to see?

OBLONG: (*Mounting the ladder to the nest on top of the tower.*) Yes Michael, I should.

MAGPIE: Hey! You're not going to take my shiny things, are you?

OBLONG: Yours, Michael? (*Peering into the nest.*) Mm. I am on the whole relieved. Silver paper, bits of glass – but there is a silver tie-pin with a fox head on it which appears to be of some value.

MAGPIE: That's all right; that's Bolligrew's!

OBLONG: (*Descending.*) It makes not an atom of difference whose it is. Stealing is *wrong.*

MAGPIE: It's no good talking to me about right and wrong, Obby. It's not in my nature.

OBLONG: I know it's difficult for Magpies, Michael, but I want you to try. Imagine the impression it would make in the Islands if it were thought that I associated with a bird – I am sorry to say this – a bird of loose principles.

MAGPIE: Awk.

OBLONG: No more stealing then.

MAGPIE: Aw...

(*There is a noise off.*)

Awk! A person!

OBLONG: Hide.

(*MAGPIE climbs to his nest. OBLONG peers off, hand on sword. A light approaches.*)

Who's that?

(*OBIDIAH enters with a lamp.*)

OBIDIAH: It's me, sir. Bobblenob the egg painter.

OBLONG: Ah, Obidiah. My poor friend, I'm sorry I wasn't able to help you in Court this morning.

OBIDIAH: You did your best sir, and I thanks you for it. That's what I come to say, sir.

OBLONG: There's no chance of your having the ten pounds by next Court Day, I suppose?

OBIDIAH: How can a poor man like me come by ten pounds, sir?

OBLONG: If I had any money myself I'd give it to you, Obidiah, willingly. But I haven't. We're not allowed to, you know.

OBIDIAH: I know that, sir. I've sometimes thought if Knights Errant were provided with proper funds, sir, they might make more of an impression, sir.

OBLONG: It's not for us to question the regulation, Obidiah.

OBIDIAH: No sir.

OBLONG: Can't you possibly make some eggs to sell at tomorrow market?

OBIDIAH: I'd need a power of eggs to make ten pounds. And then again it's fiddlin' work, sir, is egg painting, and I couldn't get 'em finished by tomorrow, sir, if I 'ad 'em.

OBLONG: No. I suppose not.

OBIDIAH: And what if I did, sir, they'd only be smashed up again like the others.

OBLONG: Have you no idea who it is that breaks into your cottage and smashes up your eggs?

OBIDIAH: I *know* who it is, sir. It's Squire Blackheart.

OBLONG: Squire Blackheart! Obidiah, do you know what you are saying?

OBIDIAH: I seen 'im at it, sir, plain as I see you. But what can I do with a great strong gentleman like that? Well, sir, you yourself – I mean, you 'esitate don't you?

OBLONG: I hesitate no longer, Obidiah. (*He paces about restlessly.*) I find myself agitated. (*He stops.*) It's Baron Bolligrew who sends him, of course?

OBIDIAH: That's right, sir. T'isn't the money he wants, sir. 'Tis my cottage he's after. When he's raised the fine to fifteen pounds or thereabouts 'e'll take the cottage instead.

OBLONG: I see. Or rather, no I don't see. What on earth does Baron Bolligrew want with a cottage?

OBIDIAH: Well, sir; this pond goes with the cottage – and there's trout in this pond, sir.

OBLONG: Aha!

OBIDIAH: Yes, sir. Baron an' Squire been keen fishermen many a year now. Mine be last trout in the Islands near enough. And finer, happier fish you never did see. I feeds 'em night and morning, sir, same as my father did before me. Friends of the family, they are, in a manner of speakin', sir.

OBLONG: (*Looking at him sharply.*) You converse with them, Obidiah?

OBIDIAH: Nothing I likes better of an evening, sir, than a quiet chat with they trout.

OBLONG: Then, Obidiah, I wish you to meet a friend of mine. (*Calling.*) Michael! Will you come here, please? A shrewd bird Bobblenob and knows the Island. Michael Magpie; Obidiah Bobblenob.

(*MAGPIE descends the ladder.*)

MAGPIE: Awk.

OBLONG: Michael, you have heard Obidiah's predicament?

MAGPIE: Awk.

OBLONG: What do you make of it?

MAGPIE: Tricky. How many eggs to make ten quid?

OBIDIAH: Two hundred 'seventy-seven.

OBLONG: And then we should have to paint designs on them you see, before tomorrow morning's market.

MAGPIE: Oh *that's* all right – I'm a dab hand with a paint brush.

OBLONG: Really? Mm – it is sad how often talent and delinquency go hand in hand.

MAGPIE: No, the real snag's getting the eggs in the first place...

OBLONG: It is indeed...

MAGPIE: (*Suddenly, to OBIDIAH.*) Hen's eggs?

OBIDIAH: Well, how...?

MAGPIE: Not heron's eggs? Seagull's? Pheasant's? Peewit's?

OBIDIAH: Very tasty, when you can get 'em.

MAGPIE: I can get 'em.

OBIDIAH: Can you?

MAGPIE: Course I can.

OBIDIAH: Two hundred 'seventy seven?

MAGPIE: Easy. Couple each. Can't count, most of 'em.

OBLONG: Michael. There can be no question of *stealing* these eggs from your friends. No Obidiah, not even for this.

MAGPIE: For this they'll give 'em, Obby.

OBLONG: Will they really?

MAGPIE: If I ask them.

OBLONG: Well there we are then! Hope, Obidiah! Do you begin to hope?

OBIDIAH: I do sir!

OBLONG: You fetch your materials; we will collect the eggs. (*To MAGPIE.*) When can we begin?

MAGPIE: As soon as the moon comes up.

OBLONG: Oh.

(*The STORYTELLER enters.*)

Ah. Would you bring the moon up?

(*A white moon ascends; bright moonlight.*)

Thank you. Now my friends, to work!

(*OBIDIAH exits in one direction; OBLONG and MAGPIE in the other.*)

STORYTELLER: For half that night they walked the island from one nest to another, and everywhere they met with success. Some birds gave their eggs because they knew Mike Magpie, many because they took a fancy to Sir Oblong, most because they detested Baron Bolligrew and wished to see him foiled. Some gave one, some gave two, some as many as half a dozen, and by one'clock in the morning the collection totalled...

(*OBIDIAH enters with painting implements and books of designs; OBLONG and MAGPIE with basket of eggs.*)

OBLONG: Two hundred and seventy-seven! Michael my dear Magpie, I have no words to express my admiration for your resourcefulness and the high esteem in which you are evidently held by these excellent birds.

MAGPIE: Awk!

OBLONG: Now, Obidiah we are in your hands. First I suppose we must boil them?

OBIDIAH: It's plain to see you don't know much about egg paintin' sir. First we paints 'em, then we boils 'em; thus preparing the egg itself for consumption and fixin' the colours used in the design. We don't speak of boilin' an egg in the trade, we speaks of fixin' an egg.

OBLONG: How interesting.

OBIDIAH: Yes. I have brought along one of my old books of sample designs.

OBLONG: Very sensible.

(*OBLONG and MAGPIE look at the book.*)

Mm. These look rather ambitious, Obidiah.

OBIDIAH: These (*Producing another book.*) are simpler designs for the use of apprentices.

OBLONG: Ah. Ah, that's more like it.

MAGPIE: Pooh. (*Takes the other book.*)

OBLONG: Well then, let's commence.

(*ALL in unison sit, take one egg, dip their brush and start work.*)

STORYTELLER: And so they commenced, each giving of his best according to his own ability. Obidiah Bobblenob produced his usual quota of highly professional eggs, Mike Magpie produced a small number of very ingenious eggs and Sir Oblong a large number of rather elementary eggs, some of which he painted bright blue all over. But when the moon went down and dawn came up, they had done.

(*The moon goes down; the light changes, during which OBLONG turns the basket about, presenting the painted side of the eggs to the audience.*)

OBLONG: Done!

OBIDIAH: And I thanks you all from the bottom of my heart.

MAGPIE: I'm tired.

OBIDIAH: Me too.

OBLONG: I'm a bit fatigued myself. However. Now we must boiler-fix them, I suppose?

(*MAGPIE falls asleep.*)

OBIDIAH: (*Settling himself comfortably.*) One thing we never does in the trade, sir, is pass straight from the paintin' to the fixin'. The hand is unsteady and the brain excited. Many a panful of eggs I've seen split from top to bottom by some unchancy journeyman for lack of forty winks.

OBLONG: (*Attracted.*) Forty winks? Have we time?

OBIDIAH: Ample time, sir. Market don't open till ten o'clock. If we takes 'em down to my cottage at nine o'clock, say we take 'em straight from the fixin' to the market and – less chance of runnin' into Squire Blackheart, sir.

OBLONG: That's well thought of. (*Lying down.*) Though I'm bound to admit I shouldn't mind crossing swords with the fellow. Upon a legitimate occasion. Do you know his father was an under footman?

(*But OBIDIAH too, has fallen asleep. OBLONG sleeps, his hands clasped on his tummy.*)

STORYTELLER: Now Squire Blackheart, owing to his habit of sleeping in his armour, slept little and rose early. On this particular morning, disturbed by a loose rivet, he rose particularly early and went for an early morning walk, with his favourite hound.

(*BLACKHEART enters downstage, preceded by a cut-out hound on wheels. He crosses and is about to exit, when he double-takes sharply, letting go of the hound, which runs off opposite. BLACKHEART tiptoes to the sleepers, inspects them, sees the eggs, reacts, looks furtively off left and right, draws his sword, raises it high in the air, flat side down, and is about to smash the eggs.*)

OBLONG: (*Still recumbent, opening an eye.*) Good morning, Squire.

(*BLACKHEART checks. OBLONG rises.*)

What are you doing?

BLACKHEART: What d'you think I'm doin'?

OBLONG: I think you are about to destroy Obidiah's eggs.

BLACKHEART: Right.

OBLONG: Not, I think, for the first time.

BLACKHEART: Right. (*Pushing OBLONG.*) Out of me way, fatty.

OBLONG: (*Resisting.*) One moment. (*Clasping his hand behind his back.*) Yesterday, Squire, you permitted yourself to insult me. Varlet and Knave, I think it was.

BLACKHEART: That's it; varlet and knave. I remember.

OBLONG: Blackheart, it is my considered opinion that you are a commonplace rogue and a disgrace to your profession.

BLACKHEART: *Eh?*

OBLONG: One moment. (*He puts his hand under BLACKHEART's nose, and snaps his finger and thumb.*)

BLACKHEART: A-aaah!

(*BLACKHEART makes a terrific swipe, which OBLONG nimbly jumps over.*)

OBLONG: Not a bad stroke, Squire. Now!

(*OBLONG draws his sword. They fight. BLACKHEART's strokes are lethal but ponderous; OBLONG fights light-weight style, great dexterity but no knock-out punch. The STORYTELLER enters and watches calmly. The whistle of*

BLACKHEART's blade and the merry clatter of OBLONG's short sword, their gasping breath, are taken up and exaggerated by a loudspeaker, OBLONG is borne backwards offstage by BLACKHEART, followed by OBIDIAH. MAGPIE hides behind the church with the basket as BLACKHEART returns.)

BLACKHEART: The eggs! Where are the blazin' eggs?

(*OBLONG enters limping but determined.*)

OBLONG: Come along Squire, we haven't finished.

(*BLACKHEART rushes at him. OBIDIAH and MAGPIE emerge. Avoiding the combatants, they collide and MAGPIE falls. BLACKHEART kicks him. MAGPIE seizes BLACKHEART's leg and nips ankle with his beak.*)

Michael, let go! One on to one! That's the rule! Let go immediately!

(*OBLONG is borne off again by BLACKHEART. MAGPIE and OBIDIAH exit on tiptoe with the basket. The noise of battle ceases on a cry from BLACKHEART off. OBLONG enters, breathless.*)

I'm getting, getting past it. One does not realise.

STORYTELLER: Would perhaps (*Nodding discreetly to the exit opposite.*) discretion be the better part of valour?

OBLONG: Run away? (*He seems tempted for a moment.*) No. There's life, life in the old dog yet.

(*BLACKHEART enters also limping.*)

BLACKHEART: Had enough, have you?

OBLONG: Certainly not. Lay on, and may the best man win!

(*OBLONG and BLACKHEART fight again, watched by the STORYTELLER. Despite their differing styles, they are well matched, but it is OBLONG who is once again borne off. The din of battle recedes. The STORYTELLER walks slowly forward. The noise dwindles, goon-fashion, to infinity.*)

STORYTELLER: It is sad but true when men fight the fight goes not to the best man but to the best fighter.

(*BOLLIGREW enters in tearing high spirits, and blows a whistle.*)

BOLLIGREW: Court! Court's in session! Draw near!

(*The MEN-AT-ARMS, PEASANTS, and the LORD MAYOR enter as before.*)

That's the spirit! Ah, there you are Bobblenob! Good market this morning? Trade brisk?

(*OBIDIAH smiles sadly.*)

Ha ha! Just my little joke, you know. (*He sits.*) Well now. (*Surprised.*) Where's me colleague?

MAN-AT-ARMS: (*Looking off.*) Coming now, my lord.

BOLLIGREW: (*Calling, cheerfully.*) Come on, Blackheart, I'm waitin'!

(*OBLONG enters limping, with adhesive plaster on his forehead.*)

BOLLIGREW: Oh, it's you. (*Grinning.*) Been in an accident, old man?

OBLONG: You might call it that. (*He sits.*)

BOLLIGREW: (*Sotto voce.*) Challenged you, did he?

OBLONG: (*Sotto voce.*) He did challenge me, yes.

BOLLIGREW: Mm. Well, you may think you've had a hiding, but he's let you off pretty lightly – compared to some of the thumpings I've see him hand out, eh, Corporal?

MAN-AT-ARMS: Yes, my lord; that gentleman 'e 'ad words with at the point-to-point.

BOLLIGREW: Blood all over the paddock.

(*BOLLIGREW and the MEN-AT-ARMS laugh reminiscently.*)

(*Irritably.*) Wonder where he is?

MAN-AT-ARMS: 'Spect 'e's 'avin' forty winks, sir.

SECOND MAN-AT-ARMS: Always likes forty winks after a scrimmage, does the Squire, sir. Makes him sleepy.

BOLLIGREW: Well I'm not waitin'. Bobblenob, stand forward. Oh, it occurs to me, Oblong, that you and I might disagree on the verdict.

OBLONG: Quite likely.

BOLLIGREW: Well, we don't want poor old Bobblenob held up by the delays of the Court, do we?

OBLONG: No.

BOLLIGREW: No. So I'll appoint another Magistrate. Corporal, you're a Magistrate. Siddown. I've been thinkin' about this case, Corporal, and I'm afraid I can't let it go on any longer. What do you think?

MAN-AT-ARMS: If 'e don't pay up today, my lord, I should put 'im inside.

BOLLIGREW: That would be *too* severe. But I'm afraid I shall have to take his cottage, you know.

MAN-AT-ARMS: If 'e don't pay up today, my lord, I should take 'is cottage.

BOLLIGREW: That's settled then. Cheer up, Oblong. Bobblenob's probably *got* the money today! Got the money, Bobblenob?

OBIDIAH: Yes, my lord.

BOLLIGREW: Well now, look here, this can't go... *Eh?* You have?

OBIDIAH: Yes, my lord. Ten pounds; the proceeds of my painted egg stall this morning. (*He holds out the money.*)

OBLONG: You seem surprised, Baron?

BOLLIGREW: Surprised? Well I – well – I – we – er...

OBLONG: We did have a little trouble getting the eggs.

BOLLIGREW: (*Staring at him, hypnotised.*) The eggs. Yes, you would.

OBLONG: And then of course the mysterious hooligan turned up.

BOLLIGREW: Oh. The 'ooligan...

OBLONG: Yes.

BOLLIGREW: You *beat* him?

OBLONG: With some difficulty, but yes, I think I may say I beat him.

BOLLIGREW: (*Tearing his eyes away from OBLONG.*) Well, that's very satisfactory! Congratulations, Bobblenob. Glad your troubles are over. (*Taking the money.*) Court will rise –

(*BOLLIGREW and the MAN-AT-ARMS rise.*)

OBLONG: One moment, Baron!

BOLLIGREW: (*Reluctantly.*) Court sit.

(*BOLLIGREW and the MAN-AT-ARMS sit.*)

OBLONG: Baron, I think we can at last establish the identity of this hooligan.

BOLLIGREW: (*Mopping his forehead with his handkerchief.*) You do?

OBLONG: Yes. He left behind him a piece of tangible evidence. (*He produces the enormous black plume from BLACKHEART's helmet.*) Do you know whose it is?

BOLLIGREW: (*Shaking his head vigorously.*) Never seen it before.

MAN-AT-ARMS: That's Squire Black'eart's, my lord.

BOLLIGREW: Idiot!

OBLONG: Well I knew it was, of course, but I'm glad to have that confirmed by our colleague on the Bench here. People's exhibit One.

BOLLIGREW: Look here, Obby old man, what exactly are you goin' to do with that?

OBLONG: I thought of sending it to the Duke's High Court on the mainland.

BOLLIGREW: High Court, eh?

OBLONG: Yes. No doubt the Squire will explain to them *why* a gentleman in his position should persecute a humble egg painter. (*As one struck.*) Unless, of course…

BOLLIGREW: Yes?

OBLONG: Unless we were to deal with the case in our own little Court here.

BOLLIGREW: I knew you were the right sort, Obby! Just – just give me that thing and – you can rebuild the church!

OBLONG: I shall do that in any case. I was thinking now of the second part of my mission: the restoration of justice here.

BOLLIGREW: Anythin' you say, old man.

OBLONG: Well, in the first place, I think Blackheart himself should resign from the Bench.

BOLLIGREW: He's resigned.

OBLONG: And then – (*Confidentially.*) – is the Corporal really suitable? I mean, has he really the legal brain?

BOLLIGREW: Complete fool. He's resigned, too. You've resigned, you numbskull. Get off the Bench!
(*The MAN-AT-ARMS rises.*)

OBLONG: And now, you see, there are just the two of us again.

BOLLIGREW: And very nice too, Obby. Couldn't be happier. Now let's have that, there's a good chap.

OBLONG: You see, there ought to be a third Magistrate in case, as you very shrewdly pointed out, you and I should disagree.

BOLLIGREW: (*Licking his lips.*) A third Magistrate?

OBLONG: What about the Lord Mayor? (*He offers the plume.*)

BOLLIGREW: (*Checking his hand.*) The…?

OBLONG: Lord Mayor. (*Withdrawing the plume.*) Other side, you see, I don't think we shall be competent to judge this case.

BOLLIGREW: (*Sinister.*) Lord Mayor – do you *want* to be a Magistrate?

LORD MAYOR: (*With a nervous giggle.*) You see, Sir Oblong, I'm delicately situated.

OBLONG: Baron persuade him.

BOLLIGREW: (*Between his teeth.*) Lord Mayor, I would take is as a personal favour if you would accept a seat on the Bench!

LORD MAYOR: (*With another giggle.*) Sir Oblong, may we take it that this morning you met Squire Blackheart in personal combat, and, er, defeated him?

OBLONG: Soundly, Lord Mayor.

LORD MAYOR: Then, Baron, I am happy to accept your invitation.

(*The LORD MAYOR sits nervously at the far end of the bench from BOLLIGREW. OBLONG offers the plume again. BOLLIGREW snatches it and glowers.*)

BOLLIGREW: Court rise!

(*BOLLIGREW leaps to his feet. The LORD MAYOR half rises.*)

OBLONG: The case, Baron.

BOLLIGREW: Eh?

OBLONG: (*Indicating the plume in BOLLIGREW's hands.*) The case.

BOLLIGREW: Court sit.

(*BOLLIGREW sits, heavily.*)

OBLONG: To my mind, gentlemen, those ten pounds belong to Obidiah Bobblenob.

BOLLIGREW: (*Stares incredulously, then.*) No!

OBLONG: Lord Mayor, what do you think?

BOLLIGREW: (*Grimly.*) Yes, Lord Mayor, what *do* you think?

(*All heads turn to the LORD MAYOR. The PEASANTS shuffle forward a step in suspense. The LORD MAYOR licks his lips, grips his knees, and avoids BOLLIGREW's glaring eye.*)

LORD MAYOR: I agree with Sir Oblong!

OBLONG: (*Beaming at him.*) Well done, Lord Mayor! Very well done indeed! (*He takes the money from BOLLIGREW's nerveless hand and gives it to OBIDIAH.*) Case dismissed?

LORD MAYOR: (*Delighted with himself.*) Case dismissed!

OBLONG: That's two to one, Baron.

BOLLIGREW: (*Snarling.*) Case dismissed!

(*Triumphal march music and cheering pours from the loudspeaker; OBLONG and the LORD MAYOR rise, cheering PEASANTS crowd round.*)

OBLONG: To the Church!

(*OBLONG leads the way, circuitously round the stage; the PEASANTS fall in step behind him. In time to the march, the segments of church are fitted into place. A bell is placed in tower, at which the cheerful pandemonium on the loudspeaker is augmented by church bells. OBLONG is carried shoulder high and all exit, OBLONG bowing and waving graciously to left and right. BOLLIGREW is left slumped sullen and motionless on the bench. Offstage celebrations dwindle to silence on the loudspeaker. BLACKHEART enters, looking nervously left and right. His plume is missing, bits of his armour have come loose and flap from him, his sword is broken short and sharply bent. BOLLIGREW turns his head and watches him sourly.*)

BLACKHEART: Has he gone?

BOLLIGREW: Ha! Me invincible Champion, battling Black'eart!

BLACKHEART: Now don't take that tone, Bolligrew! (*He limps to the bench and sits with a clatter. Aggrieved.*) Feller's a professional. Don't fight like a gentleman. Jumps about like a bally grass'opper! Can't get a decent swipe at 'im. Look at my armour – me best suit!

BOLLIGREW: (*Roaring.*) And 'oo paid for it, might I ask? 'Oo signed the whackin' great cheque for it? (*He rises and soliloquises, trembling with self-pity.*) Here am I, doing no harm to anybody! Followin' the innocent pursuits of a retired country gentleman! Along comes this interferin' little barrel of a chap from the mainland and what do *you* do? You go swaggerin' off like you always do and come back lookin' like a half-opened sardine tin! (*He sits.*) Frankly, Black'eart, I'm disappointed.

BLACKHEART: All right, if you feel so inclined, *you* 'ave a go at 'im. An' I'll lay a five-pun' note to one of your rotten cigars, you never even touch 'im!

BOLLIGREW: Now, now, Black'eart, it's no good carryin' on like that. We've got to think.

BLACKHEART: (*Dubiously.*) Think?

BOLLIGREW: That's it; because I'll tell you what, Black'eart; this chap's some sort of disguised intellectual.

BLACKHEART: Oh Lor'...

BOLLIGREW: Yes, we're in trouble. Because it's no good pretendin' that you and me are brainy blokes, Blackheart. We're not. You especially... (*He rises, he thinks.*) Got it! (*To the STORYTELLER.*) You: fetch me Secretary.

STORYTELLER: My Lord.

BOLLIGREW: We need help, Blackheart, and I think I know where we can get it.
(*A SECRETARY enters.*)
(*Rising.*) Secretary, take a letter.
(*The SECRETARY mimes shorthand while BOLLIGREW strolls about, dictating.*)
To Doctor Beelzebub Moloch, Dean of the Faculty of Magic and Regius Professor of Wickedness, at the University, Oxford. 'My dear Moloch, finding myself in a difficulty, my thoughts turn to the most distinguished living practitioner of the Art of Magic.' No, say 'the Science of Magic'. He'll like that. 'The situation is one

which I know will engage your disinterested attention, but I need hardly say that expense is no object.' No, that's a bit crude – 'disinterested attention but I shall of course expect to defray your expenses. Er, perhaps you could spare me a week or two of your valuable time during the next long vac., Yours etc. Bolligrew.'

(*The STORYTELLER enters, looking grave.*)

STORYTELLER: Baron Bolligrew, there is a letter for you.

BOLLIGREW: Oh?

STORYTELLER: It's from the Dragon.

(*All flinch.*)

BLACKHEART: (*Rising.*) The *Dragon*?

SECRETARY: D-dragon!

BOLLIGREW: How d'you know it's from the Dragon?

STORYTELLER: I know the handwriting, my lord. And – it's in an asbestos envelope.

BOLLIGREW: (*Licking his lips.*) Well, bring it.

(*The STORYTELLER exits.*)

BLACKHEART: (*Uneasy.*) Look here, Bolligrew…

BOLLIGREW: (*Excited, though fearful.*) No, wait a bit. This may be very handy.

(*The STORYTELLER enters. He carries in a pair of tongs a large grey envelope, which smokes slightly. BOLLIGREW takes it, gingerly opens it. A magnesium flash and smoke rises from envelope. BOLLIGREW blows on his fingers, extracts a paper, charred at the edges. The others watch as he reads.*)

BOLLIGREW: Ah-ha! Eh? *What*? (*To the SECRETARY.*) You get that letter off to Moloch.

BLACKHEART: What does he say?

BOLLIGREW: He says – he's hungry.

End of Act One.

ACT TWO

When the curtain rises, the stage is dark except for the spot in which the STORYTELLER stands.

STORYTELLER: When Doctor Moloch, the Professor of Magic, received the Baron's letter, he was at first reluctant to leave his luxurious rooms in the heart of an ancient University Town for so remote and uncultivated a spot as the Bolligrew Islands. But then he reflected that it would make a change from his usual routine and that the Baron, after all, was rich and could be made to pay. (*The lights come up. BOLLIGREW, MOLOCH and BLACKHEART enter. MOLOCH is a snappish intellectual; he wears an academic gown.*)

BOLLIGREW: Enjoy your meal, I hope, Doctor?

MOLOCH: Passable. Bolligrew, in the first of the month I must be back on the mainland. I am to address an important meeting of the Merlin Society. Let's get down to business.

BOLLIGREW: Right. Well, first there's this Royal Knight Errant, Oblong.

MOLOCH: Yes. You wish him made away with? Turned into a frog – something of that order?

BOLLIGREW: No! If he disappears altogether we shall have trouble from the mainland; Duke; King, maybe.

MOLOCH: Awkward. And then?

BOLLIGREW: Then there's the Dragon.

MOLOCH: Yes. This is an aspect of your matter which I don't much care for, Bolligrew. Tell me again?

BOLLIGREW: Well as you know, we 'ave this agreement. I 'ave this side of the island for grindin' the faces of the poor, and Dragon 'as that side of the Island for ravagin.'

MOLOCH: And now he says?

BOLLIGREW: Now 'e says e's ravaged it! There's nothin' more to eat there, and he's hungry.

MOLOCH: Hungry. I like it less and less, you know. And in his letter he proposes?

50

BOLLIGREW: He proposes I should let him have half *my* half! Well I can see as far through a brick wall as the next chap. Thin end of the wedge, that is.

MOLOCH: Mmm! You do realise, Bolligrew, that a spell against a Dragon would be expensive?

BOLLIGREW: Oh yes.

MOLOCH: I mean really very expensive.

BOLLIGREW: Bound to be. Not far short of ten quid, I was thinkin'.

MOLOCH: (*Amused.*) Ten pounds? Twenty-five. Guineas.

BOLLIGREW: All right. Done.

(*They shake hands. MOLOCH paces away considering.*)

BLACKHEART: Tricky situation, eh?

MOLOCH: (*With a patronising smile.*) I dare say we shall think of something, Squire. This Oblong. Unselfish? Gentle? High principles? Nice with the kiddies? Kind to animals? In short, a *good* man.

BLACKHEART: Sickenin'. He talks to animals.

MOLOCH: And they understand him?

BOLLIGREW: Seem to.

MOLOCH: Then he's very good. Unless like me he's very bad. Which isn't very likely. Excellent. Dragons like good men.

BLACKHEART: Do they?

MOLOCH: Yes, they have a flavour all of their own. Gentlemen, if the Dragon were to eat Sir Oblong, this would dispose of Sir Oblong, – pretty finally – and I don't think we need anticipate any very fevered reaction from the mainland. For a Knight Errant to be eaten is an occupational risk and common enough.

BLACKHEART: Right!

MOLOCH: If Sir Oblong had previously been treated with some reliable dragon poison – well that would dispose of the Dragon, would it not?

BLACKHEART: I must say, Moloch, when you clever fellers put on your thinkin' caps – it's a treat to listen to yer.

MOLOCH: Thank you Squire. It remains to effect a meeting between the Dragon and our victim.

BOLLIGREW: Yes it does! 'Cause I tell you Moloch, if once that beast sets foot in my half of the island...!

MOLOCH: No no, the victim will go to him. Either you as my client, or I as your consultant, will say: 'Oblong, at such an hour on such a day, be off to the Dragon's den' and off he will go.

BLACKHEART: Will he? Why?

MOLOCH: Because, my dear Squire, he will be under a spell; another rather expensive spell I'm afraid, Baron, the ingredients are very costly, very rare – snake's feet, fishfeathers, things of that sort – shall we say another twenty-five?

BOLLIGREW: Another twent...! That's fifty quid!

MOLOCH: Guineas. Bolligrew, in mine as any other profession, cheap is cheap – and your Dragon is no fool.

BLACKHEART: Somethin' in that you know.

BOLLIGREW: (*Venomously.*) All right. Agreed.

MOLOCH: Very wise. (*To the STORYTELLER.*) I shall need a small basket of apples.

STORYTELLER: I have them here, Doctor. (*He produces a basket of apples from the wings.*)

MOLOCH: These will do nicely. And now I need Sir Oblong.

STORYTELLER: (*Gravely.*) Yes Doctor, I know. (*He starts to go, then turns.*) Doctor...

MOLOCH: Well?

STORYTELLER: Are you sure you want this?

MOLOCH: You are, I think, the Storyteller?

STORYTELLER: Yes.

MOLOCH: Then you know what's going to happen in the story?

STORYTELLER: Yes, that's why I...

MOLOCH: (*Holding up his hand.*) You're certain you know what's going so happen.

STORYTELLER: Quite certain.

MOLOCH: That must give you a pleasant feeling of superiority. However, if you're quite certain you know what will happen, whatever it is will happen quite certainly.

STORYTELLER: Yes.

MOLOCH: (*Shrill.*) Then what is the good of asking me if I *want* it to happen? Like everyone else, so far as I'm able, I'll *do* what I want.

STORYTELLER: Just so, Doctor.

MOLOCH: Then, Sir Oblong?

(*The STORYTELLER exits.*)

The path to Hell is paved with good intentions. It must be very soggy underfoot. (*He turns briskly and calls.*) Mazeppa!

(*MAZEPPA, a magpie, carrying a box, books and a wand, enters behind the others.*)

BLACKHEART: Eh!

BOLLIGREW: Magpie! (*He raises his gun.*)

(*MOLOCH stamps his foot and points an imperious finger. There is a magnesium flash, the gun flies from BOLLIGREW's hand, who shakes as if from an electric shock.*)

Wh-wh-wh-wa-wa-what the bl-up-lu-blazes...

MOLOCH: (*Indifferently.*) Mazeppa my dear, prepare the ground for the mortification of apples while I look up the incantation.

(*MAZEPPA takes some chalk from the box and draws a complex caballistic pattern on floor, while MOLOCH consults a book.*)

You have had a narrow escape, Bolligrew, Mazeppa is my familiar. The bird is priceless and took years to train. Had you shot him I should probably have lost my temper and done something irreversible to you. Yes, here we are. Is all ready, Mazeppa?

MAZEPPA: Ready, Master.

(*MAZEPPA hands the wand to MOLOCH, receiving from him the book from which he reads in a low croaking monotone, circling round the pattern in which the apple is placed.*)

Bumbly-wumbly, peejly-weejly. Weejly-peejly bumbly wumbly, etc...

MOLOCH: (*Over MAZEPPA, and much clearer.*)

That Oblong with his own last breath

May be the means of Dragon's death,

Lord of Darkness hear the plea
Of Beelzebub Moloch, Phd!

Rosy apple, healthy fruit
Of healthy tree with healthy root,
I call down by magic art
The unqualified canker of the heart.

I summon up my utmost might
And plant in you the invisible blight.
That he who tastes may wish for more
Taste sweet and sound, AND HAVE NO CORE!

(*A thin column of smoke rises from the apple, as MOLOCH applies the wand to it.*)
Splendid. Clean up, Mazeppa, and make the usual entry in the journal.
(*The others come cautiously forward and peer warily at the apple.*)
It's quite safe gentlemen; what you saw was merely the virtue leaving it. *But* – any person who eats so much as one bite of this apple, becomes instant Dragon poison.

BLACKHEART: Well I call that dashed ingenious.
(*MAZEPPA exits with his props.*)

MOLOCH: A simple process, Squire, but effective. Our next task is more difficult. In order to bring Oblong in our power, I need from him some dearly prized possession.

BLACKHEART: Oblong's got no prized possessions.

BOLLIGREW: Yes 'e 'as. That purple mantle!

BLACKHEART: (*Evidently touched on the raw.*) Ah!

MOLOCH: He prizes it?

BLACKHEART: (*Resentfully.*) 'E prizes it all right. Swaggerin' up an down the 'Igh Street…

BOLLIGREW: Never takes it off!

MOLOCH: We must persuade him to.

BLACKHEART: (*Looking off.*) 'E's 'ere.

MOLOCH: I must have that mantle.
(*OBLONG enters.*)

OBLONG: Good evening, Baron.

BOLLIGREW: 'Evening, Oblong! What brings you up here?

OBLONG: I have a serious complaint to make.

BOLLIGREW: (*Listening intently.*) Oh?

(*BOLLIGREW signs to BLACKHEART, who goes behind
OBLONG and clumsily tries to detach his mantle.*)

OBLONG: Obidiah Bobblenob has been placed in the
stocks on the village green.

BOLLIGREW: Has he?

OBLONG: He has. And your men at arms are pelting him
with treacle pies. Hot, treacle pies.

BOLLIGREW: Are they now?

OBLONG: They have, as I expect you know... (*He spins
round and draws his sword.*) Blackheart, what are you about?

MOLOCH: (*Hastily coming forward; benign, ecclesiastical.*) Is it
Oblong fitz Oblong?

OBLONG: Er, well, yes.

MOLOCH: Let me take your hand sir. In these degenerate
days, a real Knight Errant of the good old school – a
privilege. My name is Innocent, Doctor Innocent, Dean
of Divinity and unworthy Professor of Goodness at the
University.

OBLONG: (*Respectfully.*) Oh. A privilege so meet *you* sir.

MOLOCH: Er – (*He draws OBLONG aside.*) – you're having
a wonderful effect here you know.

OBLONG: Things are a little better than they were I suppose.

MOLOCH: Wonderfully better, wonderfully. And you know
– (*Very confidential.*) – you're beginning to have an effect
on our friend here.

OBLONG: Bolligrew?

MOLOCH: I know. But I have been poor Jasper's spiritual
adviser many years now – stony ground, Sir Oblong,
stony ground – but there's good in the man, oh yes. And
you have set it in motion, where I failed.

OBLONG: Well I should like to think so.

MOLOCH: (*To BOLLIGREW.*) My son...

BOLLIGREW: Er, yes, Father?

MOLOCH: I want you to go and release that poor fellow
from the stocks.

BOLLIGREW: Oh. Er, very well, Father. (*He starts to go.*)

MOLOCH: And humbly beg his pardon.

BOLLIGREW: Eh?

MOLOCH: As an act of repentance. You will feel the better for it, won't he, Sir Oblong? (*He nods vigorously at BOLLIGREW behind OBLONG's back.*)

OBLONG: You will, Bolligrew, honestly.

BOLLIGREW: Oh. Well. If *you* say so, Oblong. (*To BLACKHEART.*) Comn' repentin' then? (*BLACKHEART and BOLLIGREW exit.*)

OBLONG: I must say that's very gratifying.

MOLOCH: A great gift of yours, this, Sir Oblong. Mightier than the sword I do assure you.

OBLONG: Doctor, you make me ashamed.

MOLOCH: No no. Yours is a noble calling. Ah, this is the famous purple mantle. A prized possession I imagine.

OBLONG: I must confess it is.

MOLOCH: And rightly so. Dear, dear, it's torn.

OBLONG: It's a hurly-burly sort of life, Doctor.

MOLOCH: (*Trying to take the mantle.*) Let me repair it.

OBLONG: Oh no – (*Alarmed.*) – really...

MOLOCH: (*Desisting; with a silvery chuckle.*) The workman is worthy of his hire. I was at one time, Abbot of St Clare's and there our daily task was the repair and manufacture of – oh, church vestments, altar-cloths, exquisite work; I often regret those quiet days with the needle. (*He unfastens OBLONG's mantle.*) And you will give much pleasure to a foolish old man in the evening of his days.

OBLONG: But I never – (*Faltering under MOLOCH's gentle gaze.*) never take it off – really...?

MOLOCH: (*Wagging a roguish finger.*) Never take it off, Sir Oblong. Do I detect a little vanity at work? A last little flicker of worldly pride?

OBLONG: (*Relinquishing it.*) I shall value it the more for your attention.

MOLOCH: Well! Oh – before I go, sir, let me press you to an apple. I always bring a basket for Jasper. I grow them myself in the college garden. Do tell me what you think. (*He hands OBLONG the enchanted apple.*)

(*OBLONG bites.*)

Good?

OBLONG: It's perfect!

MOLOCH: Well, you if anyone should know perfection –
even in an apple.

OBLONG: (*Delighted, deprecating.*) Oh, doctor...

MOLOCH: No false modesty I beg. (*He starts to go, then
turns.*) Let Oblong put his faith in Oblong's goodness,
and Oblong is invincible.

(*MOLOCH exits. The STORYTELLER enters.*)

OBLONG: That excellent old man came just in time!

STORYTELLER: Indeed?

OBLONG: Indeed. I was in danger of adopting violent and
even underhand methods on this mission.

STORYTELLER: And now?

OBLONG: Now I shall rely on simple goodness.

STORYTELLER: I see. Is that wise.

OBLONG: Wise? It's right! Oh how much better to have
reformed Bolligrew than merely to have conquered him.

STORYTElLER: Have you reformed Bolligrew?

OBLONG: I've made a start. (*Beaming, excited, complacent.*)
It seems I have a gift for it.

STORYTELLER: And will you reform – the Dragon?

OBLONG: The Dragon! I say that *would* be something –
after all, I reformed Michael Magpie.

STORYTELLER: Did you now?

OBLONG: Oh yes – he used to be a thief you know...

STORYTELLER: Used to be?

(*MAGPIE enters running. He skids to a halt when he sees
them. We see behind his back the twinkling LORD MAYOR's
Chain.*)

MAGPIE: Awk!

OBLONG: (*Pleased.*) Ah – Michael – we were just –
(*Noticing MAGPIE's awkwardly innocent posture.*) Michael?

MAGPIE: Awk?

OBLONG: What have you got behind your back?

MAGPIE: Behind my back? (*Elaborately he searches the stage
behind him, passing the chain from hand to hand to keep it
hidden as he turns.*)

OBLONG: Michael!

MAGPIE: Awk! (*He shows the chain.*)

(*The STORYTELLER coughs discreetly, and looks dryly at OBLONG.*)

STORYTELLER: *Now,* what will you do? (*Quickly.*) Think, Sir Oblong.

OBLONG: Think? What is there to think about? Degenerate bird!

MAGPIE: I'm sorry Obby. 'E left it in the garden you see, and the sun was shinin' and it twinkled...

OBLONG: That was the temptation. Did you resist? You did not. It twinkled, so you took it – and there we have you in a nutshell.

MAGPIE: Awk.

OBLONG: You may well say so. (*He takes the chain.*) I am only thankful Dr Innocent has not witnessed this.

MAGPIE: Awk! Well if you ask me – there's something very fishy about that old geyser...

OBLONG: So! Not content with telling untruths, with breaking your word, with thieving – you would now plant in my mind contemptible suspicions against a fine old gentleman who was once the Abbot of St Clare's! (*The STORYTELLER makes gesture of helplessness and exits.*) Michael, it pains me to say this because there is something about you, a certain – gaiety – high spirits – which has won my affection. (*He strokes MAGPIE.*)

MAGPIE: (*Bending his neck to OBLONG's caress; softly.*) Awk...

OBLONG: (*Sharply removing his hand.*) But that is superficial! You are an unworthy instrument Michael, and until my mission is accomplished, I may not regard you as my friend.

(*OBLONG exits.*)

MAGPIE: (*Stricken.*) Awk! Obby. I won't do it again...! (*Silence. He sniffs.*) Well *I* don't care. See if I do. (*He hops about stage, jaunty and forlorn, improvising.*)

Hi diddledidee,
A Magpie's life for me,

I pinched the Lord Mayor's Chain −
An I 'spect I'll do it again −
I'm happy and I'm free −
A Magpie's life...

(*His voice tails unhappily.*) Oh dash it! Obby? (*He stumps off, tearful and aggrieved.*) It *twinkled*! I *like* twinkly things! *I* can't help it...!
(*MAGPIE exits. As he is doing so, MAZEPPA, MOLOCH, BLACKHEART and BOLLIGREW enter from the opposite side. MAZEPPA carries a screen and a box. The lights dim. The air is tense. ALL keep their voices low. They stop centre stage, and ALL look towards MOLOCH.*)

MOLOCH: Twilight. I can now perform the spell to make one person subject to another. The screen, Mazeppa.
(*MAZEPPA erects the screen and carries the box inside, while MOLOCH stands tense and listening.*)

BOLLIGREW: Er, Moloch...

MOLOCH: Sh...!

BOLLIGREW: What?

MOLOCH: I want to hear an owl cry and a church clock strike the hour.
(*Instantly, a distant bell chimes, and an owl shrieks nearby.*)
Excellent. (*Moving towards the screen.*) Prized possession, Bolligrew.

BOLLIGREW: Moloch, I want to watch this.

MOLOCH: Watch? This is Grimbleboots, probably the most powerful spell in the civilised world − it is certainly the most secret.

BOLLIGREW: I want to watch.

MOLOCH: Out of the question.

BOLLIGREW: In that case, Moloch, I'll ask you for a little demonstration.

MOLOCH: Demonstration?

BOLLIGREW: That's it. Pop this in with the other prized possession, will you? (*He produces BLACKHEART's black plume from under his jacket, and gives it to MOLOCH, sweetly.*) Just to make sure I'm gettin' me money's worth, you know.

MOLOCH: Bolligrew, I find you offensive.

BOLLIGREW: Aye, most chaps do.

(*MOLOCH goes behind the screen; BLACKHEART turns.*)

BLACKHEART: 'Ave they started?

BOLLIGREW: Just goin' to.

(*Together they regard the screen.*)

BLACKHEART: (*Wistful.*) I envy these brainy blokes, Bolligrew. Must make life deuced interestin'.

(*BOLLIGREW gives an unsympathetic grunt.*)

MOLOCH: *Quiet,* please gentleman!

(*There is a short pause. Then, in the dispassionate manner of surgeons, aeroplane pilots or other practised technicians.*) Retort?

MAZEPPA: (*Overlapping.*) Retort.

MOLOCH: Burner?

MAZEPPA: Burner.

MOLOCH: Essay.

(*A thin column of illuminated pink smoke rises. MOLOCH and MAZEPPA, overlap as before.*)

Trim-spickle-tickle, trim-spickle-tickle, trim-spickle-tickle, trim-spickle-tickle, trim-spickly-wickly! Grimbleboots!

MAZEPPA: Grimbleboots.

MOLOCH: Portent?

MAZEPPA: Portent.

MOLOCH: Presto!

(*There is a soft explosion and a billowing cloud of blue smoke, brightly lit: also twangings and bashings of cymbals and harps on the loudspeaker.*)

BLACKHEART: Fascinatin'.

BOLLIGREW: Yes. Needs to be, for fifty quid.

MOLOCH: Prognostication?

MAZEPPA: Possible.

MOLOCH: Proceed.

(*Accompanied by more effects on the loudspeaker, overlapping.*)

Scrambled-shambles, pickled-winkles, frightening-lightning eevil-weevil, Knight's a nuisance, Knight's a mess; what he has is his alone and won't be Bolligrew's *unless* –

MAZEPPA: – won't be Bolligrew*'s unless* –

BLACKHEART: (*Nudging BOLLIGREW.*) 'Mentioned you then, old man.

BOLLIGREW: Shut up.

MOLOCH: (*With rising excitement.*) Shamble's scrambled –

MAZEPPA: (*With rising excitement.*) Winkle's pickled –

MOLOCH: Lightning frightens –

MAZEPPA: Weevil's evil –

BOTH: By powers of unhappiness!

MAZEPPA: (*Crying out.*) Misery!

MOLOCH: (*Crying out.*) Poverty!

MAZEPPA: Woe!

MOLOCH: (*Screaming.*) Precipitation!
(*Frantic twangings and bashings on the loudspeaker, a geyser of sparks, coloured balls, magnesium streamers, a cloud of smoke. MOLOCH emerges with the mantle.*)

BLACKHEART: First class show, Doctor. Never seen anythin' like it! Can I 'ave a squint be'ind the scenes?

MOLOCH: By all means, Squire.
(*BLACKHEART goes behind the screen. MOLOCH hands the mantle and plume to BOLLIGREW.*)

BOLLIGREW: Don't look any different to me, Moloch.

MOLOCH: I should hope not indeed. The prized possession must be returned to its owner. Only if he accepts it is he in your power.

BOLLIGREW: Oh. (*Calling.*) Blackheart!

BLACKHEART: (*Emerging.*) Terrible smell in there. Yes, old man? Me plume! Where d'you get it?

BOLLIGREW: Oh, feller picked it up somewhere. D'you want it?

BLACKHEART: (*Taking the plume.*) I should say. (*Jamming it into socket of his helmet.*) Felt 'alf naked without me plume.

MOLOCH: He is in our power, Squire…

BLACKHEART: Yes?

MOLOCH: Sit down!
(*BLACKHEART startled, collapses instantly.*)

BLACKHEART: (*Agreeably.*) Like that?

MOLOCH: Get up.

(*BLACKHEART levitates.*)

Can you dance?

BLACKHEART: Dance? Lor' no!

MOLOCH: Try.

(*A minuet is heard on the speaker. BLACKHEART dances.
BOLLIGREW is enchanted.*)

BOLLIGREW: 'Ere – 'ere – let me 'ave a go – Black'eart!

(*BLACKHEART stops.*)

BLACKHEART: Yes old man?

(*BOLLIGREW struggles with the wealth of possibility.*)

BOLLIGREW: (*In a moment of inspiration.*) Be a teapot!

(*BLACKHEART stands on one leg, one arm cranked forward
as the spout, the other crooked behind him as the handle.*)

MOLOCH: Enough, Baron?

BOLLIGREW: (*His smile fading.*) Not quite, Moloch.

Blackheart – (*He points.*) – off to the Dragon's den.

BLACKHEART: Dragon's den, old man?

BOLLIGREW: That's right, old man.

BLACKHEART: Oh. All right.

(*BLACKHEART exits, clanking.*)

BOLLIGREW: 'Ee's goin'!

MOLOCH: Yes, you'd better stop him.

BOLLIGREW: Blackheart!

(*BLACKHEART enters.*)

BLACKHEART: Yes old man?

BOLLIGREW: 'Ang on. (*To MOLOCH; delighted.*) 'E does it
all quite willing, don't 'e?

MOLOCH: Oh, the victim does not know he is a victim.
A small refinement of my own. Tell him to remove the
prized possession.

BOLLIGREW: (*To BLACKHEART.*) Take your plume off.

(*A magic effect on the loudspeaker. BLACKHEART takes off
the plume, shudders and 'comes to'.*)

BLACKHEART: Well if you ask me, Bolligrew that was in
dashed poor taste!

MOLOCH: Mazeppa, take the Squire's plume and burn it.
And Mazeppa, kindly make your entry in the journal with
more care. The one for this morning is barely legible.

MAZEPPA: Yes, Master.

(*MAZEPPA exits with his props.*)

MOLOCH: Now let's see where we are: Oblong has eaten the apple – which makes him dragon poison. You have the prized possession – which gives you power to send him *to* the dragon. It remains to enquire of the Dragon when he would like to dine.

BOLLIGREW: Aye. Right.

BLACKHEART: Er. You goin' to the Dragon's den, old man?

BOLLIGREW: That's right, Black'eart an' you're comin' with me.

BLACKHEART: Oh. When?

BOLLIGREW: Now.

(*BLACKHEART, MOLOCH and BOLLIGREW turn their backs on the audience and freeze, as the lights dim further and the STORYTELLER enters.*)

STORYTELLER: The Dragon lived in a black and silent valley which had once been green with pasture. His den looked like a railway tunnel without any signals or track. (*A black backdrop descends to cover the church, with a black archway in it.*) Those who had seen him, by moonlight, knew that he was bigger than four carthorses, and sleek, and black, and shiny. Like all black dragons he seldom came out except at night, because his eyes were weak. And in the day, these eyes were all that could be seen of him. (*Red eyes are switched on in the blackness of the arch.*) And all that could be heard of him was an occasional roar – (*The DRAGON roars on the loudspeaker.*) And an occasional complaint; for the Dragon was always discontented, and talked to himself continually.

DRAGON: (*On the loudspeaker throughout his voice is languorous, upper-class, sinister.*) I'm bored... There's no avoiding it; I'm thoroughly bored...

BLACKHEART: Look 'ere, Bolligrew. You see I've just remembered a pressin' engagement.

BOLLIGREW: Well forget it again.

(*BOLLIGREW draws BLACKHEART upstage towards the tunnel. The STORYTELLER exits.*)

Hello? Afternoon! Anyone at 'ome?

DRAGON: Do I hear the voice of a human bean?

(*On the loudspeaker, a noise between that of approaching train and cantering horse; the eyes grow larger.*)

BOLLIGREW: It's me! Bolligrew!

(*Clatter of hooves, squeal of brakes. Hiss. Smoke curls from the tunnel roof.*)

DRAGON: Oh – Bolligrew! Is that Moloch?

BOLLIGREW: Dragon, we're a bit pressed for time. This proposal of yours for takin' over half of my half of the Island…

DRAGON: Yes?

BOLLIGREW: Seems quite reasonable to me.

DRAGON: It does? That's odd! Baron, there are no *strings* attached to this, are there?

(*BOLLIGREW reels out of the Dragon's sight, mopping his brow with his handkerchief.*)

BOLLIGREW: (*Shakily.*) Strings, old chap? Don't know what you mean!

DRAGON: Moloch. *You* haven't anything up your smelly old sleeve, have you?

MOLOCH: A reasonable suspicion, Dragon, but the answer happens to be 'no'. There's something we want you to do.

DRAGON: That's better. What?

BOLLIGREW: Well, it's about this feller Oblong. I don't know if you've heard…

DRAGON: I have heard, yes.

BOLLIGREW: Well we were wonderin', if he happened to come wanderin' over 'ere, if you might like to, er, well – nosh im!

DRAGON: But Baron, people *don't* wander over here.

MOLOCH: He will Dragon, he will. We are using Grimbleboots. He will come very quietly – if you wish it, *without* his sword.

DRAGON: Understand. Is he a good man?

MOLOCH: All the way through I think. I shall be
   interested to hear.

DRAGON: Well. That's worth waiting for.

MOLOCH: Tomorrow then, at three o'clock?

DRAGON: Tomorrow at three.

BOLLIGREW: There we are then! Good-bye old chap!

DRAGON: Good-bye Baron, good-bye…

   (*The eye-lights go off. The backcloth flies up to reveal the
   church. MOLOCH, BOLLIGREW and BLACKHEART
   freeze until OBLONG enters. The lights come up again.*)

MOLOCH: Ah, there you are, sir. We have been all over
   the Island looking for you. Here's your mended mantle.

OBLONG: Oh thank you. Doctor.

MOLOCH: Turn around sir, and I'll put it on.

   (*OBLONG does so, but just before MOLOCH can clip it on
   his back, OBLONG moves away and turns.*)

OBLONG: I wonder if I should? You're right you know –
   it's only vanity and worldly pride.

   (*Consternation among the conspirators. MOLOCH recovers.*)

MOLOCH: Come sir, don't be solemn. I spoke in jest!

OBLONG: Oh.

   (*The others give an uneasy laugh. OBLONG moves back and
   MOLOCH tries again – but once more OBLONG moves
   away.*)

   Many true words spoken in jest, Doctor.

MOLOCH: (*Rather severely.*) I shall begin to think so. Did
   Gallahad refuse his suit of snow white armour?

BOLLIGREW: Yes.

MOLOCH: No. But Oblong will affect to be unworthy of
   his purple robe. Here's a vanity indeed.

OBLONG: Oh.

   (*MOLOCH and OBLONG repeat the same procedure.*)

   As a gesture of humility, you mean.

MOLOCH: Precisely.

   (*OBLONG nods, and is put into the mantle. He is struck by
   their sudden tension.*)

OBLONG: Gentlemen?

BOLLIGREW: 'Ow d'you feel?

OBLONG: (*Puzzled.*) Thank you Baron, the best of
    health…?
MOLOCH: (*Points.*) Oblong. Sit down.
    (*OBLONG sits.*)
BLACKHEART: Stand up.
    (*OBLONG obeys.*)
BOLLIGREW: On your knees.
    (*OBLONG obeys. They loom over him.*)
    Well now, you are going to be my guest at the castle for
    a day.
OBLONG: Oh, thank you.
BOLLIGREW: Don't mention is. At three o'clock tomorrow
    you are going to the Dragon's den.
OBLONG: (*Pleasantly.*) The Dragon's den?
MOLOCH: Just a social call you know.
BOLLIGREW: So leave your sword outside.
OBLONG: My sword? (*He seems to struggle for a moment.*)
    Whatever you say, Baron.
BOLLIGREW: That's it *exactly* – whatever I say. Stand up.
    Now cut down to the castle, introduce yourself to the
    butler, an' e'll show you straight to your dungeon.
OBLONG: Then I'll say *au revoir*.
BOLLIGREW: You say that.
OBLONG: *Au revoir.*
    (*OBLONG exits, BLACKHEART and BOLLIGREW watch
    him, off, fascinated.*)
BLACKHEART: 'E hasn't a clue, 'as 'e?
BOLLIGREW: Not a blazin' clue! (*Turning.*) An' will he go
    off, just like that, to the Dragon's den?
MOLOCH: At three o'clock tomorrow, just like that; no
    power on earth can stop him!
    (*BOLLIGREW, MOLOCH and BLACKHEART exit. The
    STORYTELLER enters.*)
STORYTELLER: Now, while all this was happening on the
    Island, back on the mainland the Duke and his Knights
    in armour –
    (*The STORYTELLER breaks off as the DUKE and
    KNIGHTS enter, some trundling the Round Table, others,*)

crossing them, pushing off the Church. They all sit at the table and freeze.)
– the Knights in armour were finding that the programme outlined by the Duke, and which they had so much looked forward to, was less enjoyable than they had thought.

DUKE: *(Heavily.)* Anything on the agenda, Juniper?

JUNIPER: *(Opening the minute book.)* The menu for Your Grace's birthday party; er, meringues, raspberry jelly, pickled shrimps, ginger snaps and lemonade.
(Murmur of boredom and discontent.)
(Snappishly.) If any of you gentlemen can think of something better...!

DUKE: No. No. That will do as well as anything – I suppose.
(Looking round.) Any other business?

TRUMPINGTON: There's a *rumour* going round that there's a dragon –
(On the word 'Dragon' there is a stir of interest all round.)
– down Little Gidding way.

STRONGBODY: I've seen it, gentlemen. 'T's not a dragon. 'T's a big lizard.
(ALL slump again.)

SMOOTHE: Anyone know anything about this damsel in distress at East Coker?
(ALL stir with interest again.)

FIRST KNIGHT: Went over yesterday, gentlemen. No more distressed than I am.
(ALL slump again.)
Deucedly plain girl she was, too...

JUNIPER: Well *(He sighs.)* that seems to be all, then.
(Shutting the minute book.) Musical bumps?

DUKE: Might as well.
(Music on the loudspeaker. The KNIGHTS and the DUKE tramp gloomily round the stage in a circle. Each time the music stops the KNIGHTS carefully allow the DUKE to seat himself first, then compete among themselves. The DUKE calls out the losers.)
Trumpington! Dachwood! Graceless!

(*And so on, until only the DUKE and SMOOTHE are left. The music stops, SMOOTHE assists the DUKE to the floor, where he remains, gloomily.*)

You're out Smoothe.

(*SMOOTHE returns to the table. There is a flutter of half-hearted applause from the KNIGHTS.*)

DUKE: What's the prize?

SMOOTHE: (*Bringing a box of chocolates from the wings.*) Chocolates, your Grace. (*He sits.*)

DUKE: (*Remaining on the floor.*) Don't know how it is, gentlemen. Musical bumps – hasn't got the same excitement, somehow. Nor chocolates.

FIRST KNIGHT: Not like it was in Oblong's day.

STRONGBODY: Ah.

TRUMPINGTON. Always plenty goin' on then.

DUKE: One thing after another.

JUNIPER: Best man we ever had.

FIRST KNIGHT: First class.

SMOOTHE: (*Uncomfortably.*) Oh, capital.

DUKE: (*From the floor.*) That was a dirty trick you played on Oblong, Smoothe.

SMOOTHE: Well, really!

DUKE: You thought of it.

FIRST KNIGHT: Wonder how he's gettin' on there.

STRONGBODY: (*Enviously.*) Up to his neck in it, I bet.

FIRST KNIGHT: Deuced if I don't go and see!

TRUMPINGTON: Make a change.

SMOOTHE: It would.

STRONGBODY: Hanged if I don't come with you!

SMOOTHE: So will I!

TRUMPINGTON: Me too!

JUNIPER: And me!

(*There is an excited babble; all sitting forward. The DUKE follows all this jealously then rises.*)

DUKE: Gentlemen!

(*Silence.*)

An excellent suggestion, but there won't be cabin-space for more than two – and I have had in mind for some time now to pay a State Visit to the Bolligrew Islands.

FIRST KNIGHT: (*Sotto voce.*) Well, really…!

SMOOTHE: (*Smoothly.*) I remember Your Grace mentioned that to me the other day.

DUKE: (*Surprised.*) Did I? Yes I believe I did. Smoothe, you can come with me.

SMOOTHE: Very civil of you, sir.

DUKE: I think that's all gentlemen. Meeting adjourned.

FIRST KNIGHT: Well I'll be jiggered.

(*The KNIGHTS exit with the Round Table. The DUKE addresses the STORYTELLER.*)

DUKE: Would you have my galleon got ready please?

STORYTELLER: It's ready now Your Grace.

(*The CAPTAIN enters, as before, but now his sail is purple.*)

DUKE: (*Nervously.*) If you could arrange for the weather to be better than it usually is…?

STORYTELLER: It's always the same for *that* voyage, Your Grace.

DUKE: No matter. It's not my way to be deflected from the path of duty by a little wind and rain.

STORYTELLER: No, Your Grace.

(*SMOOTHE enters with an umbrella. The DUKE 'boards the galleon'. SMOOTHE assists. Thunder and lightning crash as the 'boat' moves. BOLLIGREW and BLACKHEART enter on the opposite side.*)

BOLLIGREW: Well Black'eart, today's the day – at three o'clock this afternoon our troubles will be ov…

(*Thunder and lightning. The DUKE is seasick upstage. presenting his posterior, SMOOTHE is solicitous.*)

'Ello? Must be someone comin'!

(*BLACKHEART scans the DUKE through a telescope.*)

BLACKHEART: Oh yes. Must be somebody important.

BOLLIGREW: Oh?

BLACKHEART: Purple sails.

BOLLIGREW: Purp…? (*He snatches the telescope.*) Ber-lazes! It's the Duke!

BLACKHEART: 'Oo?

BOLLIGREW: The Duke! I'd know that face anywhere.

BLACKHEART: Ah. Duke, eh?

BOLLIGREW: Yes! 'E's comin' to see Oblong!

BLACKHEART: (*Nodding savagely.*) Very likely.

BOLLIGREW: So 'ow can we feed Oblong to the dragon?

BLACKHEART: Oh. We can't then.

BOLLIGREW: That's right, Blackheart we can't. And what's
Dragon goin' to do if we don't? I'll tell you what 'e's goin'
to do Blackheart – 'e's goin' to ravage – indiscriminate!
Whackin' great black dragon, ragin' up an' down the 'Igh
Street like as not, roarin for 'is nosh – as promised 'im,
Blackheart by you an' me – 'an that's goin' to take a bit of
explainin' too, isn't it?

BLACKHEART: Well what are we goin' to do then?

BOLLIGREW: *I* don't know! (*Mumbling to himself.*) What
are we goin' to do? (*Roaring at the audience.*) What are we
– goin' – to (*Breaking off as he sees the STORYTELLER.*)
'Ere, you, what do we do?

STORYTELLER: You consult Dr Moloch.

BOLLIGREW: Moloch!

BLACKHEART: Moloch!

BOLLIGREW: (*Calling.*) Moloch!

(*MOLOCH enters behind BOLLIGREW.*)

MOLOCH: Yes?

BOLLIGREW: Look.

(*MOLOCH scans the Duke. SMOOTHE, the CAPTAIN and
the DUKE exit.*)

MOLOCH: Dear, dear. This is an unexpected complication.

BOLLIGREW: Unexpected comp...? It's a blazin' disaster!

MOLOCH: On the contrary, a golden opportunity.

BOLLIGREW: You thought of somethin'?

MOLOCH: I have thought of a way whereby we can send
Oblong to the Dragon, and send the Duke away well
satisfied with matters here. I should not be surprised if
he conferred a Knighthood on the Squire, and on
yourself, the order of the golden artichoke.

BOLLIGREW/BLACKHEART: (*Advancing; fascinated.*) Eh?
What? 'Ow?

MOLOCH: You wish a consultation?

BOLLIGREW: 'Ow much?

MOLOCH: My consultation fee is fifteen guineas.

BOLLIGREW: Make it quids.

MOLOCH: Guineas. The Duke will be here in half an hour.

BOLLIGREW: All right – guineas!

MOLOCH: Then listen to my plot...

(*BOLLIGREW and BLACKHEART come close to MOLOCH. They all put their heads together and stand conspiratorially, with their backs to the audience.*)

STORYTELLER: It was a very wicked plan which Doctor Moloch outlined –

(*They all glance round balefully and suspiciously at the audience, then huddle again.*)

– as you shall shortly see.

(*The plotters break up, guffawing.*)

MOLOCH: So Baron, if I can handle Oblong, can you handle The Duke?

BOLLIGREW: Leave that to me – I know these bigwigs. Corporal!

(*The CORPORAL enters, running.*)

CORPORAL: Me lord?

BOLLIGREW: Duke's comin'. Turn out the population. Everyone wearin' 'is best clothes, Corporal – don't want no ostentatious poverty you understand.

CORPORAL: Yes melord.

BOLLIGREW: Issue 'em with shoes, an' everyone to 'ave one packet of paper streamers. Right gettit done. Lord Mayor!

(*The CORPORAL exits, running; the LORD MAYOR enters, running.*)

LORD MAYOR: Baron?

BOLLIGREW: Got those flags we 'ad for the Coronation?

LORD MAYOR: Yes Baron?

BOLLIGREW: Gettem up, Duke's comin'. Cook!

(*The LORD MAYOR exits, running; the COOK enters, running.*)

COOK: My lord?

BOLLIGREW: Duke's comin'. Grade one banquet, twelve o'clock sharp. Orchestra!

(*The COOK exits, running; a DRUMMER and a CYMBALIST enter, running. They meet the COOK with a thud and a crash.*)

Duke's comin'. We'll want the National Anthem an' somethin' jolly. Tune up.

(*The MUSICIANS tune noisily, augmented by the loudspeaker. The PEASANTS enter, carrying shoes. The CORPORAL follows.*)

CORPORAL: Lef-ri lef-ri lef-ri lef-riii – Alt! Siddown. Put yer shoes on. Other foot stupid!

(*The LORD MAYOR enters, backing, calling off.*)

LORD MAYOR: Lower away then! Lower away! Thank you!

(*Strings of coloured flags descend.*)

CORPORAL: On yer feet!

(*The PEASANTS rise, the CORPORAL salutes.*)

Ready me lord!

MOLOCH: Now then. (*Raising his hand.*) Oblong, by the power of Grimbleboots, be here.

(*OBLONG enters, followed unobtrusively by OBIDIAH and MAGPIE.*)

OBLONG: Good morning, Doctor, Baron. What's all this?

MOLOCH: The Duke has come to see you.

OBLONG: Oh how kind of His Grace!

MOLOCH: Yes. Sir Oblong, when you *meet* the Duke, you are to...

OBLONG: I am to what?

MOLOCH: Disgrace yourself.

OBLONG: Disgrace myself? How?

MOLOCH: Well there I thought that you might help me...

BOLLIGREW: Pitch a brick through the Lord Mayor's window.

MOLOCH: (*Hastily.*) No no. That's wildly out of character. If you did that His Grace might think that you had been bewitched!

OBLONG: (*With a deprecating chuckle.*) Good heavens, that would never do!

MOLOCH: No. Have you ever in *fact* done anything disgraceful?

OBLONG: Oh yes.

MOLOCH: What?

OBLONG: Er…

MOLOCH: …you haven't have you?

OBLONG: I do keep myself on a pretty tight rein, I suppose.

MOLOCH: Aha! I knew you'd have the answer! You have kept yourself on a tight rein now for – what? Fifty years?

OBLONG: Thereabouts.

MOLOCH: High time you let yourself go. Oblong, when you meet the Duke you will simply – let yourself go.

OBLONG: But what shall I do if I let myself go?

MOLOCH: You will do all those things which all those years you have wanted to do and have restrained yourself from doing.

OBLONG: (*With a roguish chuckle.*) Oh dear…

MOLOCH: Yes. Off you go then till you're wanted.
(*OBLONG starts to go, then turns.*)

OBLONG: Oh. At three o'clock I have an appointment with the Dragon you know.

MOLOCH: There'll just be nice time. Off with you now. The watchword is: 'Let yourself go'.

BOLLIGREW/MOLOCH/BLACKHEART: (*Softly, in unison.*) Let yourself go.

OBLONG: Well we *are* going to have an eventful day.
(*OBLONG exits. A MAN-AT-ARMS enters.*)

MAN-AT-ARMS: Duke's galleon comin' round the 'eadland now me lord!

BOLLIGREW: Right! Duke's comin'! Everybody-y-y – SMILE!
(*The drum and cymbals strike up. BOLLIGREW exits in march step, followed by ALL except OBIDIAH, MAGPIE and the STORYTELLER.*)

OBIDIAH: What d'you think of that then?

MAGPIE: What do I think? I think – witchcraft!
(*Boom of cannon and cheering on the loudspeaker.*)

STORYTELLER: The cannon fired, the people cheered, and the Duke's private galleon sailed majestically into the harbour. And then for miles around the loyal people of the Island stood smartly to attention as the band struck up – the National Anthem!

(*'Colonel Bogey' on the loudspeaker. OBIDIAH and STORYTELLER stand rigid. MAGPIE idly scratches himself until called to order by OBIDIAH, scandalised. More cheering, then 'The Lincolnshire Poacher' and a grand entrance of PEASANTS, MEN-AT-ARMS, the DUKE, BOLLIGREW, the BAND, SMOOTHE, BLACKHEART, MOLOCH and MAZEPPA. The PEASANTS are prodded by the MEN-AT-ARMS, cheerin' and throwing paper streamers over the DUKE, who is enchanted.*)

DUKE: Thank you good people! Thank you! Thank you! Well I must say, Bolligrew, I hadn't expected anything like this!

BOLLIGREW: Their own idea Your Grace. I told them Your Grace wouldn't expect any ceremony, but they would turn out. Of course Your Grace is very popular in the Islands.

DUKE: Well that's very nice, very nice. I must say Bolligrew, your people look well cared for.

BOLLIGREW: Now you couldn't 'ave said anythin' which would give me greater pleasure. That's always been my way: anythin' for the people. That's a leaf I took out of Your Grace's book I don't mind admittin'.

DUKE: Well I never. Bolligrew I'm agreeably surprised. I'd been given to understand that you were a – well rather a *bad* Baron?

BOLLIGREW: (*Sadly.*) Ah yes. I've 'eard the tales they tell about me on she mainland. That church for instance, I dare say you've been told it was a ruin?

DUKE: I had, yes...

BOLLIGREW: Well there it is, there's no stoppin' idle tongues. Blackheart, I wonder where Oblong is!

DUKE: Yes. I take it somewhat amiss, Smoothe, that Oblong isn't here to meet me.

BOLLIGREW: Oh I think we 'ave to make allowances, Your Grace. At 'is time of life we must expect a little neglect of duty. I know Blackheart here has quite a soft spot for the old reprobate, haven't you?

BLACKHEART: Er. Oh. Yes. Yes, rather. Very fond of 'im, I am in a way. Bit of a bully, of course, but...

DUKE: Oblong? A bully?

BOLLIGREW: Knocks the peasants about somethin' cruel sometimes.

LORD MAYOR: (*Pushing forward; timidly desperate.*) Your Grace!

BOLLIGREW: Yes Lord Mayor?
(*Two huge MEN-AT-ARMS close in on the LORD MAYOR.*)
Got somethin' to say?

LORD MAYOR: No, my lord.

BOLLIGREW: Oh, sorry. Thought you 'ad. Lord Mayor, Your Grace, just recently appointed 'im a Magistrate. (*Ruefully.*) Independent minded little beggar. But I like the people to take part in their own government.

DUKE: Most commendable. But, Oblong...?

BOLLIGREW: He's been goin' to seed pretty rapid since he landed I'm afraid. If it isn't wine-gums it's brandy-snaps. And it takes 'im very nasty.

DUKE: Smoothe! Do you hear this?

SMOOTHE: Yes Your Grace. As Your Grace may remember, I always had my reservations about Oblong.

DUKE: You did, yes, you did.

BOLLIGREW: A good man in 'is day, I believe?

DUKE: The best I ever had!

BOLLIGREW: (*Nodding.*) My friend Doctor Innocent 'ere – 'e's a very penetratin' observer of the 'uman scene – he tells me when you're like that, you know, keepin' yourself on a very tight rein, then you're likely to go downhill very rapid if once you *let yourself go*. (*He looks off as he says this. Cheerfully.*) And 'ere 'e is! (*His expression changes.*) Oh dear, oh dear...
(*OBLONG enters, swaggering, and carrying a packet of sweets. ALL flinch, amazed.*)

OBLONG: So! You finally got here! You backsliding old gormandiser.
(*Consternation among ALL.*)

BOLLIGREW: Oh dear, oh dear, 'e's on the winegums again.

MAGPIE: (*Amazed.*) Awk!

OBLONG: Mike Magpie. How you doin', Mike? The only creature on these Islands I would care to call my friend. (*He takes a sweet from the packet.*)

BOLLIGREW: The bird is a notorious thief, Your Grace. (*SMOOTHE utters an exclamation.*)

OBLONG: Mike, meet Smoothely – Smoothe. Slippery Smoothe we used to call him. Interesting man. Give you a sound opinion on anything under the sun and sell you his mother for threepence. (*He swaggers to the DUKE.*) Well, we've put it on a bit, haven't we? (*He chuckles, prodding the DUKE's stomach.*) How many eclairs have gone into that, I wonder? Whoops-a-daisy! (*He prods again.*)

(*The DUKE rocks, pop-eyed. There is general consternation.*)

SMOOTHE: But this is scandalous! (*He turns.*) The National Anthem! Play the National Anthem!

(*Colonel Bogey plays again. ALL rigidly to attention, eyes popping as OBLONG and LORD MAYOR break gradually into a disgraceful can-can, presenting their posteriors to the DUKE, etc. The anthem stops.*)

OBLONG: (*Very excited and breathless.*) Ha! (*He snaps his fingers at the DUKE, then gathers himself. Daringly.*) Knickers! (*Everyone claps his hands over his ears. OBLONG laughs wildly and exits, followed by the LORD MAYOR. There is a general babble. The DUKE falls fainting into the arms of SMOOTHE.*)

SMOOTHE: His Grace! His Grace is Unwell! (*He lowers the DUKE to the ground.*)

BOLLIGREW: Clear the field! Clear the field! (*The PEASANTS exit, driven by MEN-AT-ARMS. MAGPIE and OBIDIAH, 'hide', behind the church. MOLOCH waves a ginger-beer bottle under the DUKE's nose.*)

MOLOCH: His Grace revives.

DUKE: (*Weakly.*) Has he gone?

SMOOTHE: Yes, Your Grace.

DUKE: (*Seizing BOLLIGREW's wrist.*) Oh, Bolligrew, this is the ruin of a noble spirit. Oblong! There never was one like him with a dragon!

BOLLIGREW: Alas, those days 'ave gone.

MOLOCH: Gone indeed. Oblong and our Dragon are on very friendly terms.

DUKE: Friendly...! Smoothe! Can I credit this?

SMOOTHE. It's my experience your Grace that when a man fails in respect, then we may look to him to fail in anything.

DUKE: That's very sound, Smoothe. (*He scrambles up.*) And – (*Feeling his paunch.*) – failed in his respect he most emphatically has! But – *Oblong?*

BOLLIGREW: Goes over every afternoon to Dragon's den Your Grace. See it for yourself if you wish.

DUKE: The Dragon's den? What for?

MOLOCH: A purely social call so far as one can see.

BOLLIGREW: I sometimes wonder if 'e 'asn't some arrangement with the brute.

MOLOCH: Oh no.

BOLLIGREW: What other explanation is there?

BLACKHEART: Always leaves 'is sword outside.

MOLOCH: That's true, that's true.

DUKE: Gentlemen! You can *show* me this?

BOLLIGREW: This very afternoon Your Grace. I thought we'd 'ave a bite of lunch first: couple of roast oxen, three or four stuffed peacocks, nothin' elaborate.

DUKE: Chestnut stuffing?

BOLLIGREW: Yes, Your Grace.

DUKE: Then, gentlemen, to lunch and after that... Oh Oblong! Oblong! To the dragon's den!
(*The DUKE exits, followed by SMOOTHE, BLACKHEART and BOLLIGREW. MOLOCH cautiously watches them away, then turns suddenly.*)

MOLOCH: Now Mazeppa, as you see, we approach the climax.

MAZEPPA: Yes, Master.

MOLOCH: I'd be inclined to take a boat at once...

MAZEPPA: Master?

MOLOCH: But I haven't yet secured my fee from Bolligrew. Now listen carefully, my dear: go straight

down to the harbour, hire a boat, and have it standing by.
It's always possible that something may miscarry.

MAZEPPA: Yes, Master.

MOLOCH: Wait here. I'll bring our bags (*Going.*) I packed
them this morning.

(*MOLOCH exits, MAZEPPA stands down centre, looking
over the audience in an attitude of waiting. MAGPIE, and
OBIDIAH emerge from behind the church.*)

MAGPIE: What'd I tell you?

OBIDIAH: Witchcraft.

(*MAZEPPA turns. OBIDIAH hides again. MAZEPPA and
MAGPIE confront each other, MAGPIE has one hand behind
his back.*)

MAGPIE: Awk!

MAZEPPA: Awk.

MAGPIE: You're not from these parts, are you?

MAZEPPA: Me? From the Islands? (*Loftily.*) I'm from
Oxford.

MAGPIE: Go on? You attached to the University, then?

MAZEPPA: Rather depends what you mean. I am personal
assistant to Dr Moloch.

MAGPIE: (*Admiringly.*) Moloch the Magician? You must
'ave quite a head-piece on you.

MAZEPPA: I was chosen from a large number of applicants.
Yes, I keep our Journal.

MAGPIE: Journal?

MAZEPPA: Journal, yes. A record of all our spells. I often
think I could do better without Moloch than Moloch
could without me.

MAGPIE: You keep a record of all your spells?

MAZEPPA: Yes.

MAGPIE: You keep it up to date, do you?

MAZEPPA: Oh, yes. Quite up to date.

MAGPIE: (*Looking off.*) Is that Moloch coming now?

(*MAZEPPA looks to see. MAGPIE produces a monstrous club
from behind his back, and deals MAZEPPA a great blow.*)

MAZEPPA: Awk!

(*MAZEPPA falls into MAGPIE's arms. OBIDIAH emerges
from the church.*)

78

OBIDIAH: Eh, Mike, whatever are you doing – ?

MAGPIE: No time now – help!

(*OBIDIAH and MAGPIE drag MAZEPPA behind the church, just in time for MAGPIE to take up MAZEPPA's stance as MOLOCH enters carrying two cases.*)

MOLOCH: There, my dear. That one has my clothes.

(*MAGPIE takes the case.*)

This one our equipment.

(*MAGPIE takes the other case, and almost drops it from its weight.*)

Careful!

MAGPIE: Blimey!

MOLOCH: Mazeppa, do you feel quite well?

MAGPIE: Dandy! Er – yes, Master.

MOLOCH: Mazeppa, you're not going to have one of your nervous attacks, I hope?

MAGPIE: Awk. Er – no, Master.

MOLOCH: Then off to the Harbour to find a boat. Myself I'm going to get my fee from Bolligrew. At lunch I hope – if not – The Dragon's den.

(*MOLOCH exits. OBIDIAH emerges. MAGPIE rummages in the case and produces a heavy ledger.*)

OBIDIAH: My word – bit of quick thinkin' that was.

MAGPIE: (*Looking at the ledger.*) What's this?

OBIDIAH: Spells K to Z.

MAGPIE: This?

OBIDIAH: Spells A to K.

MAGPIE: Then this must be the Journal!

OBIDIAH: Right! (*He opens it.*) Here is is! 'Sunday. Performed Spell Grimbleboots. Client: Bolligrew. Victim: Oblong. Purpose: Deliver same to Dragon...' The old devil...!

MAGPIE: Look up Grimbleboots!

OBIDIAH: What for?

MAGPIE: It'll give the antidote!

OBIDIAH: The antidote! (*Flipping pages.*) 'Gattlefyg, Gollipog, Grimbleboots!'... 'Ingredients, Method, Application, Antidote!' (*A pause.*) 'No antidote exists for

79

this spell...' (*He sits.*) Baron's done some evil in 'is day. But this beats all. (*Silence.*) Pity we can't put *'im* under a spell...

MAGPIE: We can! Grimbleboots! If Grimbleboots gave Baron power over Oblong, Grimbleboots will give us power over Baron.

OBIDIAH: Stands to reason that does! Mike Magpie – it's you that should've been to that University.

MAGPIE: Ha ha! Ingredients! What are the ingredients? (*OBIDIAH reads while MAGPIE checks tins and bottles.*)

OBIDIAH. Snakes' feet.

MAGPIE: Snakes' feet.

OBIDIAH: Baking powder.

MAGPIE: Baking powder.

OBIDIAH: Fish feathers.

MAGPIE: Fish feathers.

OBIDIAH: Table salt.

MAGPIE: No table salt.

OBIDIAH: Got that at home.

MAGPIE: What else?

OBIDIAH: Er – (*His face falls.*) – oh deary, deary, me! A prized possession of the victim's. Prized possession of Bolligrew's, phew.

MAGPIE: Awk!

OBIDIAH: What?

MAGPIE: You won't tell Obby? (*Backing towards his nest.*) It was twinklin' you see. 'E left it on his dressin' table and the sun was shining, and the window was open and it twinkled, so – (*He dangles the huge gold watch.*) D'you think it'll do?

OBIDIAH: Do? Baron'll go ravin' mad when 'e misses that! That's 'is presentation piece! Well I never thought I'd live to thank a thievish Magpie! Right. Down to my cottage for the table salt. We'll work the spell and then – *A pause. They look at each other.*) – the Dragon's den. (*The lights dim; the Dragon backcloth descends as before. MOLOCH and BOLLIGREW enter hastily.*)

BOLLIGREW: Well – (*Turning to MOLOCH.*) – if those are the table-manners of a Duke, commend me to the nearest cormorant. Never 'ave I seen a man put back stuffed peacock the way 'e can.

MOLOCH: Bolligrew. I'm in a hurry.

BOLLIGREW: Aye. Right. (*He goes to the mouth of the den.*) Hello?

(*The eyes switch on. BOLLIGREW flinches.*)

Oh, there you are.

DRAGON: Here I am, where is Oblong?

BOLLIGREW: Be comin' any minute.

DRAGON: And you want me to eat him.

BOLLIGREW: Well that's easy enough isn't it?

DRAGON: It is, Bolligrew, yes. That's what makes me, just a little, wonder…

BOLLIGREW: Oh you'll be doin' me a good turn old man, don't you worry! All set then?

DRAGON: All set, Bolligrew.

(*The eyes switch off.*)

BOLLIGREW: (*To MOLOCH.*) Well. I'll go and bring up the Duke. Sorry you 'ave to go… (*He starts to go.*)

MOLOCH: My fee. Sixty-five guineas.

BOLLIGREW: (*Piteously.*) Moloch – I'm a ruined man!

MOLOCH: Rubbish.

(*BOLLIGREW pulls a bag from his pocket, but cannot part with the money.*)

BOLLIGREW: Knock off the shillings.

MOLOCH: No.

BOLLIGREW: (*Enraged.*) 'Ere you are then. (*He thrusts the bag at him.*) And bad luck to yer!

MOLOCH: Good-bye. (*He starts to go, then pauses. He weighs the money-bag thoughtfully, opens it and takes out a coin, unwraps gilt foil from it, puts the coin in his mouth and eats it carefully.*) I see – chocolate money. Well, Bolligrew, this time you've over-reached yourself! (*He goes to the den mouth.*) Dragon!

(*The eyes switch on.*)

DRAGON: Yes, Moloch?

MOLOCH: I have just found out that you are the object of a conspiracy!

DRAGON: You amaze me, Moloch. Go on.

MOLOCH: Bolligrew has given Oblong mortified apples.

DRAGON: Oh yes?

MOLOCH: Yes. I assume he got them from the mainland,

DRAGON: *Must* have done, mustn't he? Any more?

MOLOCH: I'm afraid so. When you have eaten Oblong and have fallen dead...

DRAGON: Yes?

MOLOCH: Then Bolligrew and Blackheart with some show of gallantry will come in there and cut the tail off your corpse.

DRAGON: Really. Now why would they do a thing like that?

MOLOCH: The Duke is here.

DRAGON: Understand. Ingenious scheme, Moloch.

MOLOCH: It has a certain squalid cunning I suppose. Myself I will not be a party to it. In your place I should simply claw Oblong to death, and eat the gallant dragon slayers.

DRAGON: Well of course.

MOLOCH: Oh – Bolligrew is bringing up the Duke. I must go.

DRAGON: Moloch.

MOLOCH: Yes.

DRAGON: Very grateful for the information.

MOLOCH: Not at all.

DRAGON: No, no, Moloch. Information must be paid for.

MOLOCH: Oh – (*Hesitating.*) – perhaps you'll send me a cheque.

DRAGON: Cash, Moloch.

(*There is the sound of coins on the loudspeaker.*)

Come and get it.

(*MOLOCH licks his lips and hovers at the mouth of the den, fascinated and frightened.*)

MOLOCH: Well, I – er...

DRAGON: Let's see; these seem to be ten guinea pieces. One (*Clink.*) two, (*Clink.*) three, (*Clink.*) – come in Doctor, come in –

(*MOLOCH, helplessly drawn into den, disappears from sight. His voice too comes on the loudspeaker.*)

four, (*Clink.*) five, (*Clink.*) …

MOLOCH: It's very dark in here…

DRAGON: Can you manage? I'm up here. Six, (*Clink.*) seven, (*Clink.*) …

(*On the loudspeaker there is a clatter and a little gasp from MOLOCH*)

Mind the bones. That's it. Eight, (*Clink.*) nine, (*Clink.*) – and…

(*There is a roar from the DRAGON and a shriek from MOLOCH*)

MOLOCH: Put me down! Put me down!

DRAGON: Moloch, I don't believe that *Bolligrew* thought up that little scheme.

MOLOCH. Help!

DRAGON: No. I think *you* did.

MOLOCH: Help!

DRAGON: Anyway, I'm hungry.

MOLOCH: Dragon – consider your stomach! I am the Regius Professor of Wickedness at…

(*There is a shriek, cut short. Silence, then a dreadful champing noise.*)

DRAGON: Youugh! Disgusting.

(*The DUKE, SMOOTHE, BOLLIGREW, BLACKHEART, the MEN-AT-ARMS, PEASANTS and LORD MAYOR enter.*)

BOLLIGREW: Shan't 'ave long to wait your Grace. Oblong's always 'ere 'bout tea-time. Well Sir Percy – ever seen a den as big as that?

SMOOTHE: It is very big…

BOLLIGREW: (*To the DUKE.*) You see why, up till now, no-one's cared to tackle 'im.

DUKE: Up till now?

BOLLIGREW: Yes, I think today may be the day. Blackheart's fair spoiling for it.

BLACKHEART: Just say the word, Bolligrew, an' I'll be in there an' 'ave 'is tail off in a jiffy.

BOLLIGREW: Courage of a lion, Your Grace.

(*There is an indignant roar from the DRAGON. ALL flinch.
Then BLACKHEART shakes his fist and roars back.*)

Oh yes, he's workin' up to it. Today's the day all right.

DUKE: You mustn't let him, Bolligrew! That's not a one-man
Dragon.

BOLLIGREW: One-man? Oh – I shall go in with 'im,
naturally.

DUKE: Bolligrew!

BOLLIGREW: Matter of *noblesse oblige*, Your Grace. Er, if
anything goes wrong, you'll not forget the poor and
needy of these islands, will you?

DUKE: (*Moved.*) Good Heavens Bolligrew. I'm overwhelmed.
And all this while, Smoothe, Oblong – our official
representative, is on familiar terms with the brute!

SMOOTHE: (*Drily.*) Yes, Your Grace. I can hardly believe it.

BOLLIGREW: (*Pointing.*) You'll believe your own eyes
I hope?

(*ALL look off.*)

DUKE: It is. It's Oblong. Good Heavens – he's *whistling*!
(*MAGPIE and OBIDIAH enter behind the others. OBIDIAH
prominently carries the watch.*)

OBIDIAH: Baron Bolligrew!

(*ALL turn on hearing OBIDIAH's tone.*)

BOLLIGREW: Don't bother me n... 'Ere! That's me
presentation piece! (*He takes the watch.*) Where d'you
get it?

MAGPIE: Awk...

BOLLIGREW: (*Putting the watch on.*) Oh you was it?
(*OBLONG is heard off whistling* Sir Eglamore *as he
approaches. ALL turn and, as the whistling grows louder,
shuffle back to prepare for OBLONG's entrance.*)

OBIDIAH: (*Suddenly.*) Baron, cartwheel!

(*BOLLIGREW cartwheels. ALL turn to him.*)

MAGPIE: Another!

OBIDIAH: Another!

MAGPIE: Twirligig!

(*BOLLIGREW handsprings, then crashes in a sitting position,
astounded.*)

DUKE: Bolligrew...!

(*OBLONG enters, whistling. ALL spin round towards him. He makes a brisk semicircle, then sticks his sword in the ground down centre.*)

OBLONG: Bolligrew! Smoothe. People. (*He walks briskly towards the den drawing a ginger-beer bottle from his belt as he goes.*) Have a wine-gum, Tum-tum?

DUKE: Certainly not!

OBLONG: Suit yourself.

(*OBLONG disappears into the den.*)

BOLLIGREW: See! Just as I said!

OBIDIAH: Baron, call him back.

BOLLIGREW: Come back!

DUKE: Good Lord!

(*OBLONG reappears.*)

OBLONG: (*Pleasantly.*) Yes?

DUKE: Smoothe – Smoothe – what's going on?

OBIDIAH: Your Grace. The Baron 'as Sir Oblong in 'is power. And I 'ave Baron in mine. Baron, tell 'im to remove 'is prized possession.

BOLLIGREW: Remove your prized possession.

(*OBLONG plucks the mantle from his back.*)

OBLONG: (*Coming to himself.*) Good heavens – Your Grace? Good Heavens – the Dragon's den – my sword! What's happening here? (*He finds the ginger-beer bottle in his belt, looks at it, realises what it is and throws it from him with a horrified exclamation.*)

DUKE: Oblong is himself again. Old friend. I fear you have been foully practised on.

OBIDIAH: Tell 'is Grace it is so.

BOLLIGREW: It is so.

DUKE: Oh infamous!

OBIDIAH: And tell His Grace that you, not Sir Oblong had an agreement with the Dragon.

BOLLIGREW: I, not Sir Oblong, had an agreement with the Dragon.

LORD MAYOR: And have had this many a year…!

BOLLIGREW: And have had this – you shurrup!

OBIDIAH: And tell His Grace you did it with the aid of Dr Moloch calling himself Innocent.

85

BOLLIGREW: Did it with the aid of Dr Moloch, calling 'imself Innocent, yes.

DUKE: (*Amazed by his comfortably obedient tone.*) And you confess this freely?

BOLLIGREW: Do I blazes confess it freely! This man 'ere's bewitched me somehow. 'Ere...! (*He fumbles to unfasten the watch.*)

OBIDIAH: Baron. Hands off!
(*BOLLIGREW's hands fly out at arm's length.*)

BOLLIGREW: See! See? (*He turns for all to see him.*) An' if I'm not greatly mistook, the 'ole of this is 'ighly illegal!

OBLONG: That's perfectly true. Evidence obtained by witchcraft is no evidence whatever − and rightly so. Obidiah I am deeply displeased. Tell the Baron to remove his watch.

OBIDIAH: (*Together with MAGPIE.*) But Sir...

MAGPIE: (*Together with OBIDIAH.*) Don't be daft...

OBLONG: Immediately, Obidiah.

OBIDIAH: Then Baron, take it off.
(*BOLLIGREW takes off the watch.*)

DUKE: Now Baron, repeat your story.

BOLLIGREW: I will do no such thing! Pack of lies from start to finish!

SMOOTHE: Oblong my dear man, you've destroyed your own case.

OBLONG: (*Quietly.*) I can't help that, Smoothe. I cannot countenance the use of witchcraft.

BOLLIGREW: Well I'm glad to see there's *one* honest man 'ere. Besides me! I tell you what Obby − we've been practised on you an' me! We'll 'ave the law on the lot of 'em. Uncover corruption in very high places I dare say. Black'eart saw it. 'E'll be witness!

OBLONG: Bolligrew, you are a transparent rogue and I have nothing to say to you. (*He sounds bitterly sad.*) I hope his Grace will send some worthy gentlemen to take my mission to a successful conclusion.

DUKE: Oblong, what's this?

OBLONG: Your Grace I shall never forget how I misbehaved this morning.

DUKE: But you were made to!

OBLONG: (*Quietly and sharply.*) I was not. I was made to let myself go. I let myself go and (*He turns sadly and picks up the mantle.*) I fell prey to Dr Moloch, by my vanity and pride.

DUKE: Oh Oblong, really, that's ridiculous.

OBLONG: Not at all. (*He walks towards the sword, thoughtfully, lovingly, folding and stroking it.*) I used to say I was not worthy, if truth were told I thought I was too good. Here's my sword. Well. (*Drapes the mantle over the sword.*) I will never carry a sword again.

BOLLIGREW: Eh, now look 'ere Obby...

(*Immediately ALL join, following and vociferously begging, cajoling, urging OBLONG to stay, according to their different natures. 'Be a sport Obby, don't take it like that', 'Don't leave us Sir Oblong, you're the first Knight Errant we ever 'ad and we don't wish for none better', 'Oblong, my dear fellow, this is really very fine drawn stuff; I wish you'd reconsider', 'Look man, every blessed person here is asking for you', 'Awk! Obby! Don't go of to the mainland now and leave us 'ere to Bolligrew', 'Come too Obby, place won't be the same without you', 'Sir Oblong, please – you are a familiar and well-loved figure in the Islands', 'Remember 'ow we built the church sir – what's to become of that?'*)

OBLONG: (*Drowned, so that we can only see his firmly upheld hand, and his head shaking in refusal.*) No, no, I thank you, but my mind is made up.

DRAGON: My patience is exhausted!

(*Instant silence. ALL turn to face the DRAGON.*)

I can hear human beans. I can smell human beans. And – I'm – HUNGRY!

(*The lights dim, there is the noise on the loudspeaker of the DRAGON approaching – the eyes light up and grow larger.*)

ALL: The Dragon! The Dragon is at large!

(*ALL scatter, leaving OBLONG isolated. After a moment's hesitation, he snatches his mantle, wraps it round his arm, pulls his sword from the stage and rushes into the den.*)

OBLONG: An Oblong! An Oblong!

DUKE: (*Pointing.*) Bolligrew! Redeem yourself!
(*There are loud sounds of conflict on the loudspeaker.*)
BOLLIGREW: By Jove! Tally-ho!
(*BOLLIGREW crams some cartridges into his shotgun and follows OBLONG.*)
DUKE: Smoothe – assist them! Smoothe!
(*SMOOTHE follows rather reluctantly.*)
Men-at-Arms!
(*The MEN-AT-ARMS cheer and follow.*)
Poor and needy!
(*The PEASANTS and LORD MAYOR cheer and follow. Only BLACKHEART is left.*)
(*Indignantly and rhetorically.*) Squire Blackheart! Are you a gentleman or are you not?
BLACKHEART: No, I blazin' well am not!
(*There is a climax of noise on the loudspeaker: shouts, roars, clashing swords, the banging of the shotgun. Then follows a sudden silence – and afterwards a gush of smoke. BOLLIGREW and OBLONG emerge with a huge black tail, followed by ALL the others, smoke-blackened. The lights come up.*)
DUKE: Oblong! Peerless Knight! You have surpassed yourself.
OBLONG: No, no Your Grace! The principal credit belongs to the Baron.
DUKE: The Baron?
BOLLIGREW: (*Shaking his shotgun; beaming and excited.*) Got 'im with both barrels. A left and a right! Pow! Pow! Did'n I, Obby?
OBLONG: He did. The beast was on the wing too. Beautiful shots, Baron!
BOLLIGREW: By Jove, that's what I call sport! You can keep yer pheasants. Eh – these Dragons – can you breed 'em, artificial?
OBLONG: I never heard of it. Bus there are lots of wild ones.
BOLLIGREW: Where?
OBLONG: Up North. Dragons, Goblins, Lord knows what. Very good sport up North I believe.

BOLLIGREW: Blackheart, get ready to pack.

BLACKHEART: Now look 'ere, Bolligrew...

BOLLIGREW: You'll love it, Black'eart! (*Aiming his gun at an imaginary dragon.*) Pow! pow! Eh – what's the season?

OBLONG: All the year round.

BOLLIGREW: 'Ear that Black'eart – no closed Season. Well you needn't expect to see me back 'ere for some time, if at all.

(*There is a general stir of delight.*)

No, no, I shall be missed, I know that, but me mind's made up.

(*The STORYTELLER enters. Rhyming dialogue commences.*)

STORYTELLER: Then who will rule your people when you've gone?

BOLLIGREW: Fat lot I care! Pow! Pow! Anyone!

DUKE: That timorous gentleman over there?

LORD MAYOR: (*Quailing under BOLLIGREW's appraisal.*) I thank your Grace, but I'll stay Lord Mayor.

DUKE: The bare-footed fellow showed some resource.

OBIDIAH: I'll stick to my trade, sir – thanks of course.

STORYTELLER: Excuse me your Grace, but it is getting late.

BOLLIGREW: (*Putting his arm round OBLONG.*) There's a perfectly obvious candidate!

STORYTELLER: And I ask you to name him with one voice.

ALL: Oblong fitz Oblong!

STORYTELLER: The people's choice – Sir I salute you in a world of smiles. First Baron Oblong of the Isles! And that of course concludes the play...

OBLONG: It certainly doesn't. I've something so say.

(*The STORYTELLER looks at OBLONG, struck by his indignant tone.*)

We've killed a Dragon, and mended a quarrel...

STORYTELLER: What of it?

OBLONG: What of it sir? The *moral!* (*He steps forward.*)

STORYTELLER: I beg your pardon. But please keep it short.

OBLONG: It's simply this: My dears, do-what-you-ought. When there's something you want, and you can't do without it. There are various ways of going about it...

MAGPIE: (*Righteously.*) And a very good way is to – do – what – you – *should.*

OBLONG: Exactly.

MAGPIE: But a bit of what you fancy, does yer good!

OBLONG: Michael!

MAGPIE: Awk!

(*Music plays, as the curtain falls.*)

The End.

VIVAT! VIVAT REGINA!

Characters

MARY QUEEN OF SCOTS

Overbred, refined and passionate; sympathetic, beautiful, intelligent and brave. But sensual and subjective. Born a Queen, deferred to from the cradle, it is a tribute to her nature that she is not simply spoiled. But she mistakes her public office for a private attribute.

CLAUD NAU

An elderly bachelor; gentle, learned, anxious, utterly upright, deeply affectionate.

WILLIAM CECIL

A top flight Civil Servant, reasonable, courteous, ruthless.

ELIZABETH I OF ENGLAND

Personable, wilful, highly-strung. But schooled to clear sight and tuned to self-discipline by a dangerous and lonely childhood. Commencing her reign as a natural perhaps just faintly neurotic young woman, her strength of character is such that she meets the unnatural demands of Queenship with increasing brilliance, in an increasing rage of undisclosed resentment.

ROBERT DUDLEY

A tall, hard, virile animal; unintellectual but nobody's fool.

JOHN KNOX

A pedant and a demagogue, a nasty combination. But palpably, frighteningly sincere.

BAGPIPER

DAVID RIZZIO

A likeable hedonist, affectionate and sceptical; but a lightweight; precarious.

LORD MORTON

Renaissance noble and tribal Chief; seasoned and at ease in every kind of villainy.

LORD BOTHWELL

Shrewd, coarse-natured, irresponsible; but uncomplaining as unpitying, genuinely a law unto himself; a dangerous vortex to dependent natures.

LORD BISHOP OF DURHAM
A conscientious career clergyman, a bit selfish,
a bit ignoble; but he knows that.
A CLERIC
SIR FRANCIS WALSINGHAM
A Puritan and humourless on principle, but dangerously
intelligent; a selfless intriguer, a dedicated wolf.
DE QUADRA
Walsingham's opposite, suave in manner;
equally dedicated, equally dangerous.
DAVISON
A slightly built youth of good family. Too
generous by nature for the trade of politics.
HENRY STUART, LORD DARNLEY
A tall, athletic, good-looking aristocrat; too
young, too merely pleasant to withstand the heavy
personal and public pressures bearing on him.
LORD MOR
RUTHVEN
LINDSEY
A DOCTOR
TALA
ORMISTON
A ragged Border ruffian.
Middle-aged, his moral sense quite atrophied.
A PRISONER
A scholar priest worn thin by the life of a secret agent.
SCOTS ARCHBISHOP
PHILIP, KING OF SPAIN
THE POPE
JAILERS
BREWER
COURTIERS, LAIRDS, CLERKS, SERVANTS
COURT LADIES
Pretty, flighty, privileged, young.

Vivat! Vivat Regina! was first performed at the Chichester Festival Theatre on 2 May 1970, and afterwards at the Piccadilly Theatre, London, on 8 October 1970, with the following cast:

MARY, Sarah Miles
NAU, David Bird
CECIL, Richard Pearson
ELIZABETH, Eileen Atkins
DUDLEY, Norman Eshley
KNOX, Leonard Maguire
BAGPIPER, Willie Cochrane
RIZZIO, Matthew Guinness
MORTON, Archie Duncan
BOTHWELL, David McKail
BISHOP, Brian Hawksley
CLERIC, Kenneth Caswell
WALSINGHAM, Edgar Wreford
DE QUADRA, Edward Atienza
DAVISON, Eilian Wyn
DARNLEY, Cavan Kendall
MOR, Brian Hawksley
RUTHVEN, Glyn Grain
LINDSEY, Alexander John
A DOCTOR, Ken Grant
TALA, Malcolm Rogers
ORMISTON, Jonathan Mallard
PRISONER, Malcolm Rogers
ARCHBISHOP, Maurice Jones
PHILIP, Alastair Meldrum
POPE, Kenneth Caswell
JAILERS, Adrian Reynolds, Ken Grant
BREWER, Adrian Reynolds

COURTIERS, LAIRDS, CLERKS, SERVANTS etc,
Glyn Grain, Ken Grant, Maurice Jones, Alastair
Meldrum, Adrian Reynolds,

COURT LADIES, Isabel Metliss, Angela Easton

Director, Peter Dews

Setting, Carl Toms

The action of the play takes place in France,
England and Scotland

Period – sixteenth century

A NOTE TO THE DESIGNER

I have tried to assume enough for you to work upon yet not so
much as to prevent your making a substantial contribution to
the style of production.

You will see that the stage serves at one moment for the
Court of England and at the next for the Court of Scotland.
I hope the properties will be solid and pleasurable in themselves
to look at, but that the lighting, not the properties, will create
the changes of time and place and mood. I hope the costumes
will convey the extravagances and extremes of the period, yet
not distract the audience nor tie up the actors.

I have assumed: One, a flat-topped pyramid or flight of
shallow steps, supporting a screen or curtain in the First Act
and the throne in the Second Act. Two, a table with stools.
Three, a 'pulpit', though this could be a mere lectern. Four, a
hanging or revolving cloth of State. My intention is to maintain
a smoothly continuous narrative to which changes of time and
place will seem incidental.

ACT ONE

Exterior. Dappled sunlight on leaves and fruit.

NAU stands looking up at them. Everything still.

VOICE: (*Off.*) Ho there – The Queen!
  (*Fanfare. MARY enters swiftly followed by two LADIES. She comes to a halt and looks at NAU. He goes down on one knee.*)

NAU: Your Grace?
  (*MARY stares at him a space.*)

MARY: (*Softly; shocked and pitying.*) Oh…
  (*NAU smiles.*)

NAU: Your Grace?

MARY: You are grown quite white, Claud.
  (*NAU smiles again at the note of reproach, rubs his white hair, and rises.*)

NAU: (*Ruefully.*) The winters in Scotland are frosty.
  (*MARY's faint smile vanishes. She crosses away from him.*)

MARY: Yes… Upon what care of State I wonder has my mother sent you back to France. I'm sure it is some care of State. No care for me.

NAU: (*Reproving.*) Mignon; before all else I am to tell you that your mother loves you well.

MARY: My mother does not know me.

NAU: That is her sorrow, too. The ruling of your Scottish kingdom in your name – and nothing else – has kept your mother from you. And Mignon, that is love and not the lack of it.

MARY: A kind of love.

NAU: The hardest kind.

MARY: Aye hard it is. And granite too is hard. But I have yet to hear it is a good material to make a cradle of.
  I tell you, Claud, no care of State shall keep me from my child… (*Disturbed, she controls her feelings and sits. Formal.*) Come, let me know your charges.

NAU: Mignon, your mother wonders whether presently in probability you may yourself expect a child.

97

(*MARY looks at him.*)

MARY: (*Softly.*) By Heaven I wonder she should wonder it.
By Christ – I wonder you should ask!

NAU: (*Appalled.*) Mignon…

MARY: Leave us, ladies.

(*The LADIES curtsy and exit quickly.*)

NAU: Mignon…

MARY: I was your 'mignon' when I was your pupil, sir!

NAU: (*Bewildered.*) Your Grace, I meant no disrespect…

MARY: What did you mean – affection?

NAU: Assuredly, Your Grace.

MARY: I do not understand you, Claud. (*She leaves him.*)
Have you not waited on my husband?

NAU: But now, Your Grace.

MARY: Did you not see his face? They sometimes draw the
curtains, Claud, to spare his visitors his face.

NAU: I saw, Your Grace.

MARY: And having seen his face – and having seen the
suppurating sores that batten on his poor young mouth –
and having seen his ancient eyes – sir, do you ask…? –
do you of all men dare to ask if presently in probability
I may expect a child?

(*NAU stares at her a second. Understands her misconception.*)

NAU: O-o-oh… (*He kneels.*) Pardon.

MARY: *No!* (*But seeing his pathetic kneeling figure.*) Oh,
Claud, I was a little girl, and you were all the father
and the mother that I had; you taught me how to read
and write; and when I got my lessons well – good
God, you sat me on your knee and said I was your
best of little girls!… And when I got my lessons ill
my sharpest punishment was your displeasure! And
you stood by and said no word and let them marry
me to syphilis! No, no – you shall not have my
pardon now.

NAU: My word carried no weight, Your Grace. Beseech
Your Grace believe I spoke.

(*MARY looks at him dubiously.*)

MARY: (*Suspiciously.*) You spoke no word to me.

NAU: They said it would be treason and the axe if I should speak that word, to you. And I was too afraid to do my duty. Pardon.

MARY: (*After a pause, gently.*) Pardon? For what?

NAU: Cowardice.

(*MARY crosses, and raises him.*)

MARY: I'm glad that it was cowardice. Connivance I could not have pardoned.

NAU: And am I pardoned now?

MARY: Right gladly. (*She becomes almost shy.*) I wept in puddles when you went away to Scotland, Claud.

NAU: I wept a little, too.

MARY: Truly?

NAU: I wept with due decorum but, oh yes, I wept.

MARY: (*Smiling.*) 'With due decorum.' Oh, welcome back... It was my mother offered you the axe if you should tell me, was it not?

NAU: It was.

MARY: For love of me?

NAU: She made the match for love of you. Your husband is the King of France. You are the Queen of Scots. And France and Scotland joined might get your English kingdom, too.

MARY: Would you, for fifty Englands, kiss my husband on the mouth?

(*NAU cannot meet her eyes. She moves away, NAU looking after her.*)

NAU: Can they not cure him, madam?

MARY: If prayer and care can cure him, I will do it. I do not think the doctors can.

NAU: God bless Your Grace.

MARY: Aye, bless me, Claud. I also pray for him to die.

NAU: Mignon!

MARY: Yes. And for myself to have a husband I might love.

NAU: Nay now, you must love the one you have.

MARY: I am forbid to touch him, Claud.

NAU: There is a love that needs no touching.

MARY: With such a love as that I love him. But what kind of 'love' is that?

NAU: The royal kind. The King of Heaven loves us all with such a love as that.

MARY: I know it, sir. (*She crosses herself.*) And holy nuns return his love; but then they are betrothed to Christ. My husband was betrothed to death upon the day that he was born. And I have no such high vocation as a nun.

NAU: (*Sternly.*) You ought to have; you have high office.

MARY: I know that, too, sir. (*Leaving him.*) Right well I know. (*She is abstracted.*) What is your second charge?

NAU: Nay, let us finish with the first. (*Severely.*) Mignon, do you mean to take a lover?

MARY: ...I mean to hear your second charge.

NAU: The treaty which your mother has negotiated with the English.

MARY: (*Indifferently, her thoughts elsewhere.*) Well?

NAU: The English have desired another term.

MARY: Oh?

NAU: Your Grace shows here – (*Indicating the cloth of state.*) – the lion of Scotland and the English leopard.
(*She begins to pay attention.*)

MARY: Yes?

NAU: The English now desire you to take down the leopard and show the lion only.

MARY: No.

NAU: Your Grace, it is the express desire of the English Queen.

MARY: Of whom?

NAU: Your Grace, she is effectively the Queen.

MARY: Elizabeth fitz Tudor is a bastard and a heretic and cannot be a queen.

NAU: She sits on a throne.

MARY: A dog can do that. No, I will not sign this treaty, Claud.

NAU: Then the English army will remain in Scotland, where it lives upon the people barbarously.

MARY: You are clever, Claud.

NAU: Your Grace, I hope, is pitiful.

MARY: Let her be pitiful – it is her army!

NAU: They are your people.

MARY: (*With a shrug.*) Well, I will sign it. And she is queen indeed.

NAU: In this you show more queen than she.

MARY: Aye, anything that makes me less makes me more queen, Claud, does it not?

NAU: There is much truth in that.

MARY: There is no truth at all in that. And I am sick of hearing that. Diminish me, the Queen's diminished. Starve me, and the Queen will fail. If I am sickly, she is pale. I am the Queen and more the Queen the more I am myself!

(*It is a credo, passionate. NAU looks at her thoughtfully.*)

NAU: So thinks Elizabeth.

MARY: (*With sour indifference.*) Indeed.

NAU: Indeed. She too mistakes her office for herself. And thinks that her whole duty is to do as she desires.

MARY: She has not had the advantage of your ceaseless moralising, Claud.

NAU: Perhaps that's it. For she will have what she desires and it will fetch her off the throne.

MARY: (*Startled.*) What...? Why, what does she desire?

NAU: A husband she might love.

MARY: What husband?

NAU: Her lover.

MARY: (*Incredulously.*) Robert Dudley?

NAU: She loves him.

MARY: But he's a commoner.

NAU: She loves him for himself, perhaps.

MARY: He has a wife.

NAU: He does not love his wife.

MARY: So?

NAU: (*Suddenly stern, heavy with distaste.*) So his wife must die.

MARY: ...How, die?

NAU: Violently.

MARY: Are they mad?

NAU: They see no duty but their duty to themselves. And that is mad.

101

MARY: Oh, let them do it! – let them do it!

NAU: Can you rejoice at murder?

MARY: Nay, Claud, you said yourself this thing will fetch her off the throne.

NAU: The Queen then must rejoice. I had thought *yourself* more natural.

MARY: You are my teacher still… But is it true?

NAU: Your mother thinks it true.

MARY: I'll warrant she rejoices at it. (*Then, seeing something in his face.*) What is it, Claud?

NAU: Your mother does not much rejoice at anything, Your Grace.

MARY: Why?

NAU: Your Grace, she is dying.

MARY: Oh. (*She moves, checks, then continues sharply.*) You should have told me this at first.

NAU: I was instructed to retain it till the last.

MARY: Why?

NAU: Your royal mother charged me thus: she said, 'Our daughter must think first upon these high affairs of state, not discomposed by any grief she may be pleased to feel, upon our dying.'

(*She stares at him.*)

MARY: (*Softly.*) She said that?

NAU: Your Grace.

MARY: (*Almost whispering.*) Dying, she said *that*?

NAU: Your Grace.

MARY: Oh, Claud – I would to God that I had known her!
(*Her face crumples, streaming with silent tears she raises and lets fall her arms in a gesture of utter helplessness, and goes, blindly.*)
(*MARY exits.*
NAU looks after her, then collects himself, moves quickly and calls formally.)

NAU: Ho there – the Queen!
(*There is a fanfare, as NAU exits.*
The lights change to a cold interior as the leaves and flowers move out. SERVANTS enter and place in position a table and throne. CECIL enters.)

CECIL: Ho there – the Queen!

(*There is a fanfare and ELIZABETH makes a royal entrance. The SERVANTS bow and exit as ELIZABETH sits.*)

Your Grace, even a sovereign cannot do what is impossible.

ELIZABETH: For me to marry Robert Dudley is not impossible.

CECIL: For Your Grace to marry him and remain Queen of England is impossible. (*With gentle insistence.*) He must to prison.

ELIZABETH: We do not know yet that he did it!

CECIL: It would appear that he did it. That being so it must he made apparent that Your Grace did not. Your Grace must think how such a marriage would be taken in France and Spain, as well as here at home.

ELIZABETH: Must I marry to please France and Spain?

CECIL: Your Grace, this marriage would delight them. When Mary Stuart heard of it she cried out: 'Let them do it!'

ELIZABETH: She said that?

CECIL: That and more, Your Grace.

ELIZABETH: What more?

CECIL: Such stuff as I cannot repeat to Your Grace.

ELIZABETH: She is free in her ways, that Mary.

CECIL: She can afford to be, Your Grace. She is Queen of France, and France is rich. She is Queen of Scots, and Scotland is the rear gate to England. The Catholic half of England thinks that she is Queen of England, too – and she cried out: 'Let them do it!'

ELIZABETH: Well; I would not please Mary by my marriage. Nor will I not marry to displease her! I will marry as my heart and conscience say.

CECIL: Conscience…! In Spain they are saying openly: 'What kind of a State Church is this, where the Head of the State, the Head of the Church will not only let a man murder his wife – but marry him for 't?' Your Grace, he must to prison.

ELIZABETH: But what if he is innocent?

CECIL: He must to prison pending the enquiry which will find him innocent.

ELIZABETH: Call him.

(*CECIL moves to go.*)

William.

(*CECIL stops.*)

What if he is guilty?

CECIL: In that case, too, he must to prison pending the enquiry, which will find him innocent. In neither case can Your Grace marry him.

ELIZABETH: Call him.

CECIL: Be wise, Your Grace.

ELIZABETH: As wise as I can.

(*CECIL still hesitates.*)

(*Angrily.*) I cannot be wiser!

CECIL: (*Calling.*) Robert Dudley.

(*DUDLEY strides in, carrying his rapier and belt. He chucks them down, glances at CECIL, stands bristling before ELIZABETH, then goes down on one knee. For a moment his and ELIZABETH's glances meet.*)

ELIZABETH: Well, sir, rise, and tell it.

(*DUDLEY rises, flashes a resentful look at CECIL, and sneers.*)

DUDLEY: Haven't you been told?

ELIZABETH: Not by you.

DUDLEY: No – *I* have been kept outside your door! Three days! Three nights!

ELIZABETH: Tell it.

DUDLEY: There was a fair at Abingdon. She didn't go herself. But she sent all her servants.

CECIL: So she was alone.

DUDLEY: I didn't know she was alone; I was in London.

CECIL: Why all her servants – was she so kind?

DUDLEY: ...Yes.

ELIZABETH: I never heard you say so.

DUDLEY: ...No.

CECIL: Well, sir.

DUDLEY: They came back in the evening. And found her. On the floor of the hall. Below the stairs.

CECIL: With her neck broken.

DUDLEY: I was in London.

CECIL: And your agents?

DUDLEY: What 'agents'?

CECIL: Oh come, sir.

DUDLEY: I didn't *hear* of it until that night!

CECIL: How did you hear of it?

DUDLEY: How?... God forgive me, right gladly.

ELIZABETH: Oh, Robin!

DUDLEY: And you?

ELIZABETH: God pity me, right gladly, too.

CECIL: These past six months, sir, you have put it around that your wife was sick and like to die.

DUDLEY: Yes.

CECIL: And was she?

DUDLEY: No.

CECIL: These stairs, now...

DUDLEY: Elmwood. Polished.

CECIL: Ah, polished. She slipped, then.

DUDLEY: I suppose so.

CECIL: It was an accident; she fell, from the stairs.

DUDLEY: I suppose so.

ELIZABETH: Robin, she was lying fifteen feet from the stairs – she was thrown!

DUDLEY: ...Yes! Yes. She was thrown! No, not by me. Or by my agency. She threw herself.

ELIZABETH: Herself – but why?

DUDLEY: Because she *knew* that I would hear of it – right gladly.

ELIZABETH: Oh God...

DUDLEY: I put it around that she was sick and like to die because I hoped – God damn me black – I hoped that one who loved me or desired my favour might – do it. Well, now. One who loved me and desired my favour, *has.*

ELIZABETH: ...Oh, Robin, either this is true or else you are a devil.

DUDLEY: You must decide that, madam. I've done.

ELIZABETH: But can there be such love? Robin, I would not do that for you.

DUDLEY: Well, love is never equal. I would for you.

ELIZABETH: (*To CECIL.*) Sir, I think this gentleman is innocent.

(*CECIL is unresponsive.*)

Well, speak.

CECIL: Am I to say what I think, Your Grace, or what you want to hear?

ELIZABETH: Oh, Cecil, can they never be the same?

CECIL: (*With a shrug.*) Then I say, with Mary Stuart: 'Let them do it.'

DUDLEY: What's this?

CECIL: Sir, the Queen believes you innocent – and I am ready to believe you innocent – but the Queen, alas, is not the country, nor am I. And you must understand…

DUDLEY: I understand no word you say. Can't you speak like a man?

CECIL: To speak like a 'man', sir: if the Queen takes you to bed she will lie down Elizabeth the First and rise the second Mrs Dudley.

DUDLEY: Zounds! (*He lunges for his sword.*)

ELIZABETH: Put that up! (*She gets up, goes and stands below the cloth of state.*) You may withdraw.

DUDLEY: I?

ELIZABETH: Yes, Robin.

DUDLEY: And he stays?

ELIZABETH: Yes, Robin.

(*DUDLEY stares for a moment, then snatches up his rapier and turns to CECIL.*)

DUDLEY: Cecil, you have ruined me, and I will not forget it.

CECIL: You are wrong, sir, I have saved you. And belike I have made your fortune. And you will forget it.

(*DUDLEY snatches a bow at ELIZABETH, and goes.*)

ELIZABETH: Cecil, were the summers better than they are now, when you were a child?

CECIL: Your Grace…? Yes, Your Grace, I share that common illusion. The summers then were nothing but sunshine. I and the weather have declined together.

ELIZABETH: Who raised you, Cecil?

CECIL: My father and my mother, madam.

ELIZABETH: It is not sunshine you remember; it is love.
My father killed my mother and disowned me, and
I can't remember a summer when it was not raining after
that. I was raised by cautious strangers in the shadows,
between prisons. I was taught; mathematics, Latin,
Greek, and caution, too well; and saw too soon where
love could lead. Prisons were familiar, and so I put my
heart into protective custody. But, Cecil, I mislaid the
key, and it has lain in darkness, cold and calcifying these
twenty years. And, Cecil, Robin had a magic word,
which opened doors for me. You said that you would be
my servant and my friend, and will you be my jailer?
(*CECIL is moved, but…*)

CECIL: Something of each, Your Grace. Your Grace's
Councillor.
(*ELIZABETH looks at him.*)

ELIZABETH: Aye. Well then. To Council.

CECIL: And – the gentleman?

ELIZABETH: (*Going.*) To prison.

CECIL: Your Grace.
(*She hears the discreet satisfaction in his voice and turns.*)

ELIZABETH: But, Cecil, we believe him innocent. And if
from now until your dying day, you whisper one word to
the contrary; we will punish you.
(*ELIZABETH and CECIL exit.*
The lights change. Thunder sounds.
KNOX enters in a dripping cloak. He shakes it, water falling
in a puddle at his feet. He looks up.)

KNOX: Welcome to Scotland. And welcome to St Andrew's
Kirk, but lately called 'Cathedral' – for it is nae long
since a great fat 'bishop', in 'vestments' – like a prostitute
in her undergarments – was wont to jabber forth the
Word of God in heathen Latin from that very pulpit –
tchah! (*He goes to the pulpit, flips down the cross, flips up the*
drape, is about to continue his address, then checks and sniffs.)
D'you know what I smell here? (*He sniffs again at the*
pulpit.) Aye, perfume. (*He looks round.*) The whole place
needs scrubbin'! It still reeks of Catholicism! (*He controls*

himself and walks away.) Well, well, yon fat lad'll no enjoy his 'tithes' where he is now. We hastened him where he come from (*Jabbing downwards.*) wi' a length of rope. And you'll look hard for a Catholic priest in Scotland now. Scotsmen can stand upright! We have a godly governance…! Or did until today. Today it seems once more we have a Queen amongst us. And that's my matter. (*He goes briskly to the pulpit and mounts it.*) Beloved brethren: certain of the Ancient Fathers make a question of it whether women have immortal souls like men or else like animals are morsels of mere Nature. (*He breaks off and leans forward confidentially.*) Er, this is my First Blast of the Trumpet Against the Monstrous Regiment of Women. Yes, I, John Knox that am the Father of the Kirk and spake with Calvin as a friend, regard myself as naething mair than a wee trumpet in the hands of the Almighty – and if that's not humility, I'd like to know what is. (*He resumes his formal academic manner.*) Now. If the Fathers make a question of it, then it is in doubt. Doubt is a lesser thing than certainty. It is a certainty that men have souls. So: Woman is a lesser thing than Man. (*He leans forward; impressively.*) That being so, the Regiment of women *over* men is monstrous – and we must take it as a visitation and a punishment – as was proved upon us lately by that tiger Mary Guise, as proves upon the English by that wolf Elizabeth, and as will prove upon us once again by that she-cat Mary Stuart, now unhappily amongst us following the death – the *mysterious* death – of her wee French husband. No more of that. They that have ears, let them hear. He was, they say, unable to supply her raging appetite.
(*The lights change to exterior.*
KNOX sits, disappearing.
A BAGPIPER enters, playing, followed by MARY wearing crimson. She sits. LADIES, RIZZIO and NAU follow, all in grey silk aflutter with white favours. Last come the Scots LORDS wearing black faintly relieved by sombre plaids. The entourage groups itself about MARY. The Scots LORDS stand

in a stiff line behind the solemn BAGPIPER, who plays on.
MARY and her entourage have difficulty in suppressing their
amusement. Seeing this, MORTON steps forward from among
the LORDS and jabs the BAGPIPER in the ribs. Startled,
he stops and his instrument falls silent with a long-drawn
melancholy wail. MARY registers the stone-faced LORDS.)

MARY: My lords, forgive us. Our ear is not yet tuned to this wild instrument.

MORTON: Certainly, madam, it is no lute.

(RIZZIO picks out a mocking little chord on the strings of his beribboned instrument.)

MARY: *(Sharply.)* Davie – have done. Where is Lord Bothwell?

BOTHWELL: *(Stepping forward.)* Madam.

MARY: Here, sir… *(She goes and gives him a purse.)* We thank you for conducting us from France in safety, through such storms.

BOTHWELL: *(Looking up at her.)* Were there storms, madam? I didn't notice.

MARY: Ah – a Scot can turn a compliment!

BOTHWELL: Aye – given a strong stimulus. Thank you!

MARY: Will you remain in Edinburgh?

BOTHWELL: I am the Lord-Lieutenant of the *Border*, madam.

(MARY sits again, straight-backed and formal.)

MARY: They tell me you steal sheep across the border, Bothwell.

BOTHWELL: Aye, madam, English sheep.

MARY: We would not have our cousin Elizabeth provoked.

BOTHWELL: Oh, they're not her sheep. They're Harry Percy's.

MARY: Lord Bothwell, we have come here to rule.

BOTHWELL: And welcome to Your Grace's bonny face.

(BOTHWELL exits.)

MARY: Morton, this Border raiding must be stopped.

MORTON: It can't be stopped, Your Grace. Lord Bothwell is head of the Clan Hepburn.

MARY: So?

MORTON: The Border is Hepburn country.

MARY: All Scotland is my country, my lord.

MORTON: But Your Grace has no men.

MARY: But haven't you – my Lord in Council – men?

MORTON: Aye, madam. *We* have.

MARY: Well, no doubt we will atune ourselves to both your music and your manners. Now, we will to supper.

MORTON: Now we must to kirk, madam.

MARY: 'Must' we?

NAU: (*In quick confidential warning.*) Yes.
(*MARY swallows her anger and shrugs.*)

MARY: Well then, to kirk.
(*MARY rises. The lights change. Two LORDS move the throne into position, and MARY sits in it. The LORDS and entourage countermarch into position, all looking upwards at the pulpit, on which the lights come up to reveal KNOX.*)

KNOX: You may read in Revelations of a Great Whore; dressed in scarlet; sitting on a throne.
(*There is a stir among the entourage; they look at MARY.*)

MARY: If I had known your text, good Master Knox,
I would have worn a different garment.

KNOX: Nae doubt.

MARY: Now that you have seen my garment, no doubt you will change your text.

KNOX: I have nae mind to.

RIZZIO: Then you insult the Queen.

KNOX: Signor Rizzio, they tell me you're Her Grace's favourite musician. What more ye may be to Her Grace, God knows. You're not a theologian. The Great Whore in the Book of Revelations is no Queen – though Queens may be great whores – she is the Church of Rome!

MARY: Now prove that, Master Knox, or by Heaven I will have God's Trumpet scoured – for I find it something dirty.

KNOX: Prove it, quotha! Secret murders and strange painted vices, whispering together in the shadows of the Vatican is thought by some sufficient proof.
(*There is a murmur of approval from the LORDS.*)
Screeching choirs of castratos and great bronze bells to drown the outcries of the poor is thought by some sufficient proof!

(*A louder murmur from the LORDS. KNOX is intoxicated.*)
Elaborate, blasphemous, tinkling show in place of sober
piety is thought by some... Aye, madam, you may laugh!

MARY: Marry I must. I have heard this vulgar stuff a
hundred times before and know how to refute it.

KNOX: Do so.

MARY: Shall I?

RIZZIO: Briefly.

MARY: Suppose the Holy Father and his priests are all
imperfect as you'd have them. What of that? Because
there are no perfect judges, is there no such thing as
justice? Priests are all men, and since our father Adam
fell imperfection has been part of every man's essential
nature. But it is accidental to the Church, which in its
essence is, was and always will be perfect.

RIZZIO: Brava! Multa brava!

KNOX: (*Smiling quite kindly.*) Well now, my lords, it seems
we are to have a little disputation here.

NAU: No – no...

RIZZIO: Yes. Avanti – trounce him!

KNOX: What – will you back your little fighting hen
against John Knox?

MARY: I am willing, Master Knox.

KNOX: (*Kindly.*) Good. (*He turns away, looks over the
audience, his manner musing, gentle, academic.*) What is the
essence of your Church, Your Grace?

MARY: Its essence?

KNOX: Aye. It is not the Mass?

MARY: It is.

KNOX: What is this Mass?

MARY: It is the sacrament whereat the priest offers to God
the sacrifice of Jesus Christ.

KNOX: (*Quickly, as not having heard.*) Who offers it?

MARY: ...It is a sacrament.

KNOX: Who offers it?

MARY: The priest.

KNOX: The priest... (*His voice is not quite steady on the word.
Then he continues as before.*) Without the sacrifice of Jesus
Christ, could any soul hope for redemption?

MARY: No.

KNOX: Can God refuse that sacrifice, when it is offered?

MARY: He will not.

KNOX: Can he? (*Warningly.*) Remembering that the Son who is sacrificed, the Father who is offered are both – (*Breathing hard now.*) – one God?

MARY: I see where you would lead me.

KNOX: Daren't you follow?

MARY: You are insolent!

KNOX: A very royal argument.

MARY: No. God cannot refuse the sacrifice when it is offered.

KNOX: Then God is at the mercy of the priest.

> (*There is a murmur of satisfaction from the LORDS, but KNOX ascends now to a level of frightening passion, though his voice is at first low.*)

And my soul is at the mercy of the priest. For we can only traffic at the priest's permission. Christ's sacrifice is a cold spring, put here for my soul to drink at freely – which else must perish in this *desert* of a world. But now the Church has led this spring into a tank, and on this tank the priest has put a tap – the Mass – by which he turns Christ's mercy on and off and sells it by the dram!

MARY: Hold there...

KNOX: Aye, madam, hold fast will I – for he will sell it into hands still red with the murder of a husband –

> (*MARY leaps up from her chair.*)

– hands still hot from groping, slake the thirst of carnal fever with it, ladle it down mouths still wet from filthy exercise, sell it unto Satan...

MARY: Come down from there! By God, come down or answer for your disobedience with your *head*!

KNOX: 'By God,' she says, blaspheming in His very house!

MARY: This is no house of God! This is a market – where a scurrilous low peasant brings his dirty produce – (*She whirls on the LORDS.*) – and buys treason from disloyal lords!

NAU: Madam...

KNOX: (*Tolerantly.*) Peace! She is young. (*He descends.*)

MARY: Quit us!

KNOX: And passionate.

MARY: Go!

(*KNOX moves towards the exit, the LORDS following.*)

Ourselves we will to our own chapel – to hear Mass!

KNOX: Madam, I am sorry for you; make a marriage.

(*KNOX and the LORDS go.*)

MARY: (*Crying after them.*) Save your sorrow for yourself,
John Knox! For I may make a marriage that will give
this country cause for sorrow.

(*ALL go. A fanfare sounds.*
The lights change. The fanfare modulates to an organ chord.
A BISHOP and a CLERIC enter and move to the pulpit,
plain-chanting.)

BISHOP: God save the Queen.

CLERIC: And all the Royal Family.

BISHOP: God save the Duke and Duchess.

CLERIC: And both their charming children.

BISHOP: God save all Barons, Earls, Viscounts and Baronets.

CLERIC: And the ladies they have married.

BISHOP: God bless the Squire.

CLERIC: And the Squire's wife.

BISHOP: And the Squire's Bailiff.

CLERIC: And the Constable.

BISHOP: And the Overseer of the Highway.

CLERIC: And the Overseer of the Poor.

(*During the above, they have replaced the Catholic cross and*
drape, been worried by the effect, replaced them with a more
discreet cross and drape, and congratulated each other. The
BISHOP mounts into the pulpit where he now concludes.)

BISHOP: God bless all persons in positions of authority.

(*He smiles at his congregation and begins his address.*)

Steering our course between the Scylla of Rome and the
Carybdis of Geneva, we in the Church of England
cultivate the quality of moderation. Not one of the heroic
virtues. No, compared with courage, and conviction,
moderation is a modest matter. Sometimes – as I am
aware – a laughing matter. So be it. The block and the

bonfire are not laughing matters, and I would rather be the object of your ridicule than of your fear, will gladly spend Eternity in some quite humble mansion of my Father's house if I may get there without blood or fire... And that, at this point in our history, is not so easy as you might suppose. No, I am not ashamed to lift my voice and pray: (*In plain – chant.*) God Save the Queen. (*DUDLEY, CECIL and CLERKS enter, plain – chanting a descant.*)

ALL: A-a-a-a-a-aaamen-en.

(*A blown-up contemporary print of St James, labelled, flies in over the table. DUDLEY is adjusting a new robe and chain with fierce satisfaction. CECIL smiles.*)

CECIL: Well, sir Councillor, I said I should make your fortune.

DUDLEY: And that I should prove ungrateful. There you were wrong.

CECIL: We shall see. A word in your ear. Do not seem too ready in the business I have broached to you.

DUDLEY: No.

WALSINGHAM: (*Off.*) Ho there – the Queen!

CECIL: Let me persuade you.

DUDLEY: So.

(*ELIZABETH enters with WALSINGHAM. She affects surprise at seeing DUDLEY.*)

ELIZABETH: How, Master Cecil, what does *this* fellow here?

(*ALL laugh at the Queen's little joke.*)

DUDLEY: (*Kneeling.*) He kneels, serves, loves.

ELIZABETH: Well. Come then, Gentlemen. Walsingham.

(*They sit. WALSINGHAM busies himself with papers.*)

WALSINGHAM: The new Dean for Durham. It is between Doctor Glover and Doctor Boze.

ELIZABETH: Which?

WALSINGHAM: Glover is three parts Catholic.

ELIZABETH: Walsingham for Doctor Boze.

CECIL: I also, madam. There are too many Catholics in the North already. Too close to the Border.

(*WALSINGHAM scribbles as ELIZABETH speaks.*)

ELIZABETH: To the Lord Bishop at Durham. Reverend
　　Father in God. We have heeded your request to name a
　　person. Long thought and anxious prayer alike conclude
　　in Doctor Boze. She that hath you ever in her mind and
　　care, your loving Sovereign, Elizabeth, et cetera.
　　(A CLERK goes with the letter to the BISHOP in the pulpit
　　as ELIZABETH continues, to DUDLEY.)
　　You see how we dispatch here, Councillor.
　　(The BISHOP glances at the paper.)
BISHOP: To the Queen's Majesty at St James. May it please
　　Your Grace, this Doctor Boze inclines towards Geneva
　　and the people hereabouts alas bend hard the other way.
　　We fear he will prove contumaceous. May it please Your
　　Grace to think upon the Reverend Doctor Culpepper.
　　(The CLERIC looks modest.)
　　This gentleman is moderate, learned, lowly and discreet.
　　He loves not dispute. Besides, he is known to us. *(He*
　　hands the letter to the CLERK.)
　　(The CLERK takes the letter back to the table, the CLERIC
　　and BISHOP looking anxiously after him, the BISHOP
　　murmuring.)
　　Eternally Your Grace's grateful servant Hugh,
　　Dunelmiensis.
ELIZABETH: Reverenced Father. The multiplying merits
　　of your nephew are known to us. Notwithstanding,
　　further thought and yet extended prayer confirm our
　　former choice. But we would not be peremptory.
BISHOP: It's Boze. *(He sits.)*
　　(The lights go down on the pulpit.)
WALSINGHAM: Good.
ELIZABETH: Glover is the better man.
CECIL: But Boze the better watchdog. And Your Grace has
　　need of watchdogs on the Scottish Border, now.
ELIZABETH: *(Alert.)* Why? What news from Scotland?
CECIL: It comes from Madrid, Your Grace. It is quite
　　certain that the King of Spain will marry his son to Mary
　　Stuart.
ELIZABETH: …Well then, it is certain.

CECIL: Your Grace, it must not be.

ELIZABETH: What then?

(*CECIL does not answer.*)

WALSINGHAM: It cannot be, Your Grace; war rather.

CECIL: War with Spain?

ELIZABETH: What then? Speak!

(*CECIL hesitates.*)

CECIL: Spain would not marry his son to Scotland, if he could marry him here.

ELIZABETH: Cecil, I have told you not to speak of this again.

CECIL: I spoke at your command, Your Grace.

ELIZABETH: Oh, Cecil, you are too clever to be honest...
(*She rises, uneasy.*)

CECIL: (*Pressing his advantage.*) If a Spanish army comes at us from Scotland it comes through a Catholic North, on a Catholic Crusade, with a Catholic Queen at its head. And the North won't fight...

ELIZABETH: And would the South accept a Catholic King? Walsingham, would you?
(*All look at WALSINGHAM.*)

CECIL: (*Quickly.*) No King; a Consort.

WALSINGHAM: He would not be offered the Crown Matrimonial?

CECIL: No.

WALSINGHAM: And a Protestant marriage?

CECIL: Of course.

WALSINGHAM: It is a way, Your Grace. If he will take those terms.

ELIZABETH: He will not.

CECIL: Then give him war, Your Grace, and then give even me a sword – but only then. And he would come by sea, we might resist. But if he comes by land what army can we send against those Spanish infantry? We are Sunday bowmen; and they are men of iron; and they have proved themselves of such a sort that where they set their foot no grass grows, thereafter. War with Spain is England lost.
(*It makes a silence.*)

ELIZABETH: And the Prince of Spain is a dribbling dwarf!
A diminutive monster who foams at the mouth!

CECIL: I cannot answer for his person, Majesty; I will
answer for my policy.

(*DUDLEY shifts.*)

ELIZABETH: Aye, what do you think, Councillor Robin?

DUDLEY: Too much to speak, Your Grace.

ELIZABETH: Then quit my Council.

DUDLEY: Robin thinks, war rather, death rather, let
England go. Your Grace's Councillor thinks no, let love
go; Her Grace must keep England.

(*ELIZABETH shifts and looks away.*)

ELIZABETH: (*Harshly.*) Love? Who spoke of love? (*Holding
out her hand to CECIL.*) For Madrid.

(*CECIL hands her a paper.*)

(*Glancing at it.*) Who wrote this?

CECIL: I, Your Grace.

ELIZABETH: We did not think you had such wooing terms.

CECIL: I was young once, Your Grace.

ELIZABETH: Logic compels us to believe you. For Madrid.

(*A MESSENGER exits with the letter
DUDLEY's head is sunk in apparent gloom.*)

Cecil, what can I do for this gentleman?

CECIL: There was an Earl of Leicester once in England.

ELIZABETH: Earl...? You are very sudden friends.

CECIL: I hope it truly, madam.

DUDLEY: Your Grace, I am not worthy.

ELIZABETH: Then be so, Lord Earl. (*Raising her voice.*) We
will receive the King of Spain's reply at Hampton.

(*CECIL and DUDLEY rise and bow. St James flies out as
Hampton Court flies in. CECIL and DUDLEY meanwhile
meet downstage, while ELIZABETH and WALSINGHAM
'freeze'.*)

CECIL: Well, sir, I had not thought you were so politic.

DUDLEY: Neither had I. I do not relish this.

CECIL: We dig for gold because we relish gold, sir. Not
because we relish digging. Do you want to break off?

DUDLEY: No.

CECIL: (*Moving to go.*) Come, then.

DUDLEY: What is my part this time?

CECIL: Perfect silence. Come.

(*They approach the table, bow together, then speak together.*)

CECIL/DUDLEY: (*Together.*) Your Grace.

(*CECIL and DUDLEY sit.*)

ELIZABETH: You arrive together, Gentlemen.

CECIL: We met on the road, Your Grace. Is the Spanish Ambassador come?

ELIZABETH: (*To a CLERK.*) Admit him.

(*DE QUADRA enters. He goes swiftly to ELIZABETH and kisses her hand with affectionate respect.*)

De Quadra.

DE QUADRA: Your Grace.

ELIZABETH: How does your master?

DE QUADRA: Your Grace. His Catholic Majesty is all transported. He thinks Madrid a little town in Paradise. And only fears to have curtailed his future lot by tasting Heaven here.

ELIZABETH: We thank His Majesty. And, His Majesty's fair son?

DE QUADRA: His son! Your Grace, a heart of thistledown. He floats.

ELIZABETH: Then we shall float together; for we are even as you say he is.

DE QUADRA: *Madam...*

CECIL: What dowry does His Majesty propose?

DE QUADRA: Ah, Cecil, my good friend, the King would dower such a match with the whole world...

CECIL: But failing that.

(*DE QUADRA whips out a roll of paper and places it deftly into CECIL's hands, gliding on to ELIZABETH in the same movement.*)

DE QUADRA: This – (*Showing a locket.*) – is a likeness of the Prince.

ELIZABETH: His Highness is well favoured, if this speaks true.

DE QUADRA: Would it might, Your Grace, but alas it is not the handiwork of a god.

ELIZABETH: De Quadra, such a face presages a strong mind.

DE QUADRA: Even so.

ELIZABETH: Deal honestly, de Quadra.

DE QUADRA: Your Grace, His Highness, it is true, is –
highly-strung. But there, what would you? The spirit of a
giant in a little human frame.

ELIZABETH: How little?

DE QUADRA: His Highness is compact, Your Grace.
I would not say little…

ELIZABETH: Would you say tall?

DE QUADRA: Tall… Alas, Your Grace, how tall is tall?

ELIZABETH: (*Indicating DUDLEY.*) This gentleman is tall.
(*DUDLEY rises. CECIL looks up from the scroll.*)

CECIL: This is well.

DE QUADRA: I think so, too, sir.

CECIL: Yet not so well that it could not be better. What is
this of Spanish galleys in our Channel ports?

WALSINGHAM: What? That sounds more like war than
wedding!

DE QUADRA: Ah, Master Walsingham, how do you do?
(*To ELIZABETH.*) The galleys are for use against His
Majesty's rebellious subjects in the Netherlands.

WALSINGHAM: Our best trade is with the Netherlands,
Your Grace.

DE QUADRA: It will be better, when the Netherlands are
pacified.

WALSINGHAM: The Netherlanders are good friends to
England, and to God.

DE QUADRA: With deference, Master Walsingham, they
may be your friends, God selects his own. And as for
England – are rebel subjects anywhere good friends to
any sovereign?

ELIZABETH: Spanish galleys in our ports might make me
rebel subjects here, Your Excellency.

DE QUADRA: Well, well. The galleys are a lesser matter.

ELIZABETH: You have a greater?

DE QUADRA: The form of marriage.

CECIL: English.

DE QUADRA: With a Catholic marriage first. (*It is half a question, half an assertion.*)

CECIL: After.

DE QUADRA: Then immediately after.

WALSINGHAM: Why immediately?

DE QUADRA: (*With a shrug.*) The same day.

WALSINGHAM: Why the same day?

DE QUADRA: (*Testily.*) Before the *night*, good Master Walsingham. In Catholic eyes your English form of marriage would be – (*He spreads his hands, delicately.*) – a form.

WALSINGHAM: As would the Catholic form in English eyes.

DE QUADRA: *Some* English eyes. (*He says this significantly and looks at CECIL.*)

CECIL: Immediately after.

DE QUADRA: Excellent. The – er – form of the form is important too. Your Grace must know – for I alas am told to tell Your Grace – my master will not have his son's soul jeopardised by any form which makes a mock of God.

ELIZABETH: Then tell your master that we think ourselves as careful of our soul as any king in christendom and would permit no form which mocked at God!

DE QUADRA: Your English Church is – er – flexible, Your Grace. Here it is one thing, there another. Here a priest who is almost a Catholic, there is a priest who is no-one knows what. There have lately been some church appointments, as that of Doctor Boze at Durham, which have much dismayed my master.

ELIZABETH: Zounds, sir, will you make our church appointments now?

DE QUADRA: Oh dear! Of course these vexious questions would not be, if His Highness were to wed some Catholic Queen. (*He lets it hang.*)
(*CECIL and DUDLEY look at ELIZABETH. She sighs and raises her voice.*)

ELIZABETH: To the Lord Bishop at Durham!

(*The lights come up on the pulpit, where the BISHOP is attentive.*)

Reverend Father in God. We have considered your wise words concerning Doctor Boze. The man is disputatious. If, therefore, it is not too late, appoint instead the Reverend Doctor Glover...

BISHOP: Glover! Your Grace, the man's a rampant Papist!

ELIZABETH: You see from this that weighed against her care for you and for the spiritual welfare of her realm, no sacrifice of vain consistency is too much for your loving Sovereign Elizabeth, et cetera.

BISHOP: The woman's mad!

(*The BISHOP sits. The lights fade on the pulpit.*)

DE QUADRA: Excellent. And who can say but that the tender influence of love will heal up these unhappy differences, his golden dart transfixing two young hearts make one of two great kingdoms. The galleys are a matter for negotiation, naturally.

CECIL: Naturally.

DE QUADRA: May I enjoy your company tonight?

CECIL: Tonight I am engaged, Your Excellency.

DE QUADRA: Tomorrow then?

CECIL: Tomorrow I shall be in Canterbury.

DE QUADRA: Well, let us not delay too long. Youth will be served. Your Grace, I go now to write that which will transport my master; would I had words worthy of my theme. (*He makes a graceful bow and continues to CECIL, backing.*) Next week, perhaps?

CECIL: Your Excellency's servant.

DE QUADRA: Madam, you have made me happy. (*He gives another bow.*)

ELIZABETH: Then we are quits.

DE QUADRA: Madam. (*He gives another bow: he is almost gone.*)

ELIZABETH: Your Excellency –

(*DE QUADRA stops.*)

– we had thought your Prince had lost his heart to the Queen of Scots.

DE QUADRA: The...? Your Grace, the Queen of Scots: who remembers the pale moon, when the great sun rises?
(*DE QUADRA gives a final bow, and is gone.*)

ELIZABETH: Well, Cecil, will it do?

CECIL: I do not know, Your Grace.

WALSINGHAM: Nor I, Your Grace. I think they mean to make us clients.

ELIZABETH: I think it will not do. And thank God for it.

CECIL: Madam, it must seem to do; until the Queen of Scots has married elsewhere.

ELIZABETH: Then let her marry soon.

CECIL: I think she will.

ELIZABETH: Perhaps we can arrange a marriage for her.

CECIL: That would be best, Your Grace. I have intelligence from Scotland coming to Nonsuch.

ELIZABETH: Mp. To Nonsuch, then.
(*The Hampton cloth flies out and the Nonsuch flies in. DUDLEY and CECIL move downstage. ELIZABETH and WALSINGHAM 'freeze'.*)

CECIL: Well, my lord, the dice are falling in our favour. Are you ready for your final throw?

DUDLEY: Cecil, why are you doing this?

CECIL: Because it is good policy for England.

DUDLEY: And what is it for Cecil?

CECIL: Good policy, too. You have her heart and always will.
(*DUDLEY grips him hard by the arm and growls desperately.*)

DUDLEY: Then why may I not marry *here*?

CECIL: That, over my grave; the other I will help you to. Will you have it?

DUDLEY: (*Dropping his hand.*) Yes.

CECIL: To it, then. You that way, I this.
(*CECIL and DUDLEY approach the table from different directions and meet there.*)

DUDLEY: (*Sitting.*) Well met, Master Cecil.

CECIL: (*Sitting.*) My lord.

ELIZABETH: How is de Quadra?

CECIL: He languishes a little, but we keep him in good heart. We feed him promises.

ELIZABETH: 'We'?

CECIL: My lord had dinner with de Quadra and myself the other day.

ELIZABETH: You are grown quite intimate.

CECIL: (*With a little laugh and half bow to DUDLEY.*) Oh, I – would not say 'intimate'.

ELIZABETH: You sound like de Quadra. Admit the messenger from Scotland.

WALSINGHAM: Davison!

> (*DAVISON enters. He kneels. ELIZABETH regards him approvingly, and motions him to rise.*)

ELIZABETH: So, sir, the Spanish embassy to Scotland is gone home.

DAVISON: Yes, Your Grace.

ELIZABETH: And how likes that the Queen of Scots?

DAVISON: She is enraged, Your Grace.

ELIZABETH: (*With a grunt of satisfaction.*) Ha. And does her rage become her?

DAVISON: Yes, Your Grace. (*Defiantly.*) All moods become her.

> (*ELIZABETH stares.*)

ELIZABETH: God's death, send no more *young* ambassadors to Scotland, Cecil. (*She rises, goes and examines DAVISON as an object of deep, half-amused interest.*) Describe her, then.

DAVISON: Your Grace, I cannot.

ELIZABETH: Cannot? Is she tall?

DAVISON: As Your Grace.

ELIZABETH: Thin?

DAVISON: As Your Grace.

ELIZABETH: We are twins?

DAVISON: No, Your Grace.

ELIZABETH: What colour is her hair?

DAVISON: Your Grace, her hair is shadow coloured.

ELIZABETH: God's death, he's written poetry. Her eyes?

DAVISON: Her eyes change colour with her moods, Your Grace.

ELIZABETH: You seem much taken with her moods. Has she many?

DAVISON: Yes, Your Grace. Sometimes she is right childish, and sometimes... (*He breaks off.*)

ELIZABETH: Well?

DAVISON: Right royal, Your Grace.

ELIZABETH: Hoo! And sometimes, as we hear, she is sportive, hey? Gallante, hey? Wanton?

DAVISON: Yes, Your Grace. And cruel and wilful and unfair. But then there come such sudden sinkings, such declension into soft submission, as sets a man on a high horse. (*His voice vibrates with an emotion too serious to laugh away.*)

(*ELIZABETH leaves him, on a shaky laugh.*)

ELIZABETH: God's death, it ought not to be hard to find a suitor for the lady, Cecil.

(*She turns to find CECIL and DUDLEY making furious faces at DAVISON, CECIL with his fists raised above his head. He converts the motion hastily into a stroking of his hair as she turns, but she is not deceived.*)

What? What's this? (*She looks at DAVISON.*) What? (*She gives a snort of mirth.*) You think we are jealous of this moon calf? (*She seats herself, and continues more formally.*) What is this mountebank, Rizzio?

DAVISON: Her playfellow, Your Grace.

ELIZABETH: No more?

DAVISON: Her Councillor, Your Grace.

ELIZABETH: No more?

DAVISON: I do not know, Your Grace. But I do not think he is the man that she would love.

ELIZABETH: Why not? Come, we are not angry with you. (*She smiles.*) Why is Signor Rizzio not the man that she would love? Is he ugly?

DAVISON: It is not that, Your Grace. (*He looks at her and ventures a half-smile in response to hers.*) He is small.

ELIZABETH: Ah – like you.

DAVISON: Yes, Your Grace.

(*ELIZABETH goes to him and rubs his hair.*)

ELIZABETH: The Queen of Scots likes tall men, does she?

DAVISON: Yes, Your Grace.

ELIZABETH: Poor boy. (*Briskly, cheerfully.*) Well then, Master Cecil, it seems that we are looking for a tall... (*She breaks off and freezes. The life drains from her motionless body. She looks at CECIL, at DUDLEY, back to CECIL. CECIL bows his head. ELIZABETH comprehends it all. She looks away. White-faced, she breathes out.*) O-o-o-oh... (*She looks quickly at DUDLEY with a last flash of hope. But now he too bows his head.*) (*Again.*) O-o-o-oh... (*Her empty eyes wander to DAVISON.*) You, sir, get you gone; you are lovesick. (*DAVISON goes.*) Oh, Cecil.

CECIL: Your Grace...

ELIZABETH: I see it, Cecil, I *see* it's very good. Protestant, English, loyal, a nobleman to boot – Earl of Leicester. And tall. It should do well – eh? Robin?

DUDLEY: Your Grace, I am green in Council – these gentlemen are better able...

ELIZABETH: Faugh! (*She gestures.*) Go. (*DUDLEY moves to go.*) Go both. (*DUDLEY goes. CECIL follows. They escape like schoolboys.*) (*Gently contemplating.*) Oh, Robin... (*WALSINGHAM discreetly gathers his papers and moves to go.*) You are going, sir?

WALSINGHAM: I thought Your Grace might wish to stay this business until... (*His voice tails.*)

ELIZABETH: Do you presume to know what we might wish? (*He sits, very quietly.*) What business?

WALSINGHAM: A conspiracy against Your Grace's life, of Catholic gentlemen, in the County of Durham.

ELIZABETH: Against my life?

WALSINGHAM: Yes, Your Grace.

ELIZABETH: Well. Tell Cecil.

WALSINGHAM: Your Grace. (*He rises and moves to go.*)

ELIZABETH: In the county of Durham?

WALSINGHAM: Yes, Your Grace.

>*(ELIZABETH nods.*
>*WALSINGHAM goes.*
>*ELIZABETH looks at DUDLEY's empty chair.)*

ELIZABETH: Oh – Councillor… *(She raises her head and softly begins to speak.)*
>*(The lights softly come up on the pulpit and the gravely listening BISHOP there.)*

To the Lord Bishop at Durham. Good Father, we trouble you too much. But both the gentlemen that we have named are too extreme, for this time, and that place. Therefore, let it be your kinsman's. For you tell us that he is a man of balance. And we are like a sleep-walker who wakes to find herself on a high roof, in darkness – and without a hand to hold her. Forgive, Elizabeth, et cetera… *(She is going out on the last words, her hand just momentarily placed on DUDLEY's chair before passing on.)*
>*(The BISHOP hurries down from the pulpit, subdued but urgent.)*

BISHOP: May it please Your Grace, my nephew is gone from here and is presently in Bristol where…

ELIZABETH: *(Ringingly.)* Lord Bishop! *(She whirls.)* Do as we command or by God we will unfrock you! *(She takes a great gasp of air and almost shouts.)* Elizabeth! *Queen!*
>*(A fanfare sounds. ELIZABETH exits.*
>*The Nonsuch cloth flies out. The lights change.*
>*MARY enters. She is on CECIL's arm. NAU, RIZZIO and LADIES follow. MARY seats herself.)*

MARY: Cecil, you are very welcome. We hear you are the wisest Councillor in Christendon. We think our cousin kind to part with you. The more so, as we know her pleasant purpose.

CECIL: Your Grace, her purpose is most pleasant, yes.

MARY: Aye, for you are sent, we hear, to crack a joke with us. But we must warn you, sir, the edge is off it, for it is foretold.

CECIL: A joke, Your Grace?

MARY: Oh. Davie, we are misinformed. Forgive me, sir. There was a waggish fellow here the other day who said your purpose was to offer me the hand of Robert Dudley.

CECIL: Madam, that is my purpose.

MARY: How straight he keeps his face. Excellent, sir. If you were not a Councillor you could be a comedian.

CECIL: Indeed, Your Grace, I so lack comedy I cannot understand how you find the offer comic.

MARY: Sir, do not persist. Your offer is an insult...

CECIL: Your Grace?

MARY: Cecil, was Robert Dudley unfit for Elizabeth? And yet fit for me?

CECIL: Nay, now I am quite confounded. Unfit for my mistress? She never thought of him, Your Grace. He has her high regard indeed, but no, no, not her heart.

MARY: No, that she has given to the Prince of Spain.

CECIL: That is correct, Your Grace.

MARY: We wish him joy of such a heart. We wish her joy of such a husband. And for her comfort tell your mistress that we have given our heart to an Englishman.

CECIL: ...May I know his name?

MARY: His name is Darnley.

CECIL: Now it is Your Grace who jests, I hope, for if this is not jest it is high treason.

MARY: Sir, I am a sovereign and can commit no treason unless against myself.

CECIL: You will find that you have done that, madam, if you wed Lord Darnley. I have seen the man, Your Grace has not – he is a lady-faced horseman, empty and idle.

MARY: Oh – it is on our account that you oppose it? We thank you for your care.

CECIL: My opposition matters nothing, madam, but my mistress has forbidden it; for reasons you know well.

MARY: I do not study Elizabeth's reasons. But can guess them. Lord Darnley is a Catholic.

CECIL: Yes, madam.

MARY: And bears the Tudor blood.

CECIL: Yes, madam.

MARY: Aye – and better Tudor blood than hers because it is legitimate.

CECIL: Madam, you forget yourself.

MARY: I forget nothing. England remembers more than you suppose, and Europe knows that any child of mine by Darnley would be heir to the English throne. These are Elizabeth's reasons. And mine.

CECIL: Well, madam, I am sorry for it. And I council you to put it from your mind. Lord Darnley is forbidden to quit England and will not come if you call him.

MARY: (*To NAU.*) Call him.

(*DARNLEY enters.*

CECIL is aghast, then speaks softly.)

CECIL: You fool...

MARY: Quit Scotland, sir, you are an uncouth messenger! (*CECIL bows curtly and starts to go, but is stopped by MARY continuing.*)

And tell your mistress that I have one reason more than she. (*She takes DARNLEY's hand.*) I love this bonny gentleman.

CECIL: I think you are deceived, Your Grace. I think that you are angry with my mistress. That bonny gentleman is light. And I think that when you are undeceived Your Grace will find his passing heavy.

MARY: God's death, sir, have you finished?

CECIL: That is for Your Grace to say.

MARY: You have finished.

(*CECIL goes, escorted by NAU and RIZZIO.*)

Well, if that was Cecil, Elizabeth is welcome to him. Good Lord, I think she must have run him up from odds and ends left over from a funeral.

DARNLEY: I thought he spoke well.

MARY: He is a politician, Harry, speaking well's his trade. You were not moved by what he said?

DARNLEY: Weren't you?

MARY: I have forgotten what he said.

DARNLEY: He called me a fool and said I was not fit for you.

MARY: The more fool he.

DARNLEY: Nay, all the world accounts him wise – and me unfit for you.

MARY: My love, I have not found you so...

DARNLEY: You have not wished to find me so.

MARY: You are too thoughtful, sir.

DARNLEY: I never was accounted that.

MARY: Then what has made you so? Is it my rank?

DARNLEY: My breeding fits me for your rank. Yourself has made me thoughtful.

MARY: Oh. If thought is all I have roused in you, I have wasted many pains.

DARNLEY: Nay, you have roused my love.

MARY: Be careless then, not thoughtful. You know that I love you.

DARNLEY: I know you would.

MARY: Harry, I have told you, and I swear before the saints: I'll have a husband I can love, or else I will have none at all.

DARNLEY: Would you have loved the Prince of Spain?

MARY: Nay, do not shame me, love. That was to have been a stroke of State. Yet Harry, even him I would have tried to love.

DARNLEY: And now you are trying to love me.

MARY: My lord, we were so born that we must choose fit marriage mates politically. It is God's generosity that we have found fit mates we naturally love. We are not to scrutinise his generosity, we are to love. If we attend to love, my lord, both dignity and reputation will come begging to our door.

(*Uplifted, he goes to her. They kiss.*)

Oh come, my love – and let's be married!

(*Bells ring, cheering is heard, and the sound of cheerful organ music. MARY takes DARNLEY by the hand and leads him towards the upper level.*

The ARCHBISHOP enters and awaits them. RIZZIO, NAU and LADIES enter from one side, the LORDS from the other. MARY and DARNLEY kneel, facing each other. The

ARCHBISHOP makes the Cross over their heads. They rise and kiss. The Court applauds in a crescendo of sound. But the LORDS deliberately straddle their legs and fold their arms, glowering. MARY and DARNLEY descend, acknowledging the applause. MARY kisses her LADIES, who curtsy. They turn to the LORDS.)

MARY: My lords, will you not rejoice?

MORTON: We have no cause here to rejoice.

MARY: Are even weddings not rejoiced at, then, in Scotland?

MORTON: Your Grace is wedded to a Catholic boy.

DARNLEY: Call me 'boy' and you shall have cause to regret, Lord Morton.

(MORTON laughs.)

What, sir, do you laugh?

MORTON: Yes, I laugh.

DARNLEY: I never endured insult when I was a private man, Lord Morton; do you think I will endure it now?

MORTON: Why, what are you now?

DARNLEY: By God, sir, am I not your lord?

MORTON: You are this lady's laddie; and no more.

DARNLEY: Zounds...! *(He steps forward.)*

(MARY stops him.)

MARY: Harry...! No...!

DARNLEY: What, am I to rule Scotland and must eat such stuff as this?

(There is a little silence.)

MARY: *(Awkwardly.)* You are to rule me, my lord, not Scotland.

(DARNLEY glares at her, bows stiffly, turns his back, and goes.)

(Half starting after him.) Harry...

(MORTON laughs again. MARY whirls.)

Lord Morton. My consort and myself mean you no harm. And we will give ourselves one season in which to show we mean no harm. Thereafter, we expect to see you smile. Harry!

(MARY hurries after DARNLEY, the Court following pell-mell.)

MORTON: Ten English pounds to ten Scots pennies, they're at one another's throats within six months.

RUTHVEN: No bet.

(The LORDS go, laughing. The lights change.
ELIZABETH enters at speed, CECIL after. She checks. He
is diffident and soothing.)

CECIL: *(Placating.)* Your Grace of course may marry whom you will.

ELIZABETH: Oh...! You are full of news this morning, sir.

CECIL: Within what's reasonable. And this petition, which your loving Commons most respectfully present –

ELIZABETH: – is no petition, but an admonition! I am admonished, by the Commons, to marry – now. Not when I would, nay, nor to whom I would, but to one of these that they have named, and get a child by him – and now!

CECIL: The Princes they have named they have enquired into most...

ELIZABETH: Enquired, sir? Are they kennelmen and I their breeding bitch?

CECIL: You are their mistress, madam, and this country's Queen.

ELIZABETH: In this I am no more than any other woman, Cecil. And I tell you that I have no mind, nor heart, to marry now.

CECIL: Your Grace, it would be very prudent, now. The Queen of Scots expects a child.

ELIZABETH: *(Alert.)* How do you know?

CECIL: I have it from Lord Morton, madam.

ELIZABETH: He has written?

CECIL: He is here, Your Grace.

ELIZABETH: Fetch him.

(CECIL gestures quietly offstage.
MORTON enters.)

Is this true?

MORTON: Yes, Your Grace.

ELIZABETH: She has not announced it.

MORTON: No doubt she expects to make some use of the announcement.

CECIL: She'd be a fool if she did not expect to make some use of it. It is a useful thing.

ELIZABETH: If it is so.

MORTON: I have it from a friend who is a friend of a close lady-friend of Signor Rizzio.

(*ELIZABETH picks up the petition thoughtfully.*)

ELIZABETH: Is he still close friends with your Queen?

MORTON: He's been no more than that since she was married. But he is still that. It's true enough, Your Grace.

ELIZABETH: I thought that Mary and her husband were no longer bed-fellows.

MORTON: They're not, not since he took to whores. But they were busy bed-fellows at first.

(*CECIL looks at ELIZABETH, expecting her to follow the main issue. But she is looking down and now looks up.*)

ELIZABETH: It's true, is it, that he has taken up with whores?

MORTON: Oh aye, and common brothel whores at that.

ELIZABETH: Why?

MORTON: He's a king in a brothel. In Council he's a clown. She boxed his ears and sent him packing from the Council in the end.

ELIZABETH: She boxed his ears?

MORTON: She all but pitched him off his seat.

ELIZABETH: (*With a shrug.*) No wonder then he took to whores.

MORTON: Her wits go out the window when she's in a rage. And she was in a hellish rage. He showed so cocky and so daft, you see, so brainless – overbearing, and so greedy for his own. And she, then, was in love with him.

ELIZABETH: She never was in love with him.

MORTON: Oh, yes, she was, Your Grace.

ELIZABETH: She was infatuated.

MORTON: Your Grace may call it what you like. I saw it. She hung upon him like a pedlar's bag. And sometimes when they danced, she had a look upon her face, that showed as much of her as if she had been naked... (*He is lost for a moment.*) No woman ever looked at me like that... (*CECIL coughs. MORTON comes to.*) She's three months gone.

CECIL: And she is nightly on her knees, Your Grace, and praying for a son. And praying for her son to be a wise and potent Prince. Of Scotland and of England, too. As he is like to be, and soon, Your Grace, unless Your Gr…

ELIZABETH: Enough, enough, I am not blind. (*She looks at the petition.*) This is not ill-considered neither. But here they name three Catholic Princes and three Protestants. (*She puts down the petition.*) And if I go courting any one of these, I lose the love of one half of my people.

CECIL: Your Grace may find that one half of your Court is paying court in Edinburgh presently.
(*She looks at him.*)

ELIZABETH: …Do you pay court in Edinburgh?

CECIL: No, madam, I do not.

ELIZABETH: The time may come. Meanwhile tell the Commons that we will not marry, yet, but that we thank them for their care. And will remit some portion of the taxes due to us this coming year. I go a-courting with my people, Cecil. (*She moves to go.*)

CECIL: (*Irritated and anxious.*) And the son that she is praying for?

ELIZABETH: Why, on your knees, good William, and pray for it to be a girl. Three Queens on the run should finish any country.
(*She goes, leaving CECIL perplexed.*)

MORTON: That lassie has a long head on her shoulders.

CECIL: (*Preoccupied.*) Yes – the problem is to keep it there.

MORTON: Well, that may be a problem for us all, quite soon.

CECIL: It will.
(*He looks at MORTON, who says nothing.*)
So what do you intend to do, Lord Morton?

MORTON: (*With a wolfish grin.*) Me, Master Cecil? D'you really want to know?

CECIL: Perhaps not. Good day to you, Lord Morton. (*He moves to go.*)

MORTON: Good day to you.
(*CECIL goes.*)
You creepy wee creature.

(*The Scots LORDS enter. MORTON turns and joins them. The LADIES, RIZZIO and NAU enter opposite. A fanfare sounds and MARY enters. They all bow. She mounts to the upper level and addresses the LORDS, smiling graciously.*)

MARY: My lords, we have assembled you to hear a happy thing. You were right melancholy wedding guests, but now I think you will rejoice. My lords, we are with child.

MORTON: And why should we rejoice at that?

MARY: Because you are loyal Scots.

MORTON: Aye, we are Scots. And we should have a Scottish King.

MARY: If God grants me a son, you'll have a Scottish King.

MORTON: His mother for a start is French.

(*MARY turns away impatiently, but then turns back.*)

MARY: My father bore the blood of Bruce. And I was born at Lithgow Castle. When I was five years old I do confess I went away to France and got my breeding there. Forgive me, it was an error of my youth. If my manner is offensive so be it and good night. I can do no more. It is not for myself I ask your loyalty. My child, on whose behalf I do demand your loyalty, will be both born and bred in Edinburgh – and fully Scots as you.

MORTON: And will he so?

MARY: By parentage it's true he'll be a little French on one side and a little English on the other...

MORTON: And will he so? By parentage?

MARY: I do not think I understand you, sir.

MORTON: I think you do. Where is Lord Darnley?

MARY: I do not know, sir, where he is.

MORTON: It's odd that he's not here.

MARY: It's very odd. I did desire him to be here.

MORTON: What means his being elsewhere then?

MARY: I cannot guess his meanings, but by Heaven I will come at yours.

MORTON: My meaning is the same as his. And you can come at it in any pub in Edinburgh. This child, my lords, will be a little French on one side, aye, but on the other – (*He glares at RIZZIO.*) – half Italian!

(*MARY raises a hand as though to strike him, controls herself and turns away.*)

RIZZIO: My lords, I swear by all the saints...!

MARY: What? Will you protest it? Lord Morton, leave us. You infect the air.

(*MORTON and the LORDS bow and go. MARY turns.*)

Well, Claud, I have tried the patient way...

RIZZIO: ...Maria. (*He points warningly.*)

(*MARY turns to find that BOTHWELL has lingered and stands now looking at her. She is a bit startled.*)

MARY: Lord Bothwell.

BOTHWELL: (*Bowing gravely.*) Your Grace.

MARY: What do you want?

BOTHWELL: A private audience.

MARY: Private? Why so?

BOTHWELL: Don't be frightened.

MARY: Frightened, sir? What should I fear? Leave us, gentlemen.

NAU: (*Anxiously.*) Your Grace, it is not...

MARY: Nay leave us, Claud.

RIZZIO: (*Dubiously.*) Maria...

(*NAU, RIZZIO and the LADIES go.*

MARY and BOTHWELL cross, slowly eyeing each other.)

MARY: Well?

BOTHWELL: Puir wee lass.

MARY: (*Amused and startled.*) What?

BOTHWELL: You're going to have a hard confinement. You're too thin for it, though.

MARY: Indeed?

BOTHWELL: I know what I'm talking about, too. You just bide quiet awhile. Don't ride so much; and don't ride so wild. And mind what you're eatin'. And altogether be a bit more sensible; and treat yourself more kind.

MARY: Well, thanks; I will.

BOTHWELL: Guid. When's it due?

MARY: The time of our confinement is a thing we will announce when we are minded to, Lord Bothwell.

BOTHWELL: July.

MARY: Who told you that?

BOTHWELL: Your husband has been spending himself elsewhere since November, has he not?

MARY: If you will speak of him, sir, you will study your respect.

BOTHWELL: Let's speak of something else, then. You'd have to study hard to speak of Darnley with respect.

MARY: I think this insolence is studied. Leave us.

BOTHWELL: Look, I have matter which you ought to hear.

MARY: I will not hear your matter.

(*BOTHWELL shrugs and is about to go.*)

Unless you can attain a minimum of manner, too.

BOTHWELL: (*Mimicking her.*) If my manner is offensive, so be it and good night. I can no more.

MARY: Oh, Jesus, are we there again?

BOTHWELL: I like your manner fine.

(*She looks at him.*)

It's very pretty.

MARY: Good heavens, my lord, that is the second compliment within these same four years.

BOTHWELL: Now fancy you rememberin' the first.

MARY: Remember it? How not? A compliment in Scotland is a memorable thing. It stands out like a lily on a heap of dung.

BOTHWELL: That's no' a bad description of yourself in Scotland.

(*She looks at him cautiously. They exchange a little mocking bow.*)

MARY: I'll hear your matter.

BOTHWELL: It's men and means you want, I think?

MARY: It is.

BOTHWELL: You do not mean to meddle with the Kirk?

MARY: The Kirk, sir? Are you pious?

BOTHWELL: When the Kirk threw down the Catholic Church I got some fine broad meadow land; that used to belong to the Catholic Church. I'm awfu' pious about those meadows.

MARY: If I got men and means from you I could not meddle with your meadows.

BOTHWELL: That's true enough. What terms are you offerin'?

MARY: No terms. I have taken out an option on the future Bothwell; and you have wit enough to see it.

BOTHWELL: (*Smiling approval.*) You're no fool, are you?

MARY: No, sir; did you think I was?

BOTHWELL: You married Darnley.

MARY: …What is it in me, Bothwell, that provokes you and your fellow lords at every turn and all the time to strip me of my dignity? Is it merely that I am a woman?

BOTHWELL: A bonny woman.

MARY: So?

BOTHWELL: Worth strippin'.

MARY: Is that another compliment?

BOTHWELL: Yes.

MARY: Your vein of courtesy's exhausted. Go.
(*BOTHWELL moves to go.*)
It was a compliment for a courtesan.

BOTHWELL: Am I to go or stay?

MARY: You'll change your ways, sir, if you stay.

BOTHWELL: I have no mind to change my ways. We're very much alike.

MARY: You'll not tell me that's a compliment.

BOTHWELL: Oh, I steal sheep and you steal revenues. Otherwise we're much alike.

MARY: By God, there is another difference –

BOTHWELL: There is.

MARY: – I am a sovereign. And you, sir, are a subject.

BOTHWELL: No. You are a woman. (*He approaches close.*)
Why don't you send me packin' now?

MARY: Oh, sir, I am fascinated by your rough provincial masculinity.

BOTHWELL: I think you are, a bit.

MARY: Go!
(*BOTHWELL moves to go again.*)
You are unfit for our purpose.

BOTHWELL: Why, what was that?

MARY: What, sir, do you smell promotion?

BOTHWELL: Do I?

MARY: A high promotion, Bothwell; you might come by further meadows.

BOTHWELL: What is it?

MARY: We had thought to make you Lord Protector to our child.

BOTHWELL: Oh. (*He pulls at his beard, thoughtfully.*)

MARY: Ay. Now I think he'll change his ways.

BOTHWELL: You'd want a Catholic for that.

MARY: So change your church and be a Catholic. It would not cost you much.

BOTHWELL: It would not cost me anything, to be a Catholic, for I am not a Christian. I will not do it, though. For if our ways are different and you would like our ways to match – you must change your ways! To mine!

MARY: By Heaven, Lord Bothwell, I have heard about your ways. Even in Scotland your name is morbid. You are a bloody villain, sir, a tyrant and a sodomist, an enemy to innocence, a vampire and a demonist! It's only in your better moments, Bothwell, that you are a thief.

BOTHWELL: So *that's* what fascinates you.

MARY: Go!

(*BOTHWELL goes.*)

And go for ever – be banished to Dunbar – you will never see my face again!

BOTHWELL: You're wrong, I think.

MARY: Go!

BOTHWELL: I was goin' – you keep stoppin' me.

(*BOTHWELL has gone. MARY glares after him.*
Unseen behind her, NAU and RIZZIO enter.)

MARY: Lout!

RIZZIO: Bothwell?

MARY: Yes. (*She turns to him with a little laugh.*) I do believe he thinks he's a lady's man!

RIZZIO: Astonishing.

MARY: No fooling, sir; I am not in the mood.

(*The light begins to concentrate into a small conspiratorial area at the table, surrounded by shadow. MARY sits.*)

(*To NAU.*) Did any other of the lords come forward, Claud?

NAU: No, Your Grace.

MARY: (*Dipping her pen.*) Well – (*She writes, rapidly.*) – I will try my way now.

(*NAU sits and watches her unhappily. RIZZIO, too, draws near.*)

NAU: You write, Your Grace?

MARY: Yes, sir, I write.

RIZZIO: (*Peeping.*) In Latin, too.

NAU: To whom does Your Grace write?

RIZZIO: He'll have difficulty reading it, whoever he may be.

MARY: (*Writing.*) So you will make it fair. And you –
(*Looking up at NAU.*) – will carry it to Rome.

NAU: (*Sadly.*) Oh, madam, Rome?

MARY: And when you have got means, in Rome, I will send to Milan for mercenaries. Loyalty does not grow in Scotland, so I will import it.

(*DARNLEY enters, uncertainly, hanging off in the shadows. He carries a bottle.*)

RIZZIO: My lord.

DARNLEY: (*Eagerly.*) Good evening, Claud – Signor Rizzio.

RIZZIO: My lord.

(*NAU and RIZZIO withdraw respectfully as DARNLEY drifts towards MARY, who, after one glance round, one stare, returns to her writing. He sits and watches her.*)

DARNLEY: Good evening, Mary.

MARY: What do you want?

DARNLEY: Might I not simply have come home, like any other man?

MARY: You might. It seems improbable. (*She does not look up from her flying pen.*)

DARNLEY: (*After a pause.*) Are you writing a letter?

MARY: Yes.

DARNLEY: Who to?

(*She thrusts it towards him at full stretch. He looks at it.*)
It's in Latin.

MARY: Yes.

DARNLEY: I can't read Latin.

MARY: No. (*She pulls it back and goes on writing.*)

DARNLEY: You're cruel, Mary.

MARY: Oh, Harry, go away.

DARNLEY: Mary, I'm sorry.

(*It is touching in its sincerity, pathetic in its infantile inadequacy. She shifts restlessly and stops writing, but does not look up, exhaustedly impatient.*)

MARY: Have you been drinking?

DARNLEY: I'm not drunk.

MARY: You're maudlin.

DARNLEY: It isn't drink that's made me maudlin. Not this evening.

(*He waits. She struggles against it, but speaks at length, still without looking up.*)

MARY: What is it then?

DARNLEY: (*Pathetically.*) Mary...

MARY: (*Exasperated.*) *What?*

DARNLEY: Look at me.

(*She blows out an angry sigh, throws down her pen, and raises her glowering face. But seeing him, her expression alters. She rises, staring, and backs away.*

RIZZIO and NAU come forward, alarmed. DARNLEY averts his face from them.)

NAU: Your Grace.

MARY: There are sores on his mouth... Harry, look at me – what are those sores on your mouth?

(*Her reaction has appalled DARNLEY. He rises, stares wildly at RIZZIO and NAU, then speaks defiantly.*)

DARNLEY: It's the frost!

MARY: By God I know that frost.

DARNLEY: Mary... (*He approaches her.*)

MARY: Stand off!

DARNLEY: Mary...

MARY: Sir, will you stand off? You are unclean...!

(*DARNLEY almost runs to the exit, then turns.*)

DARNLEY: (*In a voice shaking with feeling.*) God save me from a loving woman.

(*DARNLEY goes.*)

MARY: (*Starting after him.*) Harry... (*She checks.*) Oh, Jesus – the child...!

(*RIZZIO goes to her, alert and calm.*)

RIZZIO: When was the child conceived, Maria?

MARY: Four – four and a half months.

RIZZIO: And have you seen the sores before?

MARY: No?

RIZZIO: The child is safe.

MARY: Oh, Davie, do you really know?

RIZZIO: Cherto! In Padua this useful branch of knowledge was the most highly regarded of my many accomplishments. I was greatly in demand. But do you know I have never been so greatly in demand as I have since we came to this godly city of Edinburgh? I think it is the cold, you know, it brings people together. Ah good, you smile. And the child is safe.

MARY: Thank God for Davie.

RIZZIO: I do, frequently.

(*She smiles again, but then her smile fades.*)

MARY: And him?

RIZZIO: Your husband. Hm. The English have a saying: You have made your bed and you must lie in it. Myself I have never seen the need for this; when there are other beds.

(*She drifts towards the exit, then turns and looks at him.*)

MARY: (*Softly.*) Davie, bring your lute.

(*MARY goes.*)

RIZZIO: (*Rising; delicately.*) Aha!

NAU: Signor Rizzio – don't go to her!

RIZZIO: Oh come, Claud, the Queen needs – (*He makes a deliberately ambiguous gesture.*) – comfort.

(*RIZZIO goes after MARY. NAU goes separately. The LORDS enter and tramp across to the table. MORTON picks up the letter.*)

MORTON: Who here has lands from the old Church?

ALL: I.

MORTON: Well, you're to lose them.

RUTHVEN: Ach, she hasnae the men.

MORTON: Oh, she'll have taken thought for that. It'll be Frenchmen maybe, or maybe mercenaries, but no, no,

141

she thought of that before she did this. (*He puts the letter down.*) So what's to do?

RUTHVEN: Fight.

MORTON: It's gey expensive fightin'. An' you can always lose.

RUTHVEN: What then?

(*From behind the curtain at the head of the shallow pyramid of stairs, the sound of the lute is heard, playing RIZZIO's tune. They turn and look. The light begins to gather, ominous.*)

MORTON: I'm getting to like that instrument. Verra seductive. Aye – a bagpipe's gey stirrin' on the moors but it's no help in a bedroom.

RUTHVEN: What are you talking about?

MORTON: Her husband, you gowk.

LINDSEY: Why, what can *he* do?

MORTON: Nothing while he's only that. But suppose he was the King. And suppose he was bound to us. Bound hard. Our man.

LINDSEY: He's no a man at all.

MORTON: Well, call him a man for courtesy. D'you see it?

RUTHVEN: No.

MORTON: Well, I do, Ruthven. I see it clear. So either come with me or take yourself off and be damned.

RUTHVEN: I'll come with you.

MORTON: Right, here he is.

(*DARNLEY enters, as before but without the bottle.*)

(*Urgently, sotto voce.*) Give him a bow, give him a bow.

(*The LORDS bow. DARNLEY stops uncertainly.*)

DARNLEY: My lords…?

MORTON: You look sick, sir. Are you?

DARNLEY: Yes.

MORTON: And so are we, sir, of the same disease.

DARNLEY: What?

MORTON: Domination! Domination by a woman. That we are sick of, and so is Scotland.

DARNLEY: By God, you are right, Morton; that is my sickness.

MORTON: We know it, sir. We have watched you. And we think you are too patient. We think the husband of the Queen should be a King.

(*DARNLEY looks at them, breathing hard, pulling at his opened doublet, trying to sober up.*)

DARNLEY: Well?

MORTON: And you would be the King, sir, you must play the leader.

DARNLEY: Leader?

MORTON: Aye. And if you'd be a husband, you must play the man!

(*The lute is heard again and a low laugh from MARY.*)

Ha! They're vigorous enough, heh? They're diligent, heh?

DARNLEY: Wha'...?

MORTON: God's death, my lord, they're going *to* it – now!

DARNLEY: Who...?

MORTON: The monkey – and your wife!

DARNLEY: *Whaaa*-aa...! (*He reels towards the steps.*)

(*MORTON grips him by the arm and wheels him round and back.*)

MORTON: (*With an admiring chuckle.*) Did I not say there was a kingly spirit in this man? But see, Your Majesty, these things must be done majestically. I have here a wee paper. Which all of us will sign. (*He puts it on the table and gives a curt nod to his colleagues.*) Sign.

(*The LORDS sign.*)

DARNLEY: (*As they do so.*) What is it?

MORTON: Our warrant.

DARNLEY: Warrant?

MORTON: Aye – or say a promise which we make each to each other, aye and God Almighty too, that what we purpose here is a naething mair nor less than justice for yourself and David Rizzio; nae mair for you, nae less for him. The crown for the King, death for the adulterer. Now you sign. (*He thrusts the pen into DARNLEY's hand.*)

DARNLEY: Sign?

MORTON: Kneel, my lairds.

(*The LORDS kneel.*)

This is a solemn moment in the history of Scotland.

(*Still DARNLEY hesitates. MARY's low laugh comes again. He turns and looks up at the curtain.*)

They're going to it now, my lord! Laughing! Making comparisons!

(*DARNLEY whirls back again and signs. The LORDS rise. MORTON takes the papers, grunts, satisfied, and puts it away. He pushes DARNLEY aside as done with. All draw daggers.*)

Right, my lords. Quick and quiet.

(*In a swift padding rush they are up the steps and tear down the curtain, revealing MARY and RIZZIO.*)

Signor Rizzio!

(*He grabs RIZZIO and throws him to the others. They fall on him like a pack of dogs.*)

MARY: (*In the uproar.*) Ho there! Rescue! Treason! Bothwell! Bothwell!

(*The mangled corpse is let drop. MARY falls in shock. DARNLEY is hanging off, appalled and nerveless. MORTON is angry.*)

MORTON: Dagger him, man!

(*DARNLEY is paralysed. A LORD leaps down to him, snatches his dagger and throws it to MORTON, who plunges it into the corpse. MARY gives a cry of horror.*

BOTHWELL and NAU enter at the run. They check as the LORDS present daggers, crouching. BOTHWELL spreads his empty hands, approaches and looks at the corpse.)

BOTHWELL: God's death, my lords, you're very thorough. Lord Darnley, I think this is yours. (*He tosses the dagger to DARNLEY.*)

DARNLEY: (*Piteously.*) Mary, I...

(*DARNLEY dashes from the stage.*)

MORTON: Now, Lord Bothwell, are you here to hinder or to help?

BOTHWELL: Neither, Lord Morton.

MORTON: Then you're in my road.

BOTHWELL: Then may I get out of it?

MORTON: Right out of it, Bothwell, out of Edinburgh now.

BOTHWELL: (*To MARY.*) Your Grace.

(*MARY raises her head and looks at him.*)

It seems that I must leave you to God's care. I'm for Dunbar.

(*BOTHWELL goes.*)

MORTON: Now, madam, though this was rough yet it was justice.

(*MARY descends unsteadily, NAU hovering anxiously at her side. She crouches at the corpse and sees the wounds.*)

MARY: Oh, God...(*She rises, bewildered.*) He was my friend. (*She feels faintness coming over her, reaches for support, and swoons.*)

(*NAU catches her and lowers her to the ground. MORTON looks on gloomily.*)

NAU: Good God, my lord – what have you done?

MORTON: Our duty. Naething more.

(*MORTON moves to go. The LORDS follow. MORTON snarls at them.*)

Shift it!

(*MORTON and the LORDS go, dragging the corpse. MARY watches covertly.*)

MARY: (*When they have gone.*) Morton, Ruthven, Lindsey, Douglas, Glencairn, Falconside and Kerr...

NAU: (*Startled.*) Madam...?

MARY: Remember them! Remind me every day that they must die.

NAU: Oh, madam, this is wild! The castle is full of their men!

(*She looks about, then rises from her knees.*)

MARY: So we must quit it.

NAU: There is a guard on every door!

MARY: There will be no guard on the kitchen door. Come. (*She moves to go.*

NAU follows her, shaken, bewildered.)

NAU: But, madam, where?

MARY: Where? To the Border – Dunbar!

(*They go.*)

End of Act One.

145

ACT TWO

The throne is on top of the pyramid now. At the foot of the pyramid stands an ornate golden casket three feet high, with carrying handles.

When the curtain rises KNOX is discovered in the pulpit. MORTON, RUTHVEN and LINDSEY, all gloomy, stand below.

KNOX: Lord, Lord, what tribulations we have seen. What marching, counter-marching, lying down in the wet heather, rising in the night, what ambushes, what wounds, what death... (*Descending; plaintively.*) The execution of the adulterer Rizzio was a very godly deed, you might have thought that it would prosper. But no, no, Man proposes, God disposes. (*Bitterly.*) Aye, and the Devil looks after his own. This, an't please you – (*He indicates the carpet.*) – is a christening font. Aye – it's no ornament from a brothel, it's a christening font. Gurnia, gurnia, solid gold.

CECIL: (*Off.*) Ho there, the Queen!

MORTON: Now for God's sake, Master Knox, and you must speak, speak small. For our cart has no wheels and the woman's rampant.

(*ELIZABETH, WALSINGHAM, LEICESTER and CECIL enter.*)

ELIZABETH: Are these the murderers?

KNOX: There was no murder, madam.

ELIZABETH: What then?

KNOX: Godly execution.

ELIZABETH: I do not think I know a godly execution. But I know the difference between execution and murder. It is the Royal Warrant.

MORTON: We had it, madam.

ELIZABETH: (*To WALSINGHAM; contemptuously.*) Darnley's 'warrant'.

KNOX: No, madam, God's.

ELIZABETH: Oh – did he sign it, too?

KNOX: That's verra blasph...

146

ELIZABETH: Peace, Master Knox. We are no Edinburgh housewife. Morton, how came the Queen to escape?

MORTON: She spoke me fair, madam – God help me, she seemed – (*Indignantly.*) – remorseful.

ELIZABETH: You mean she fooled you.

MORTON: Your Grace, the woman is a verra serpent!

ELIZABETH: Poor Adam. Poor, thick-witted, bloody-handed, Scottish Adam. What do you expect of me?

MORTON: Your mercy, madam.

KNOX: And your aid, madam.

ELIZABETH: For our mercy, it is universal and you have it. For our aid: we tell you here before the world, we aid no rebels. For royalty and rebellion both, are indivisible. Go. (*KNOX, MORTON, RUTHVEN and LINDSEY go.*) Walsingham. Give them money.

WALSINGHAM: Yes, Your Grace. How much?

ELIZABETH: As little as will keep them rebellious. Cecil, talk to Lord Morton.

CECIL: Your Grace.

ELIZABETH: Robin, you have the hardest task.

DUDLEY: Your Grace?

ELIZABETH: Listen to Master Knox. Now leave us. (*DUDLEY, WALSINGHAM and CECIL go.*

ELIZABETH approaches the font and looks at it carefully.) (*To herself.*) She escapes – down little stairs and greasy passages, she escapes, through the kitchens. I do not know where the kitchens are. And then in the dark, in the sweet smelling stables, she saddles her own horse; he knows her, he is quiet. *I* cannot saddle a horse. And then she rides, down rocky screes, through mountain rivers, two days and nights, two hundred miles, she must have ridden without sleep. And *I* am sleepless, I am spent. And then, this Bothwell – raises men, half-naked men whose whole wealth is a sword, and drives her enemies from Edinburgh – and for what? Why, for herself... And now she returns, but easily now, easily. (*Harshly.*) For she is big with child. And that child is my heir, for I am a barren stock! (*She ascends to the throne.*)

147

ROBERT BOLT

*(MARY, LADIES, two LORDS, BOTHWELL, the
ARCHBISHOP, MOR and NAU enter.
MARY carries a baby. She goes to the font.)*
(Calling.) Your Grace – your rebel subjects came here
and appealed to us. But we have given them a sour reply.
And for a further token of our love, we send you this.
(She indicates the font.)

MARY: Your Grace, we guess what manner of reply you
gave our rebel subjects. Your Grace may guess our
gratitude. And for this further token of your love – why,
we will put it to good use!
(The ARCHBISHOP dips into the font.)

ARCHBISHOP: In the name of the Father, Son and Holy
Ghost: James Stuart, Prince of Scotland, Ireland, and
England!
*(A fanfare sounds. ELIZABETH exits above. The
ARCHBISHOP exits, followed by the two LORDS bearing
the font.
MARY takes the child, peering at it delightedly, taking it
back towards BOTHWELL.)*

MARY: Hey, boy, shall we ride? Hey? Shall we ride
together, you and I – hey, boy? Shall we then…? Oh!
(She laughs up at BOTHWELL.) He sneezed.
(BOTHWELL nods coldly.)

BOTHWELL: He's very talented, no doubt about it.
(MARY smiles.)

MARY: *(To the baby.)* And so he is. No doubt about it.

NAU: Your Grace must now appoint the Lord Protector.

BOTHWELL: The job is spoken for.

MARY: What needs he with a Lord Protector? He will make
shift with a Queen Protector – won't you, boy, hey?

NAU: Madam, these are not the times to break an ancient
custom; beseech you to decide upon some valiant and
sober gentleman who…

BOTHWELL: Are you deaf, man? The job's spoken for.
*(MARY looks at BOTHWELL thoughtfully, a little sadly,
then down again at the baby.)*

MARY: *(Softly.)* Lord Mor.

(*MOR steps forward. BOTHWELL watches darkly.*)

Lord Mor, I give into your guard this most precious burden.

MOR: It is a trust that I will answer for to God himself, Your Grace.

MARY: (*Smiling, ready to weep, relinquishing the baby.*) I ask no better.

(*MOR goes with the baby. The LADIES follow. MARY's eyes and body yearn after them.*)

Bring him to me, ladies, before supper.

(*All go except MARY and BOTHWELL.*)

BOTHWELL: (*Quietly.*) So you don't trust me.

MARY: (*Frightened, placating.*) With myself I trust you.

(*BOTHWELL looks away from her and gloomily grunts.*)

BOTHWELL: Mebbe.

MARY: I have no choice but trust you, being your slave.

BOTHWELL: Don't you know yourself better than that? You're nobody's slave.

MARY: It is you who do not know me. See. (*She goes down, clasping his legs, abased.*)

BOTHWELL: That's just extravagance. Let go my legs. You want it both ways, Mary. Like – you'll feed me food on a fork. But I must eat it whether I've a mind to it or not, or you'll sling the plate across the room. You've a bluidy awful temper, d'you know that?

MARY: Yes.

BOTHWELL: And you were my wife, I'd have taken a whip to you before this.

MARY: Well, I would be your wife in anything I can.

(*She smiles up sideways and catlike, but he leaves her.*)

BOTHWELL: (*Soberly.*) I doubt that. With me to your bed here in Edinburgh, and Darnley to your husband away there in Glasgow, you have it both ways, the way you want it. I doubt you'd be my wife.

MARY: I have given you no cause to doubt it.

BOTHWELL: There's an easy way to prove it. Fetch him here.

(*She rises, wretched, and looks away.*)

(*Sadly, bitterly.*) You're playing, Mary. You play at everything. You think that life's a game and you the only

149

one allowed to cheat. Well, it's no game and you canna cheat, for there are no rules. It's real. But you're no a real woman.

MARY: You lie.

BOTHWELL: Yes, I lie. Come here.

(*She goes to him. He kisses her, quite gently. Her response becomes fierce. Deliberately, he holds her away.*)

Do you fetch him?

(*She searches his face.*)

MARY: Jamie; do you know what you are asking?

BOTHWELL: Yes; everything. Ought I to ask for less?

MARY: I'll fetch him.

(*MARY goes.*)

BOTHWELL: (*Calling.*) Ormiston!

(*ORMISTON enters, peeling an apple.*)

Well?

ORMISTON: Well – I have forty-five pounds of it; in three wee kegs. It should suffice.

BOTHWELL: To hell with should; will it?

ORMISTON: It's no just the verra best powder I've seen; it has a sort of greyish look, guid powder's black. And Kirk o' Field's a gey strong house. Aye, strongly built. What like did you want with the house?

BOTHWELL: I want it lifted off the earth.

ORMISTON: Forty-five pounds'll no do that.

BOTHWELL: Get more then.

ORMISTON: That's a' verra well. It's not easy to come by, not quietly. And there's enough folk ken what you're about already.

BOTHWELL: Who?

ORMISTON: That's hard to say. But since she went to Glasgow there's been a sort of gathering in the air. Have you not noticed?

BOTHWELL: Yes.

(*TALA enters with a letter and gives it to BOTHWELL.*)

TALA: A letter, Laird, from herself in Glasgow.

BOTHWELL: How is it?

TALA: You're in deep water, I would say. He's awfu' sick. She's sorry for him.

BOTHWELL: Hell. (*He opens the letter and reads.*)
(*The two men look over his shoulder.*)

ORMISTON: It's a guid hand is that.

TALA: It's a French hand.

ORMISTON: Is that right?

BOTHWELL: Off, you dogs! (*He reads.*) 'Being absent from him who has my heart…' mp. (*He turns several pages impatiently.*)

TALA: It's a long letter.

ORMISTON: Why wouldn't it be? It's a love letter.

BOTHWELL: (*Reading.*) 'His sickness abates yet he has almost slain me with his breath though I came no nearer than the bed's foot. For Rizzio he says…' Curse what he says, is he coming? (*He reads.*) 'Alas, my lord…' (*With an impatient growl he turns another page.*) 'I cannot sleep because I cannot sleep…' Hell and damnation, is he coming or not? 'Summa. He will not come except… And so I have promised. We come' – (*He turns a page then breathes out, satisfied.*) – 'tomorrow.' Ormiston, how much to make it certain?

ORMISTON: Another hundred pounds.

BOTHWELL: Get it from the armoury.
(*He throws a ring of keys which ORMISTON catches.*)

ORMISTON: (*Dangling them; dubiously.*) It's awfu' obvious.

BOTHWELL: (*Scanning the letter again.*) Do it.

ORMISTON: You're the master; I'm the man.
(*ORMISTON goes, with TALA.*)

BOTHWELL: (*Reading again.*) 'It is late, I am alone, I desire never to cease writing, yet now must cease for lack of paper and so end my letter. Read it twice or thrice. Burn it.' Burn it? Oh, no, my love; this is my warrant.
(*MARY enters above. She is alone.*)
Where is he? Have you not fetched him?

MARY: Yes. Jamie, what do you mean to do?
(*He looks at her hard.*)

BOTHWELL: Don't ask me what I will do. You've done your part.

(*DARNLEY and a DOCTOR enter above. DARNLEY wears a weird white mask, white gloves and slippers, a fanciful white dressing-gown.*)

DARNLEY: Mary...

(*BOTHWELL turns and stares.*)

BOTHWELL: What's this?

MARY: James – he is defaced.

BOTHWELL: Defaced? Why, it's only a touch of the pox, my lord. Let's have a look...

MARY: Leave him alone, Jamie!

(*BOTHWELL turns and stares at her grimly.*)

DARNLEY: Bothwell – the Queen and I are reconciled.

BOTHWELL: Yes, I see you are. (*He turns back to DARNLEY; cheerfully.*) And I'm very glad of it, my lord. I have your room prepared at Kirk o' Field.

DARNLEY: What, am I not for the castle?

BOTHWELL: The doctors say the air at Kirk o' Field is healthier. Is that not right, Doctor?

DOCTOR: The air at Kirk o' Field, Lord Bothwell, is humorous, the place being...

BOTHWELL: My doctor says it's healthier. (*To DARNLEY, cheerfully again.*) And we've everything made ready there. But we can shift you to the castle in the morning if you like.

(*During the above MARY, staring at BOTHWELL, comes to stand protectively near DARNLEY, behind his chair.*)

DARNLEY: Well... (*To MARY.*) Will you come with me?

MARY: (*Looking over his head at BOTHWELL defiantly.*) Yes.

BOTHWELL: Well, you cannot go tonight, Your Grace. The dance is tonight.

MARY: The dance?

BOTHWELL: Your guid friend Bastien's – (*Unseen by DARNLEY he jabs his thumb at his own chest, identifying 'Bastien'.*) – wedding dance.

MARY: I will excuse myself.

BOTHWELL: Well, you can do that if you like – but I fancy it's the last you'll see of Bastien, if you do.

MARY: (*Dully.*) I will come to you, Harry, after the dance.

BOTHWELL: Kirk o' Field, Doctor! Good night, my lord.

DARNLEY: (*Going.*) Mary...?

MARY: I will come to you, Harry, after the dance!

(*DARNLEY and the DOCTOR go.*)

(*Dully again.*) Is it tonight?

BOTHWELL: Is what tonight?

MARY: I do not know, sir.

BOTHWELL: (*Gently.*) That's right. So dance.

(*Music. BOTHWELL takes her hand. They dance the Pavane. The lights fade. Shadowy figures enter behind, dancing two by two. MARY is in a bright spot, puppet-like under BOTHWELL's compelling stare. He leaves her. She makes an involuntary gesture to retain him, then dances on alone, her face frightened.*

The music ceases. A solitary drum taps out the time. Then a child's voice is heard on the speaker.)

CHILD'S VOICE: 'Mary, Mary, quite contrary, how does your garden grow? With silver bells and cockle shells and...'

(*The stage rocks in blinding light. A distant explosion follows. Uproar – the dancers scattering, bells and crowd roaring. KNOX dashes on, beside himself, and stands in the spot vacated by MARY.*)

KNOX: Did I not warn you? Did I not say? Did I not prophesy? Was not the very face of Heaven dark the day she set her foot on Scottish soil?

(*The lights come up.*

The dancers are revealed as ELIZABETH, WALSINGHAM, CECIL; LADIES, DE QUADRA, PHILIP; the POPE and a PRIEST. The Scots LORDS are on the lowest step of the pyramid, looking up like everybody else at MARY seated on the throne, BOTHWELL by her. Both are composed but desperately tense.)

How long, guid people of Edinburgh, how long? Are you God's children and the nurslings of the Kirk, and will you have a bloody-handed strumpet for your Queen?

MARY: John Knox, you are a traitor and a...

BOTHWELL: Hold hard, the world is watching you.

MARY: Good Master Knox, we have no quarrel with you – or our people.

KNOX: By Heaven we have a quarrel with you!

ELIZABETH: Your Grace, we should not do the office of a cousin and a friend unless we urged Your Grace to clear yourself. Repudiate that man – bring him to trial!

MARY: We thank Your Grace, but this gentleman has stood his trial and is found innocent.

KNOX: We know the manner of that trial, and if he's innocent, why so is Satan!

MARY: The law stands over all of us, and we think as the law does, that the gentleman is innocent. In proof of which know, all the world, that we are married.

KNOX: That does not prove his innocence – it indicates your guilt!

POPE: A Protestant pantomime, my child, no marriage. Repudiate him.

MARY: Your Holiness, although the form was empty yet our hearts were in it; I account us married in the eyes of God.

PHILIP: Poor fool, poor *fool!*

KNOX: Oh my, what sympathy these Catholics show for their own kind. The King of Spain now. Thinks himself a verra pious man. The ladies of his Court must dress just so, no hanky-panky in the Prado, no, a verra nunnery they say. Well, here we have adultery, and bigamy, and murder! And what says His pious Majesty? Why, not a word.

PHILIP: We nothing doubt but that the lady was involved against her will and merits leniency.

KNOX: The woman is a common criminal and merits death.
(*The Dancers go.*)

MARY: Lord Mor – give me my child.
(*She half descends to meet MOR, who moves to meet her, but MORTON speaks.*)

MORTON: Give her the child, you give it to Lord Bothwell, Mor. Is that how you'll discharge your trust?
(*MOR hesitates.*)

MARY: Lord Mor...!

MOR: I cannot, madam, while that man is by your side.

MORTON: So let us have Lord Bothwell and you can have your child.

MARY: What mean you with Lord Bothwell?

MORTON: We mean to hang him.

(MARY kisses her fingertips and tenderly extends her arm towards her child.)

MARY: Farewell, child...

(MOR goes. MARY watches him off.
BOTHWELL grins at MORTON.)

MORTON: You're makin' it hard for us, Your Grace, but you're makin' it gey harder for yourself. To me, Bothwell.

(MORTON and the LORDS draw their daggers.)

BOTHWELL: Ormiston!

MORTON: We've hanged him already.

BOTHWELL: Tala! Bowton! A Hepburn! A Hepburn!

MORTON: You're wasting your breath, man – you have a sort of plague. Are you coming down or must we come up?

(BOTHWELL draws his dagger. MORTON sighs.)

Verra well, my lords – quick and quiet.

(The LORDS start for the steps.)

MARY: Stop!

(The LORDS stop.)

Lord Morton, if I submit myself to you, will you let Lord Bothwell go?

(MORTON considers, then nods, pleased.)

MORTON: Done.

(The LORDS protest.)

Peace, you fools. What's one Border bandit more or less? Bothwell, you have three days to quit Scotland.

(BOTHWELL kisses MARY and moves to go.)

MARY: Be true!

BOTHWELL: I only met one woman in my life; d'you think I'll no come back for her?

(BOTHWELL goes.
MARY looks after him, radiant, then turns to MORTON relaxed, smiling, almost dreamy.)

MARY: Now you may do your worst, Lord Morton.

MORTON: Well, I ask myself what I am to do with you.

(*His tone is quite friendly, but KNOX is alert and threatening.*)

KNOX: Morton, will you parley with this harlot?

MORTON: I will, John. Yes.

KNOX: Then I will go and parley with the People.

(*They measure glances.*)

MORTON: You do that, John.

(*KNOX goes. MORTON watches him, then sighs.*)

Gurnia, gurnia, troubled times... The way of it, Your Grace, is this: we cannot and we will not have Lord Bothwell for our King. You must see that? But neither would we have the People for our King. A Queen, you see, is a great convenience to the nobility – and vicky versa. Now, you're not tied to Bothwell very hard. The way I see it, that marriage was no marriage. Because, the way I see it, you was forced. So you see, Your Grace, if you'll just say that you was forced, repudiate the man, why then, we're all in step again.

MARY: And what if I refuse?

MORTON: Now what would you gain by that? He'll no come back.

MARY: He will come back.

MORTON: If he comes back we'll put him to the horn and hunt him down like any other outlaw, and he knows it. There's no 'chivalry' in Bothwell.

MARY: Still you have not told me what, if I refuse.

MORTON: Prison. And I do not mean 'confinement' in some bra' house – no, no – I mean a Highland keep. I mean one small, strong, room, for the rest of your days. And you're young yet.

MARY: And that is my choice?

MORTON: It is; d'you want time to think?

MARY: No. For prison, I will quit it. And then woe to you; woe to this country. For Lord Bothwell – (*Her voice falters on it, then she continues strongly.*) – my lords I would follow him to the edge of the earth – in my shift!

MORTON: (*Angrily.*) ...You obdurate shrew. Awa' wi' her!

(*He shoves MARY into the arms of the LORDS.*
The LORDS run her offstage, MORTON looking after.
The lights change. ELIZABETH, WALSINGHAM and
CECIL enter. WALSINGHAM carries a purse of coins.)

ELIZABETH: To the edge of the earth...?

MORTON: Aye, Your Grace. In her shift.

ELIZABETH: Well... Where is she?

MORTON: (*Complacently.*) We have her fast. (*With grim satisfaction.*) At Loch Leven.

ELIZABETH: What is that?

MORTON: A keep, Your Grace; the keep on an island, the island in a lake.

ELIZABETH: Her jailer?

MORTON: (*With a chuckle.*) Dinna fash about that, Your Grace. He'd as soon break her neck as look at her. Black Douglas is his name.

ELIZABETH: Who has the child?

MORTON: (*With a sour smile.*) One George Buchanan, a verra godly friend of Master Knox.

ELIZABETH: (*With a nod.*) Will the Queen see the child?

MORTON: She will not.

ELIZABETH: Well.

(*WALSINGHAM gives her the purse of coins.*)
Rule Scotland wisely, Morton, till the little King grows up. (*She hands MORTON the purse.*)

MORTON: (*Unctuously.*) I will rule as Your Grace would wish.

(*DAVISON enters.*)

DAVISON: Your pardon, Your Grace. Master Cecil, this presses. (*He gives CECIL a letter.*) From the Border, Your Grace. It concerns Lord Morton somewhat.

MORTON: Me?

DAVISON: Yes.

CECIL: (*His eyes on the paper.*) Yes. Yes, rather more than somewhat. The Queen of Scots is free, Your Grace.

ELIZABETH: Free?

CECIL: Yes, Your Grace, it...

MORTON: I dinna believe it!

CECIL: (*Still scanning the paper.*) It would appear that your misogynistic friend Black Douglas has a son, of a more impressionable temper.

MORTON: What...! (*He snatches the letter and peruses it, breathing hard.*)

(*ELIZABETH laughs suddenly.*)

CECIL: (*Continuing.*) And the keep had a window. And the lake had a boat.

(*ELIZABETH laughs again. MORTON looks up.*)

MORTON: What, madam, are you merry?

ELIZABETH: All men are merry for a moment, Morton, to see a bird go free. There, my merriment is over.

MORTON: I think so, madam. She is in England.

CECIL: What?

MORTON: (*Cheerfully.*) Aye – she's in Carlisle, Master Cecil, lodged with the Earl of Westmoreland...

WALSINGHAM: (*To CECIL; alarmed.*) Westmoreland!

MORTON: Aye – and other Catholic gentlemen are flocking there – 'flocking', that's the word here. To cap it a', she throws herself on Your Grace's mercy and asks audience.

(*ELIZABETH takes the letter from MORTON and stares at it.*)

ELIZABETH: (*Almost to herself, in a voice almost of dread.*) Why me...? Why my mercy...? We are enemies.

(*CECIL watches her carefully.*)

CECIL: Yes, Your Grace. If you see her, Your Grace, you will seem to condone the murder of Lord Darnley.

WALSINGHAM: That woman alive in England is a Trojan horse. Execute her!

ELIZABETH: It would not be seen as the execution of a murderess, good Francis, it would be seen as the elimination of a rival.

CECIL: Yes... It would *be* the elimination of a rival, of course.

ELIZABETH: No.

CECIL: I wonder if the matter is not Scottish domestic...

ELIZABETH: Good. (*Smiling.*) Lord Morton, you may take our sister back to Scotland and – (*Her smile goes flat and expressionless.*) – do with her what you will.

MORTON: (*With a reproving grin.*) Oh, no, Your Grace. She's yours. An' Your Grace is welcome. Where she is, there is no safety.

(*MORTON goes. They look after him.*)

WALSINGHAM: There is no safety for Your Grace's person *while* she is. She has connived at murder once and will again.

CECIL: I would that we had proof that she connived at it.

WALSINGHAM: I have a letter here, would hang her in a common court. She wrote it from Glasgow. It was taken from among Lord Bothwell's papers.

(*ELIZABETH takes the letter, is troubled, and thrusts it at CECIL, who takes it eagerly.*)

CECIL: (*With mild curiosity.*) Is it genuine, Master Walsingham, or forged?

WALSINGHAM: Read it.

ELIZABETH: Aloud.

CECIL: (*Reading.*) 'Being absent from the place where I left my heart, I was like a body without a heart...'

(*ELIZABETH shifts fractionally. CECIL registers it and speaks to WALSINGHAM.*)

Poetic; hardly proof.

WALSINGHAM: Read the portions I have marked.

CECIL: (*Reading.*) 'Alas, my lord, you have sent me here to do a work I much detest...' er 'Certainly he fears the thing you know of and for his life. But I had but to speak two or three kind words and he was happy. Then he showed me so many little courtesies so seriously and wisely that you would be amazed. Alas, alas, and I never deceived anybody...' er 'It is late and yet I cannot sleep because I cannot sleep as I desire, that is in your arms, my dear life...'

(*ELIZABETH shifts again. CECIL stops reading and lays down the letter.*)

More of the like.

ELIZABETH: Finish it.

CECIL: Madam, the rest is... (*He waves the rest away.*)

ELIZABETH: Finish it.

(*CECIL picks the letter up and reads the rest in a tone which tries to drain it of emotion and therefore heightens it.*)

CECIL: 'Now God forgive me and God give you, my only love, the fortune which your humble faithful love desires for you. It is late. I am alone. I desire never to cease writing to you, yet now must cease for lack of paper. And so I kiss your hands and end my letter. Read it twice or thrice. Burn it.' (*He lays it down and waits for her response.*)

(*It comes flatly.*)

ELIZABETH: And he kept it.

WALSINGHAM: Happily, madam, yes.

ELIZABETH: Well, that is no forgery. (*She rises, not looking at them.*) Bring her as far south as Sheffield Castle. Confine her there. But as a Queen.

WALSINGHAM: She may correspond?

ELIZABETH: She may do anything a Queen may do. Except leave Sheffield Castle.

WALSINGHAM: It is not wise, Your Grace.

ELIZABETH: It is our will! (*She turns at the exit to say unconvincingly.*) We fear the French connexion.

(*ELIZABETH goes.*)

WALSINGHAM: (*Severely.*) Her Grace is too merciful!

CECIL: I do not think that this is altogether mercy. I think our Queen sees Mary in the mirror.

WALSINGHAM: You are grown so subtle, Master Cecil, you will shortly be invisible.

(*WALSINGHAM goes, impatiently. CECIL follows.*
The lights change. NAU and a SERVANT enter separately, the latter puts down a small keg.)

SERVANT: There, sir, from Lord Shrewsbury's own hopyards. The best beer in England.

NAU: Lord Shrewsbury is a kindly jailor. Thank him.

(*The SERVANT goes.*
MARY enters slowly, in a simple riding habit, carrying a whip.)
Your Grace. Where did you ride, Your Grace?

MARY: To The North Gate, Claud. (*She somnambulates past him, then stops.*) And then back to the West Gate – and so to the South Gate – and back to the Castle.

NAU: Are you unwell?

MARY: I am in the best health possible, for prison. This morning I am cured of hope.

NAU: Madam?

MARY: I met a person in the park. A Catholic gentleman. He said, 'God Bless Your Grace.' And gave me news of my lord Bothwell. He will not come back, Claud. He is in Denmark.

NAU: Perhaps he waits his time, Your Grace.

MARY: He has taken service with the King of Denmark.

NAU: He must provide for himself somehow.

MARY: He has bought a house.

NAU: He must have a roof.

MARY: There is a lady in the house.

NAU: How did the gentleman know all this?

MARY: He has seen it.

(*NAU has no answer. He looks at her in pity. She gives him a pale smile.*)

He only told me what you told me long ago. And what my own heart has been heavy with these twelve slow months. I think the months will seem to pass more swiftly now. (*She looks at him.*) Claud, I do not ask that you should share them.

NAU: An't please Your Grace, I will share them.

MARY: Henceforth you are the only man that I will trust. (*With bitter self-recrimination.*) Besides the man I ought to have staked my life on from the start.

NAU: What man is that, Your Grace?

MARY: The little man in Scotland, Claud.

NAU: It is cruel they do not let you see him.

MARY: I see him every night. We talk before we sleep.

NAU: What does he say?

MARY: That he loves me right well. And forgives me. And that when he is of age he will come out of Scotland like a second Tamurlaine! With bloody punishment in either hand for these water-hearted, beer-drinkers! (*She makes a swift tour of the stage, mindless as an animal.*)

NAU: Oh, Madam, be patient!

MARY: Well, I will.

NAU: You must, Your Grace.

MARY: I must. (*She comes now to a halt with her whip flicking restlessly.*)
(*NAU looks at her uneasily. There is a silence, then, indicating the keg at his feet, he offers.*)

NAU: (*Cheerfully.*) Myself, I have learned to *like* the beer.

MARY: It is an accomplishment.
(*The whip flicks again. He eyes her again.*)

NAU: Show patient, madam, and the English may at length show kind.

MARY: By God, they'll show unlike themselves then.

NAU: There is kindness in the circumstances they allow you here. And Mignon, you would need less patience if you would make more use of them.

MARY: I use the park. (*She shows him the whip.*)

NAU: Your riding to and fro like one demented half the day serves but to remind you that the park has walls. There is a wide world in the library.

MARY: I'll come more often to the library.

NAU: There are some fine romances there.

MARY: (*After a pause.*) I have done with romances. (*She pauses again.*) Henceforth I'll study policy.

NAU: Patience now is your only policy.

MARY: No.

NAU: What other?

MARY: Claud, this gentleman whom I met riding in the park. He will carry letters, secret letters, they will not be overlooked.

NAU: Oh, no...!

MARY: He is waiting for me now.

NAU: Waiting for...? Oh, madam, madam – who is this gentleman? What do you know of him? Think! Your life lies every morning in the Queen of England's hand.

MARY: She does not dare.

NAU: And if you give her just occasion she will dare! Be patient! And *preserve* yourself!
(*She considers it, then speaks reasonably, quietly.*)

MARY: For what?

NAU: For quietness. Your Grace, in quietness we save our souls. You have some need of quietness.

MARY: Sir, do you think I do not know, what state my soul is in? (*It is said quietly and with a wealth of inner suffering which rebukes him.*) But listen now. God gives each one of us a different life to live. And if we live it well He gives us everlasting life in Heaven. And if we live it ill, as surely I have lived right ill, yet still may Heaven be merciful. But if we live it not at all, nay then I think Heaven has no mercy. And God made me a Queen! I did not beg to be so born. And maybe I was not equipped to be so born. But since I was so born – (*She collects herself.*) – by Heaven I will so live! And all my means, my whole machinery of state, is this one doubtful gentleman.

(*She goes out where she entered, striding fast. NAU goes separately.*

The lights fade to a spot as an echoing cry of anguish is heard.)

PRISONER: (*Off.*) No – no – no – no...! (*After a pause.*) Oh, God – help me!

(*The PRISONER is dragged into the spot by JAILERS. CECIL and WALSINGHAM enter as the lights come up. They do not look at the PRISONER. WALSINGHAM, who carries a file, sits. CECIL addresses the audience.*)

CECIL: The Pope of Rome is a dangerous simpleton, thanks be to God. And he has had letters from the Queen of Scots which I fear dangerously misrepresent the situation here. For here I have his Papal edit 'Regnan in Excelsis', which releases English Catholics from allegiance to the Queen. Nay more – it makes meritorious in English Catholics to assassinate the Queen. And more again – it calls for a crusade to invade the territories of the Queen. So now our English Catholics have to choose, between his Holiness and her Majesty. Well, his Holiness is far away and her Majesty is close at hand and we, her Ministers, are – (*With a half-glance at the PRISONER.*) – busy. How would you choose? Yes, and so do most of they. Not all, though – no, not all. (*To the JAILER.*) Well, I see that you have racked him.

JAILER: Yes, sir.

CECIL: Can he stand?

JAILER: No, sir.

CECIL: A chair then.

> (*The PRISONER is seated. CECIL looks at him unwillingly. His silvery old man's voice is courteous, dispassionate and fatal.*)

Now, sir, again, who are you?

PRISONER: I am Nicholas Benson. Cloth merchant, of Amsterdam.

CECIL: No, sir. You are –

> (*WALSINGHAM gives him a paper.*)

– Father Edward Fenton, and you are a Jesuit priest. You were trained at Douai and sent here from there. While you were in prison at Norwich you administered the Sacrament of 'absolution' to a man you took to be a fellow prisoner awaiting death. And you told him all this. One Peter Blunt.

PRISONER: Oh. Was Peter not a prisoner?

CECIL: No, he was an instrument of Master Walsingham's.

PRISONER: Oh. (*Without much feeling.*) I am undone then.

CECIL: Now, your letters… (*He reaches for them.*)

PRISONER: They are not my letters.

CECIL: The letters which were found beneath the floorboards of your room. They implicate you in a plot, which we already know about. (*Gently, pleadingly.*) We know about it, sir.

PRISONER: What need to question, then?

CECIL: I should like to understand you if I could. Did you know that your associates intended to assassinate her Majesty?

> (*No answer.*)

Did you know that, following that, one hundred Catholic gentlemen would seize the port of Norwich while two thousand Spanish troops were landed there – on English soil?

WALSINGHAM: To make that bloody-handed harlot Mary Stuart, England's Queen? And do you call this a Crusade? And yourself English?

PRISONER: God made Mary Stuart England's Queen. It is not for me – or you – to question it.

WALSINGHAM: Ho! 'God' quotha! Lackaday what Christianity is this!

CECIL: Look, sir, you know that you must die…

PRISONER: I do; and God be thanked am ready to.

CECIL: I see you are. But you can die by burning, as a priest. Or, for treason, quickly by the axe. That choice I can give you. Now. I want to know if Mary Stuart instigated, or approved, or knew about your plans… Sir, I have seen death by burning, in Mary Tudor's time. I know which I would choose.

PRISONER: (*Smiling faintly.*) But then I have a higher calling than yourself. I am a priest. And I will die as one. (*There is a momentary pause, then CECIL motions with his hand.*

The JAILERS remove the PRISONER and his chair.

CECIL's face is pinched and wrinkled with distaste. WALSINGHAM is gloomy. CECIL sighs and moves. Both men put on wigs: WALSINGHAM's is grey, CECIL's is white and thinning at the top. CECIL smiles apologetically at the audience and explains.)

CECIL: One grows old quickly at this work.

(*ELIZABETH enters. She, too, is older than before. Her face, framed in an extravagantly flaring collar, is more obviously painted. She growls suspiciously at CECIL.*)

ELIZABETH: What do you say, Cecil?

CECIL: That I am growing old, Your Grace. It is only Your Grace who has the secret of eternal youth, and shines on like the morning star when all the rest have fled, a rainbow among clouds, a rose in winter.

ELIZABETH: Leave flattery to courtiers, Cecil. You give good measure but the quality is coarse. Well; what have you found?

WALSINGHAM: We have found the same as always, madam: Mary Stuart. Mary Stuart and Catholic Conspiracy, Mary Stuart and a Spanish rescue, Mary Stuart and Your Grace's death. Your Grace was to have

been shot down with muskets in the knot garden at
Hampton Court, on Tuesday next.

ELIZABETH: Muskets? In the knot garden…? God's death,
how long does this go on?

WALSINGHAM: As long as Mary Stuart lives, Your Grace.

ELIZABETH: Have you proof of her complicity?

WALSINGHAM: No proof, Your Grace, but no doubt either.

ELIZABETH: I will not do it without proof.

(*She says it stubbornly, as something said before, and
WALSINGHAM looks at CECIL.*)

CECIL: Your Grace, there is news from Spain. The Duke of
Parma is appointed to command the Spanish armies in
the Netherlands.

ELIZABETH: Parma!

(*DAVISON enters.*)

DAVISON: Your Grace, the Spanish Ambassador asks
instant audience.

ELIZABETH: Tomorrow.

(*DAVISON goes.*)

Parma for the Netherlands.

CECIL: Yes, Your Grace. He will be followed by fifty
thousand infantry.

ELIZABETH: Oh… This is not for the Netherlands.

WALSINGHAM: No, Your Grace, it is for England. And it
will find the country in two minds – because it contains
two Queens!

ELIZABETH: I cannot do it without proof!

(*WALSINGHAM goes.*

ELIZABETH rises, energy beginning to flow from her visibly.)

Yet, Parma. Something I must do.

CECIL: Yes, Your Grace.

ELIZABETH: What?

CECIL: May I speak without fear?

ELIZABETH: I do not know that; you may speak.

CECIL: Recall the Earl of Leicester.

ELIZABETH: Nay, you had done better to be silent.

CECIL: Your Grace, he is a soldier.

ELIZABETH: I have other soldiers.

CECIL: But none so fit.

ELIZABETH: Fit? And he were Hannibal he were not fit. He is treacherous!

CECIL: Madam, marriage is not treachery.

ELIZABETH: But secrecy is treachery! Speak no more of Leicester, he is ruined! What – ten months the slippery villain plays it out with 'Yes, Your Grace,' and 'No, Your Grace,' and then, 'A trifle I would tell Your Grace – I am married these ten months'!

CECIL: Madam...

ELIZABETH: Speak not, Cecil! I will not hear!

CECIL: Or let me speak or let me leave your service, madam.

ELIZABETH: Nay, leave it then.

(*CECIL goes.*)

Come back.

(*CECIL comes back.*)

Suffolk?

CECIL: Too old, Your Grace.

ELIZABETH: Mountjoy?

CECIL: Too young.

(*ELIZABETH goes to the throne and calls formally.*)

ELIZABETH: Recall the Earl – of Leicester!

(*DAVISON and DUDLEY enter. He also is older than before.*)

My lord.

(*DUDLEY kisses her hand and rises.*)

Are you well?

DUDLEY: Well indeed, Your Grace. Now.

ELIZABETH: And your wife?

DUDLEY: Well, too, Your Grace.

ELIZABETH: You are happy?

DUDLEY: I am a husband, madam.

ELIZABETH: You make it sound little. (*She looks away.*)

What more would you be?

(*DUDLEY snatches a look at CECIL, who nods.*)

DUDLEY: Your Grace – this summer – I hope to be a father.

(*She looks at him.*)

ELIZABETH: Take your place, my lord.

(*CECIL and DUDLEY sit.*)

CECIL: My lord is acquainted with the occasion.

(*She returns from her abstraction.*)

ELIZABETH: Oh, yes, the occasion. What do you think?

DUDLEY: I think we might shock them, if we had time to muster, and if the country were united.

ELIZABETH: ...And what do you think might unite the country?

DUDLEY: The death of Mary Stuart.

ELIZABETH: (*Softly.*) By God, time was you had other plans for Mary Stuart.

DUDLEY: (*Uncomfortably.*) Time has changed, Your Grace.

ELIZABETH: And you with it. I hope you will prove a constant soldier, Robin; for Heaven knows you're an unsteady swain. (*There is a silence, then she throws it off and continues briskly.*) How long to muster?

DUDLEY: Three to muster, three to train.

ELIZABETH: Six months in all. And Parma's veterans have not been out of iron for six years – and he will shock them. Cecil, this fifty thousand – will they come overland? (*She sits bolt upright and expressionless during what follows, a political computer gathering information.*)

CECIL: They will, if France will let them through, Your Grace.

ELIZABETH: And will France let them through?

CECIL: Not if Your Grace will make the French alliance.

ELIZABETH: Meaning the French marriage.

CECIL: Yes, Your Grace.

ELIZABETH: Walsingham, has Spain ships enough to carry fifty thousand?

WALSINGHAM: Your Grace, there is such hammering in the Spanish ship-yards that Spain shakes.

ELIZABETH: Have we ships enough to sink them?

CECIL: Not yet, Your Grace.

ELIZABETH: And you require six months in all.

DUDLEY: Yes, Your Grace.

(*A CLERK enters.*)

CLERK: Signor de Quadra, as Your Grace appointed yesterday, asks audience again today.

ELIZABETH: Again tomorrow.

(*The CLERK goes.*)

(*Turning to DAVISON.*) You, sir, tell the French Prince we
will have him.

(*DAVISON goes.*)

WALSINGHAM: He is a Catholic, Your Grace, your
people will not have him.

ELIZABETH: Nor will we; so send a hundred thousand
crowns to him, to keep his relish for our person keen.

(*WALSINGHAM goes, while CECIL gasps.*)

CECIL: A hundred thousand crowns, Your Grace!

ELIZABETH: Our person needs some flavouring. Sell
Crown lands to the value of two hundred thousand.

CECIL: Madam – sell Crown land?

ELIZABETH: There is a time when thrift becomes
extravagant, old man, and this is such a time! The other
hundred thousand send to Plymouth. Sir Francis Drake
will tell you it will build six ships, tell him it must build
me ten. If he must use green timber, so. These ships
must float till Parma's great Armada comes, thereafter
they may sink for me.

(*CECIL starts to go.*)

(*To DUDLEY.*) You, sir –

(*CECIL stops enthralled to see the last of the firework display.*)

– raise volunteers and send them to the Netherlands to
occupy the Duke of Parma there awhile.

DUDLEY: Yes, Your Grace.

ELIZABETH: And muster.

DUDLEY: Yes, Your Grace.

ELIZABETH: And train.

DUDLEY: Yes, Your Grace.

ELIZABETH: And, Robin…

DUDLEY: Yes, Your Grace?

ELIZABETH: I am glad to see you.

(*DUDLEY goes.*)

CECIL: Madam…

ELIZABETH: What?

CECIL: You are a greater monarch than your father.

(*She looks at him.*)

And he was a man among men, Your Grace.

ELIZABETH: Our very thought.

> (*CECIL goes.*
> *There is perfect stillness for a second. ELIZABETH's face remains rigid but her body crumples; she is exhausted.*
> *DAVISON enters.*)

DAVISON: Your Grace, Signor de Quadra demands instant audience!

ELIZABETH: (*Revivified.*) Nay and he demands it, let him have it.

> (*DAVISON goes.*
> *ELIZABETH descends.*
> *DE QUADRA enters.*)

DE QUADRA: How now, Your Grace!

ELIZABETH: How now, de Quadra, where have you been?

DE QUADRA: Been? This fortnight I have been outside Your Grace's door – with heavy business for Your Grace.

ELIZABETH: Oh, would that I had known; this fortnight I have been so idle that hours have seemed like fortnights.

DE QUADRA: By Heaven, Your Grace – your shipbuilders aren't idle!

ELIZABETH: (*As accepting a compliment upon her people's industry.*) I am very glad to hear it. Nothing so conduces to the welfare of the State as an industrious artisan.

DE QUADRA: My master would know what your shipbuilders do!

ELIZABETH: Well, sir, I am not familiar with that business, but I take it they build ships.

DE QUADRA: For what?

ELIZABETH: Why, to go a-sailing in.

DE QUADRA: Well, certainly Your Grace's talk is idle.

> (*She blinks then recovers.*)

ELIZABETH: Then let us talk of something else.

DE QUADRA: I am to ask Your Grace why there are suddenly a thousand English volunteers who fight against my master in the Netherlands.

ELIZABETH: Fashion, de Quadra, simply fashion. Our young men like to say that they have fought against the

Duke of Parma as their silly sisters like to say that they have fetched their ruffs from Pads.

DE QUADRA: I notice that Your Grace has taken to French ruffs.

ELIZABETH: Oh, thank you. Do you think it is attractive?

DE QUADRA: I think it might attract a Frenchman.

ELIZABETH: Alas, there is none here.

DE QUADRA: I hear Your Grace has sent a hundred thousand crowns to Paris – from your privy purse!

ELIZABETH: (*After a little pause.*) For ruffs.

DE QUADRA: Your Grace, if you will make no weightier replies to these my master's just complaints, I fear lest the amity between yourself and him may wither, and enmity ensue.

ELIZABETH: Are you instructed to say this?

DE QUADRA: Yes, Your Grace.

ELIZABETH: I'm sorry. (*She calls.*) Walsingham!
(*WALSINGHAM enters with a pile of dossiers, which he places on the table.*)
Walsingham, the King of Spain complains that we make ready to defend ourselves against his Great Armada. This gentleman complains that I make light replies. Furnish him with something heavier.

WALSINGHAM: Well, sir, this is something heavy. (*He dumps into DE QUADRA's arms the topmost of the piled dossiers.*)
(*DE QUADRA raises his eyebrows.*)

DE QUADRA: Heavy, yes; what else is it?

WALSINGHAM: That, sir, is the evidence concerning Father Edward Fenton, who conspired to assassinate Her Majesty and proclaim Mary Stuart in her place – by Spanish force of arms.

DE QUADRA: I know of no Father Fenton.
(*He is about to put back the dossier, but WALSINGHAM whips another on top of it.*)

WALSINGHAM: Nor Thomas Throgmorton?

DE QUADRA: Nor Thomas Throgmorton.

WALSINGHAM: Ha! Nor Roberto Ridolfi, I suppose? Nor Henry Cockeyn, nor George Douglas, nor George Gifford, Creighton, Paget, Parsons, Holt?

(*WALSINGHAM reels off the list of hated names, dumping dossiers in DE QUADRA's arms the while until DE QUADRA can barely see above them, but the latter keeps his dignity.*)

DE QUADRA: (*Flatly.*) No.

WALSINGHAM: Now that is strange, for they say they know you.

DE QUADRA: Men under interrogation will say anything. (*WALSINGHAM picks up the dossier which he brought in with him.*)

WALSINGHAM: Then do you know Anthony Babington?

DE QUADRA: No.

WALSINGHAM: Now that is passing strange. For here are letters to him in your hand. (*He adds the dossier to the others.*)

ELIZABETH: Well, sir, is the answer heavy yet?

DE QUADRA: Too heavy, madam. I am not a sideboard. (*He drops the dossiers.*) And His Majesty my master will not have his servants mocked. I'll go, and tell him of this strange proceeding.

ELIZABETH: Do, de Quadra.

(*DE QUADRA moves to go, when she arrests him.*)

And, de Quadra – think us lenient that we let you go.

(*DE QUADRA goes.*)

(*Quietly.*) Ye Gods, Cecil, I think it comes soon.

CECIL: I think so, too, Your Grace.

ELIZABETH: What is this Babington?

WALSINGHAM: He is a Catholic gentleman who plots Your Grace's death on Mary Stuart's behalf.

ELIZABETH: What manner of death has this gentleman provided?

WALSINGHAM: Poison, madam.

ELIZABETH: Hell and damnation, may I not eat? (*She thinks, she sags. To WALSINGHAM.*) What can you show?

WALSINGHAM: Why, letters, madam, secret letters, which have passed between them hidden in the backs of books, the soles of shoes – and other guilty tricks!

ELIZABETH: A pox on how they passed – are they proof?

WALSINGHAM: Not proof *pedantic.*

ELIZABETH: Proof is pedantic, Walsingham. And Scotland is her son.

CECIL: The King of Scots. It is a very calculating boy, Your Grace, and relishes the crown. Your Grace might hint...

ELIZABETH: Hint what?

CECIL: That if he proved well-governed, in the advent of his mother's death – and if Your Grace were not herself to marry and happily deliver of a child – Your Grace might hint that he might look one day, one distant day, to have the Crown of England, too.

ELIZABETH: Oh, Cecil, you care for me so thoroughly that you have even made ready my winding sheet.

CECIL: Madam...

ELIZABETH: Do it – hint...! (*She moves to go, then pauses to add.*) But hearken, Cecil, no more than hint. I may yet prove a freak in nature. (*To WALSINGHAM.*) And you, my other friend, get proof. Get proof pedantic. (*She moves to go again but is arrested by WALSINGHAM's words.*)

WALSINGHAM: That is more easy said than done, Your Grace!

ELIZABETH: I do not ask that you should do it easily. (*ELIZABETH holds WALSINGHAM's eyes for a moment, then goes.*)

CECIL: Now I think you could get proof.

WALSINGHAM: Instruct me, sir. Mary Stuart is cunning.

CECIL: But mainly she's courageous. And courage is a passion.

WALSINGHAM: So?

CECIL: What luxuries does she enjoy?

WALSINGHAM: The luxuries our Queen allows her. Her state, her visitors, her daily riding in the park.

CECIL: Well then.

WALSINGHAM: No; deprivation would not quench her courage.

CECIL: No, it would inflame it. Passions feed on deprivation. And courage is a flame which, fed enough, will burn the house down in the end. What does she think of her son?

WALSINGHAM: She thinks him loyal and loving.

CECIL: Yes, I think you could get proof.

WALSINGHAM: (*Calling.*) Davison! (*To CECIL.*) Will you give me authority for this?

CECIL: Oh, I think you have it, good Francis. If you are not to do it easily, presumably you are to do it hard.
(*DAVISON enters.*)

DAVISON: Sir?

WALSINGHAM: Where's Babington?

DAVISON: Still under interrogation, sir.

WALSINGHAM: Well, tell them not to break his fingers.

DAVISON: Very good, sir.
(*DAVISON goes.*)

CECIL: Why are they not to break his fingers?

WALSINGHAM: Because he is to write.

CECIL: Ah, well, sir, I will leave you.

WALSINGHAM: Yes, sir, I expect you will.
(*CECIL and WALSINGHAM go, separately.*
A stable clock chimes, rustic and melancholy.
NAU enters, an old man now in sloppy slippers, He is carrying a beer keg which he puts down and anxiously regards, drumming his fingers on it.
MARY enters, older too, without head-dress or ruff, keys and scissors hanging from her waist, and carrying an embroidery frame. She walks slowly and sits.)

MARY: Claud, is it hot or cold today? I cannot tell. Even the weather here prevaricates. What would I not give for one day of honest French weather? (*She notes his preoccupation.*) What is it, Claud; are you troubled?

NAU: Nay, what should trouble me? (*He looks over her shoulder at her work.*) Unless the fine embroidered scarf which was to have been mine last Christmas. And I see has made no progress since the spring.

MARY: The heron had no legs last spring.

NAU: (*Peering.*) His legs are something insufficient now.

MARY: There was an excellent slave-master lost in you.
(*There is a little silence, he glancing again at the keg, she sewing.*)

I saw a heron in the park today. I came so close he hopped into the air all arsy-varsy and asquawking. But then he wafted up, and sailed away, right quietly. No marvel birds do not have souls. If they had souls as well as wings they had been blessed as angels, had they not? (*She looks up.*

Feeling her regard, he turns.)

NAU: Madam?

MARY: (*Putting down her frame.*) Nay what a devil *is* it?

NAU: I do not know if I should tell Your Grace.

MARY: Then tell me. And I will tell you if you should have told.

NAU: Look, Your Grace – (*Going to the barrel and plucking out the bung.*) – there is a place in here.

MARY: A place?

NAU: A leather pocket, and in it, this. (*He takes out a folded letter.*)

(*She holds out her hand for it.*)

MARY: Well, we have seen the like before; though seldom so ingenious.

NAU: Read it, madam; it's from Babington.

MARY: (*More interested.*) Oh. (*She reads.*) 'Your Grace,
I have acquainted these with the design you know of:
Westmoreland, Darcy, Cumberland, Arundel,
Hamilton...' Hamilton? Good...

NAU: Read on.

MARY: 'They are ready to join it, but only on Your Grace's sure approval. Your Grace's signature to this sets fire to the fuse...' (*Slowly.*) My signature to this...

NAU: Yes, Your Grace.

MARY: 'Else all fails. Your Grace's humble loving servant, Anthony.' Nay, this is something too ingenious. Did that come from the castle brewery?

NAU: I do not know.

MARY: Is this his hand?

NAU: I cannot tell.

(*They peer together at the paper.*)

MARY: (*Murmuring.*) Nor I – I have ruined my eyes, on your poxy scarf...

(*There is a noise off. She folds the paper quickly; he quickly puts the barrel on the floor.*

WALSINGHAM enters. He takes an arrogant stand and looks at her.

MARY stares, astonished.)

What...? (*Calling.*) Roget!

WALSINGHAM: I have instructed your people to let us alone.

MARY: And who the devil might you be, sir, to instruct my people?

WALSINGHAM: My name is Walsingham.

(*MARY freezes, then speaks steadily and mildly.*)

MARY: Welcome, Sir Francis. You are most timely.

WALSINGHAM: Indeed?

MARY: Yes, for I desire your opinion of this keg of beer.

WALSINGHAM: Of what?

MARY: This keg of beer, sir. Taste it, for I think it tastes oddly.

WALSINGHAM: Madam, I have not come thus far to sample beer...

MARY: Yet taste it. For I think it tastes of leather.

(*WALSINGHAM frowns, then gives it up and shrugs.*)

WALSINGHAM: Look, lady, don't think to beguile me with some little arbitrary wantonness as if to say that you were nothing worse than childish. I know you what you are. Here, madam, letters for you.

(*Thinking over his evident indifference to the keg, she picks up the packet he throws down. She sees the letters blatantly opened and thinks hard again before speaking.*)

MARY: (*Cautiously, flatly.*) Walsingham, these letters have been opened.

WALSINGHAM: Henceforth all your letters will be opened. For I have opened those which you have dropped at certain times and certain places, riding in the park.

MARY: I have dropped no letters, riding in the park.

WALSINGHAM: You lie.

NAU: Sir!

(*MARY's head flies round.*)

WALSINGHAM: 'Tis no matter. Henceforward you will ride no more.

(*MARY is appalled.*)

Nor walk outside these rooms.

MARY: ...Nay, let me understand you, sir...

WALSINGHAM: I have poor opinion of your understanding, madam, but it should suffice for this – you are to be confined!

NAU: You are not serious?

WALSINGHAM: Who's this?

NAU: I am Her Grace's secretary, sir...

WALSINGHAM: Then hold your tongue. (*He turns again to MARY.*)

MARY: He is my secretary and my friend!

WALSINGHAM: Still let him hold his tongue. For I have also read the letters which your friends have carried hence when they have visited. In consequence of which, henceforward you will have no visitors.

NAU: No visitors...!

WALSINGHAM: And three servants only –

NAU: Three, sir...?

WALSINGHAM: – of my choosing. There is another thing...

MARY: (*Gripping the arms of her chair.*) What thing is that?

WALSINGHAM: (*Pointing to the Cloth of State.*) That thing – it comes down. Now I am for London, where I have material matters to attend to.

MARY: Walsingham, come here.

(*He stands before her.*)

Do you tell me that I am to be mewed up and deprived of all my retinue?

WALSINGHAM: I do.

MARY: Then you have done your office, get you gone. (*She points to the Cloth of State.*) That stays!

WALSINGHAM: Nay, don't attempt the Queen with me...

NAU: Attempt, sir? Do you dare...?

WALSINGHAM: (*Looking at MARY.*) Why, what's to dare? Her State's all gone, and God knows in herself I see no Majesty.

NAU: Do you address my lady thus upon authority?

WALSINGHAM: I need no authority for whom do I address?
(*Satisfied by MARY's reaction, WALSINGHAM goes briskly.*)

NAU: (*Tremulous with shock and pity.*) Oh, madam…
(*She holds up her hand. Her face is white and twisted but not wild.*)

MARY: Now am I learning self-commnand or losing self-respect? Time was I'd rather have been crucified than sit and suffer censure from a Jack-in-Office such as that! (*The memory of it gets her to her feet.*) An unqualitied dull cypher such as that! (*She controls herself.*) But no, good Jack, I think this persecution is too gross, too arbitrary – and too hellishly well aimed!

NAU: Madam?

MARY: You know me well. Would you not use me, point by point as he has done, if you desired me to do something desperate? (*On the last word she produces the letter.*)

NAU: (*Horrified.*) Oh, madam, burn it!
(*She considers it a second, then tosses it on to the table.*)

MARY: Aye… (*She sits.*) He'll do as he has said though, Claud.

NAU: Aye; that was hatred.

MARY: 'Twas worse; he is a Puritan, and that was disapproval. He'll save my soul by keeping me walled up. Claud, if I am to be kept walled up I think I shall run mad… (*She stares about. Her glance falls on the paper.*)

NAU: Nay. That is your death warrant.
(*He grabs for the paper, but she is too quick for him.*)

MARY: If it is genuine it is my release and her death warrant. By God, it were a pity to burn that.

NAU: It is not genuine.

MARY: The odds are even – and what now should I weigh against it?

NAU: Weigh my love against it!
(*She looks at him and wavers.*)
Weigh your son against it!
(*She looks away from him; she sags; she lets the letter fall from her fingers on to the table. Then she breathes out a terrible sigh and rests her face upon her hand, her eyes covered.*)

Oh, my poor Mistress…
(*WALSINGHAM enters, carrying a basket.*
MARY rouses, growling.)
MARY: We thought you had gone, sir.
(*WALSINGHAM dumps the basket on the table.*)
Another thing?
(*He lifts the lid of the basket. Her face changes as she takes
from the basket a selection of child's toys. Her voice wavers.*)
These are the presents, I have sent to my son.
WALSINGHAM: And your letters. (*He takes out and dumps
down a wad of letters, taped.*)
MARY: He – he has kept them?
WALSINGHAM: He has never received them. (*He tilts the
basket.*)
(*She takes out two more billets like the first.*)
MARY: Never received…? Small wonder that he never
wrote to *me*!
WALSINGHAM: He has no wish to. Nor to see you. He
knows you.
MARY: He…?
WALSINGHAM: He has been instructed, madam, in the
manner of your life; and in the manner of his father's
death.
MARY: (*Incredulously, whispering.*) You – have – blackened me?
WALSINGHAM: How blacken black?
MARY: Nay, I think this is some practice, Master
Walsingham; you would provoke… (*She fawns on him.*)
WALSINGHAM: Upon my soul it is the truth!
MARY: (*Incredulous, pleading.*) But of all my letters – not one?
WALSINGHAM: Madam, you have had no communication!
It is my mistress who has played the mother's part.
(*WALSINGHAM goes.*
*NAU watches in horror and pity as MARY, motionless, slides
helplessly into tears which she makes no attempt to hide. Then
her face darkens and her voice shakes with passion.*)
MARY: Oh, she… She-ee…! She-ee…! *Elizabeth*! (*She speeds
to the table and snatches up the pen.*)
NAU: Oh, madam, you will sign away your life!

MARY: Or hers!

NAU: Aye, madam – murder or suicide – think upon your soul!

MARY: Nay, God may think on that, it's his! (*Calling.*) Roget!

NAU: Oh, what a summing up!

MARY: I have no choice!

NAU: Cowardly, madam – always we have choice!

MARY: What choice – huh? Six rooms, no sky, and after thirty years maybe lie down and quietly die – and she to have my son? Roget!

(*A BREWER enters and stands silently.*)

Where is my gentleman?

BREWER: Your gentleman's without, Your Grace. He said Your Grace had made complaint about a keg of beer I sent from the brewery.

(*She points to the keg. He goes, takes out the bung, looks in, finds nothing, looks at her, all very deliberately.*)

MARY: Who are you, sir?

BREWER: I am an English Catholic and Your Grace's loyal subject. I am to take a matter from Your Grace to Father Flint in Chesterfield.

MARY: And he to take it where?

BREWER: We are a chain of trust, Your Grace. Each knows his neighbour and no more.

MARY: Take it then.

(*He comes and takes the letter she is holding out and moves to go.*)

But if you take it to Elizabeth…

(*He spins round indignantly.*)

BREWER: Nay, now you wrong me!

MARY: Be reasonable, sir, it may be so. And if it is we only ask that you should tell our sister that before we die we'd have one day – nay one half-day – of conversation with our son. Ask this of her charity.

BREWER: (*Angrily.*) Nay and you suppose I take this to Elizabeth I will not take it anywhere.

(*MARY licks her lips, then speaks.*)

MARY: Sir, I have made my choice. (*She moves to the exit.*) And you – whatever choice it is that you have made – (*Half an order, half a desperate appeal.*) – make haste!

(*MARY goes, NAU following.*
The lights change. WALSINGHAM and CECIL enter:
WALSINGHAM goes to the BREWER and takes the letter.
ELIZABETH enters slowly, dressed in fantastic black.
WALSINGHAM turns and plonks the letter on the table
before her.)

WALSINGHAM: Proof, madam.

(*ELIZABETH looks down at it. CECIL puts a document*
before her.)

CECIL: The warrant for her execution.

(*ELIZABETH glances unwillingly at it.*)

ELIZABETH: (*To the BREWER.*) Did she say anything?

BREWER: She said I was to ask Your Grace if...

ELIZABETH: What? She knew that you would bring this *here?*

BREWER: She did suspect it, madam; and she asked...

ELIZABETH: Nay – then do not tell me what she asked.
(*She dips the pen. She licks her lips and looks round for a*
reprieve. To CECIL.) Is there nothing from Scotland?

CECIL: (*Handing her a letter.*) This, Your Grace. It is the
most discreet, far-sighted child I ever met.
(*She takes the letter and waves them all off.*
ALL go.
Alone, ELIZABETH looks at the letter, then looks up from it.)

ELIZABETH: Oh; little boy... (*She puts down the letter, takes*
up the pen and signs, calling.) Davison!
(*DAVISON enters, in black.*)
Do you see that?
(*DAVISON looks at the signed warrant.*)

DAVISON: I see it, Your Grace.

ELIZABETH: What will you do with it?

DAVISON: I will take it to Lord Shrewsbury, Your Grace.

ELIZABETH: You will do it without authority and I shall
put you in the Tower for it.

DAVISON: May I know for how long, Your Grace?

ELIZABETH: Until such time as the world recognises that
it was not my desire.

DAVISON: I do not think the world will be deceived by
this, Your Grace. (*With a flick of resentment.*) Nor by Your
Grace's mourning.

(*ELIZABETH looks at him fathomlessly for a moment.*)

ELIZABETH: The world is deceived by nothing. It must be given something by which to seem to be deceived... Well, sir, do it. (*She mounts towards the throne.*)

(*DAVISON picks up the warrant.*)

DAVISON: I think you burden me too much, Your Grace. Your Grace must tell me what to do.

ELIZABETH: Why, man – your office. (*She sits on the throne.*) (*Drums roll, the Cloth of State is eclipsed by a black cloth of mourning.*

Two black-clad SERVANTS unroll a black carpet.

MARY enters with ATTENDANTS, NAU and a PRIEST, all in black. MARY stands at the head of the carpet and looks along it, her head high but held sideways as though unable to look directly at what is at the end of it, offstage.)

MARY: So there they are, the axe and block. How practical they look. (*To NAU.*) Love, you have stayed with me long. Spare yourself this last?

NAU: And it please Your Grace, I'll stay a little longer yet.

MARY: Here then; a memento of my idleness; your still unfinished scarf.

(*Taking the scarf, NAU breaks down.*)

Hush now!

DAVISON: Are you ready, madam?

MARY: (*Formally.*) I claim God's fatherly protection for my son; and Christ's incomprehensible compassion for my soul.

ALL: Amen.

MARY: I'm ready now, sir.

(*She moves, but DAVISON kneels quickly before her.*)

DAVISON: Pardon.

MARY: For what?

DAVISON: I brought the warrant.

(*He looks up at her. She frowns.*)

MARY: Is it not Davison?

DAVISON: Your Grace.

(*She touches his hair absently.*)

MARY: Be comfortable, William. The thing you brought was nothing much. A death-warrant requires a royal signature. And I signed my own. (*She moves, looks off again at the axe and block, isolated.*) And if your Great and Virgin Queen should wonder why I signed it, you are to tell her this: There is more living in a death that is embraced than in a life that is avoided across three-score years and ten. And I embrace it – thus! (*She throws off the black, revealing scarlet from head to foot.*) Davison.

DAVISON: Madam?

MARY: Now.

(*MARY plunges off along the carpet. The others tumble after her, taken by surprise.*

A drumbeat sounds, then stops convulsively.

CECIL enters. He looks at ELIZABETH, cautiously.)

ELIZABETH: She was an adulterous, disorderly, lecherous, strumpet!

CECIL: Yes, Your Grace.

ELIZABETH: She was a *fool!*

CECIL: Yes, Your Grace.

ELIZABETH: She was – nay there are no words for saying what she was. Only words for saying what she was not.

(*CECIL approaches the foot of the throne.*)

CECIL: (*Seriously, persuasively.*) As: worthy, thoughtful, self-denying; diligent; prepared.

(*She looks at him, attentive, mistrustful.*)

Your Grace, next year or the next, Spain sends against us his Invincible Armada. And we shall astonish them! And as their great ships founder and they drown, they will cry out: 'How? How is this possible?' And our cannon will tell them: 'Elizabeth! Elizabeth made it possible!' And they will hear it across Europe in Madrid! Aye, madam, they will hear it across Europe – and down centuries.

(*In the ringing silence left by his rhetoric her voice comes hard and dead.*)

ELIZABETH: Very like, Master Cecil; very like… (*She almost snarls.*) And then?

(*She rises painfully, and makes towards the exit. A triumphant fanfare sounds. She ignores it, as the curtain falls.*)

The End.

STATE OF REVOLUTION

Principal Characters

LENIN

His physical appearance is sufficiently well-known from photographs – the short, strong body, the alert head with the jutting beard and vivid, narrow eyes. It is the head of a leopard on the body of a little bull. There was something of the leopard in his character too. A merciful man could not have done some of what Lenin did or caused to be done. But he was not gratuitously cruel. Gratuitous cruelty indeed disgusted him. But so did tolerance, which he regarded as morally sluggish. He was certain of his purpose. And because he was completely given over to it he was completely integrated, which gave him a terrible energy, and completely unselfconscious, which gave him a terrible charm. He was awesome and naïve. Friends and enemies alike were afraid of him but even his worst enemies never seriously debited him with a dirty motive, and his friends as Lunacharsky says were half in love with him. He was an affectionate friend when time permitted, quick to see a need and insistently attentive. But friendship went by the board when revolutionary duty called, and it constantly called. After winning an argument – and he always won by fair means or foul – Gorky describes him as habitually adopting 'a strange and rather comical stance, throwing his head back, inclining it to the shoulder, thrusting his fingers under his armpits, in his waistcoat. There was something delightfully funny in that posture, something of the triumphant fighting-cock, and in that moment he beamed all over, a large child in this accursed world, a splendid man who had to sacrifice himself to hostility and hatred so that love would at last be realised.' But for all his warmth, flashes of charm and abiding personal simplicity Lenin was a deeply serious man with a dangerous intention. I think we must remember first and last his overwhelming, ruthless will.

TROTSKY

Handsome, brilliant, brave. 'An eagle', said Lenin after their first meeting. There were moments when their colleagues thought him Lenin's equal or superior. But only moments. Where they speak of Lenin's character, they speak of Trotsky's style. He was very aware of style – a thing of which Lenin was barely conscious. In his amazing many-sidedness, a man of action, orator, scholar and thinker, he is more like a renaissance man than a man of our own times; but he had that renaissance arrogance too. He was, to be blunt, a conceited man. It breathes in all his books. And the fact that his conceit was justified by his performance did not make it easier to take. He made enemies needlessly and, as it proved, fatally. But there is something admirable even in that; his own preoccupations were so lofty that he could not be bothered by the more base preoccupations of more ordinary men. He measured himself against History. He was not, except in this ultimate sense, pretentious. Rather he went in for careless elegance and wit. But his wit was stinging, and I do not know that he ever turned it on himself. However, he was not, like many witty men, cold-hearted. His accounts of the Revolution are full of emotion – not only his own. He really did share in the emotion of the revolutionary troops and workers he commanded and he elicited their devotion. So: a daring, somewhat daunting, charismatic man, but too swiftly articulate, not gladly suffering fools and a little condescending even in his friendship. The only person he looked up to was Lenin and that was because Trotsky too, for all his self-esteem, was dedicated to the revolutionary cause. The difference perhaps is this: one can imagine Trotsky as a brilliant success in any number of careers; one can't imagine Lenin as anything but what he was.

STALIN

Significantly, reliable *personal* accounts of Stalin simply do not exist. He had no friends before he came to power; thereafter he had only sycophants. He seems to have had no capacity for personal affection. His wife committed suicide, his son took to drink and his daughter fled. From start to finish he was alone; it is entirely possible that he was lonely. His manner of life at the end of his life was wretched and restless like that of some unhappy and dangerous animal. Alone among the Bolshevik leaders he was of plebeian birth and neither widely travelled nor well-read. He was and felt himself to be inferior in every way but one: his revolutionary dedication was primitive, well-grounded in resentment, not dependent on his understanding and so not to be shaken by argument nor inhibited by bourgeois scruples. In formulating Party policy he was slow to commit himself and when he had to commit himself early was often an embarrassment. Yet Lenin thought so highly of him that at the time of Lenin's death Stalin (again alone among the leadership) had a seat on every important organ of power. Lenin took for granted the high purpose of the Party and mistrusted too much talk about it. The respect which he felt for Stalin was the respect which he felt for the downtrodden masses, who had learned their revolutionary function not from Marx but from their own intolerable treatment by society as it stood. A proletarian who thought a little was a more reliable revolutionary than an intellectual who thought a lot. Stalin would do what needed doing. After Lenin's death Stalin did what needed doing to collectivise the land and industrialise Russia, thus completing the basic (that is economic) Marxist programme, the declared programme of the Party. In doing it he turned the Party and the State machine into a sort of bloody treadmill with himself as the plodding horse. Whether Lenin would have done the same or left the programme incomplete is the unanswerable question which one cannot help asking. And whether Lenin came to understand that motives of resentment, however natural, are negative, and cannot be satisfied by any positive achievement, I do not know and rather doubt. What is certain is that Lenin came to understand that Stalin was no mere wheel-horse at the service of the Party but an envious, sly and implacable enemy of anyone and anything which stood between himself and the ultimate reassurance of ultimate power. But he came to understand this only when it was too late. And Stalin proved to be as brutal and malevolent against his revolutionary peers as he had been against the erstwhile ruling class. Nobody survived his rancour. To achieve prominence and popularity was to be marked down for death. But this came later. At the period covered by the play he is a limited, slow-burning, solitary man, not more than half aware of his own malignant appetite, not Machiavellian but instinctively cunning, carefully filing each affront, hoarding his hatred. Trotsky describes his glance as 'yellow-eyed' and hostile. His expression in the photographs is shut. Except for his blue-black hair and Caucasian moustaches he was neither physically nor facially striking. But like Peter the Great this man took Russia by the scruff of its neck and tore it from one epoch to another. His death, as described by his daughter, has a sulphurous operatic grandeur, a touch of Ivan the Terrible. He cannot at any time have been merely a clown; he must have had a dangerous dormant strength as well as dangerous limitations. I think this part needs to be cast and played with that in mind.

GORKY

In appearance and character everyone's ideal Russian. He was tall and strongly built, but early privations had inflicted the disease which at length killed him. His face was primitive and powerful, with a broad forehead and high cheek-bones, but rendered complex by the melancholy eyes. His writing is not (as was later claimed) proletarian but picaresque. He had immense compassion for the suffering of the poor but what he chiefly dwelt on was the unpredictable eccentricity, passive or violent, which such suffering engenders. He was not, though Lenin thought him so, a sentimentalist. He had no illusions, as Lenin had, about the regenerative powers of popular vengeance. Peasant vengeance in particular he feared. He loved and respected Lenin but he was not afraid of him. And Lenin, though he violently resented Gorky's violent criticisms of the Bolshevik regime, never threatened Gorky nor would permit him to be threatened. Gorky was a long-time champion of the Revolution, its 'stormy petrel'; he had put his purse and reputation at its service. Also, they were friends. They quarrelled, when they did, as equals. And for all that Lenin scoffed at Gorky's agitated indignation, he coveted his good opinion. Gorky had a knowledge of life at the lower depths which Lenin never came near; he had risen from those depths with an inner moral dignity which commanded the respect of such disparate and perceptive persons as Tchekhov and Tolstoy.

He was fascinated by humanity, knowing it at its worst, longing for it to be better, but concerned for it as it was, not as it might become. So: humour, quick appreciation, moral strength held in reserve, courtesy and – perhaps most important – a certain detachment. After all he was, finally, an artist not a politician.

LUNACHARSKY

John Reed in his book *Ten Days that Shook the World* describes him in October as flashing-eyed and student-like. Contemporary photographs show a man in early middle-age, untidily dressed, with a big sedentary body and a mild, kind, thoughtful face, a bit like a good doctor. He had no gift for violence but was, after Lenin and Trotsky, the most popular of the October leaders. He thought the Revolution a new dawn and he communicated his high expectations with a candour and enthusiasm which endeared him to his armed and starving audiences, whose experience of life had not been so uplifting. Lenin never talked about the New Jerusalem, Lunacharsky never stopped. He it was who burst into tears and resigned from the Council of Commissars when it was learned in Petrograd that in the course of the coup in Moscow, the beautiful domes of the Kremlin had been shelled. Lenin persuaded him to resume his post when it was later learned that only two shells had struck, one of which had failed to detonate and the other done minor damage to a part of the palace of small architectural interest. He was intimate with the *avant-garde* among the poets, painters and musicians of revolutionary Petrograd and was often to be seen in their company, walking rapidly, talking excitedly, overcoat flapping. As Commissar for Education and Enlightenment he made himself their patron. But he had a deep respect for traditional culture and opposed the iconoclasm of those who demanded 'a Cultural October'. The educational policies of the Commissariat under his regime were both humane and practical but came to nothing, mainly from the desperate poverty of Russia at that time, but partly from his own ineptitude. Stalin's educational policy was ruthlessly utilitarian and Lunacharsky ended his days as a sort of roving ambassador in Europe, which he loved. His defence of Stalin's

Russia was sad and half-hearted but unwavering; he was, he insisted, a Bolshevik before anything else. What he particularly and predictably admired in Lenin was his strength of will. Lenin regarded Lunacharsky with alternate pleasure and exasperation. There was nobody, according to Krupskaya, whose company Lenin more enjoyed, but in serious matters he found him 'soft' – a severely opprobrious term.

DZERZHINSKY

He turned from his aristocratic background to the Revolution as a youth. He was constantly in prison. At once fastidious and romantic, he was the kind of man who gets caught. He was too sensitive and too high-minded for his own or anybody's good. He had lyric expectations of the socialist revolution, which he confided in his diary, and only these, he said, restrained him from despair and suicide. He is a man then who suffers but, being a gentleman, keeps his suffering to himself. Inwardly gentle and diffident, his outward manner will be severe – one of those men whose controlled and frosty features dissolve into a smile of touching innocence, and take you by surprise. He took an active part in the October coup and was appointed to be Commandant of the Bolshevik and Soviet Headquarters in the Smolny Institute. He performed this modest function in an exemplary way, treating all arrivals, important or obscure, with the same quiet, courteous suspicion. It was not until he was appointed to the Cheka that he became a figure of fear. Precisely because he hated the work he did it without pity, conscientiously. I imagine a sharp change in his outward manner here; he is trying to reduce himself to the status of a thing, a weapon. Even his colleagues became a bit afraid of him and at the time of his death he was pathetically and rather awfully concerned to assure himself of their affection. As the apparatus of the Cheka grew he was increasingly absorbed in keeping it clean and efficient. At no time did he use the power which was accumulating in his hands for any but its proper purpose – the enforcement of the Party's will. Because of that the Cheka came to be regarded as inviolable and unquestionable. And because of that it could of course be used for any purpose. His death was much lamented. With good reason. He was succeeded first by Yagoda and then Yezhov, a swift descent from the puritanical to the perverse. The only picture I have seen of this 'Perfect Knight of the Revolution' shows a strong, round, hairless head, the face severe but calm, the eyes untroubled behind rimless spectacles.

KRUPSKAYA

In her youth she was, I would say, very nearly beautiful, with strong but feminine features, a slightly scornful mouth and marvellous truthful eyes. Her expression is not aggressive but quite fearless; one understands that this would not be a person lightly to cross on a matter of principle. Later she thickened, and was inclined to be dowdy. As a girl she wrote to the great Tolstoy a letter which is worth quoting (condensing) because it reveals the fundamental sweetness and steady fervour of the later woman: 'Esteemed Lev Nikolaevich!... Recently I have felt more and more keenly that up to the present I have benefited by the labour of others... When I read your letter to the young ladies of Tiflis I was so glad! I know that the work of correcting books which the people will read is serious, that great ability and knowledge is needed for this, and at eighteen I still know too little... But I appeal to you with this request because, perhaps, through my love for the work I shall succeed somehow in helping my lack of ability and ignorance... Pardon me for having disturbed you with this request, I took you from your work... But surely it will not occupy you for specially much time. N Krupskaya.' Her devotion to Lenin was absolute but not uncritical. On their first meeting he mocked her 'Good Works' among the proletariat and she noted 'something evil and arid in his laugh' and she insisted in recording that impression in her famous *Memoirs of Lenin* after his death. When they arrived in Russia together in 1917 and Lenin shattered the Bolsheviks with his demand for immediate, red revolution Krupskaya turned to a nearby Comrade and mildly observed, 'It appears that Vladya is out of his mind.' In the years preceding, in their wandering exile, not only had she uncomplainingly cared for her leonine husband but had acted in effect as Secretary to the mainly conspiratorial Party using amateur codes and invisible ink. (This ink was made visible by the application of a flame and their apartment was full of the smell of burning paper.) But after the Revolution she was relegated to comparatively unimportant work in the Commissariat for Education and held no important post except, willy-nilly, the post of First Lady. Most likely Lenin thought it would smack of nepotism for his wife to hold high office in the Party of the State. Like him, she remained personally modest, even in her case a bit diffident. After his death she became a sort of mother-figure to the Russian masses, receiving daily scores of pleas for help and intervention. Stalin brought every kind of pressure to bear upon her but she never became, as did most of the others, Stalin's creature. She was forced to re-edit her *Memoirs* with the assistance of a Chekist secretary but she refused to exaggerate Stalin's part in the Revolution or to put into Lenin's mouth Stalin's abuse of Trotsky. She had that fastidious, lady-like strength of character which one sometimes still encounters in surviving suffragettes. She retained to the end not only her courage but her humour. Books, particularly children's books about her late great husband, were commonly submitted to her approval. On one such occasion 'If this is another one saying that Uncle Vladimir wants them to clean their teeth and do their homework, I won't read it,' she said. One last anecdote to illustrate their relationship. When in 1914 the socialists of the Allied and the Central Powers signified their support for the Imperialist War, Lenin was at first incredulous and then disgusted and enraged. He was reading an equivocating statement made by the German Socialist leadership. 'These people are shit!' he exclaimed. From the open kitchen door came a mild, reproving 'Vladya!' Lenin hesitated, looked towards the kitchen and repeated 'Shit!', on a note of defiance.

KOLLONTAI

She was a novelist, a poet and free-thinker. In particular she believed in free-love. In theory all the early Bolsheviks eschewed marriage as a bourgeois device for turning women into property and all believed in free-love. But Kollontai, unlike

Krupskaya in this instance, practised what she preached. 'There are only two real Communists in Russia', said the Menshevik leader Martov, 'Lenin and Kollontai'. (When Lenin heard of this he laughed and then, wistfully, 'What a clever man Martov is,' he said. They had been close colleagues and friends in the early days and now were political enemies.) When Trotsky announced to the Workers, Soldiers and Peasants of the Soviet, the success of the October coup, Kollontai stood with tears streaming down her face as the desperate audience rose and rendered first *The Marseillaise* and then *The Internationale.* She wept again when, as Commissar for Social Assistance, she had to use troops to take over the Tsarist Ministry building and funds. But she was highly and joyously intelligent as well as highly emotional, and her view of her colleagues, even of Lenin, remained drily and dauntlessly personal. She was popular with everybody. She became a leader of the short-lived Democratic Opposition to Stalin's dominance of the Party and after Lenin's death Stalin found diplomatic duties for her, outside Russia.

State of Revolution was first performed at the Birmingham Repertory Theatre, subsequently at the Lyttelton Theatre, London, on May 18 1977, with the following cast:

LUNACHARSKY, ANATOLE VASSILYEVICH, Stephen Moore

DZERZHINSKY, FELIX EDMUNDOVICH, John Normington

LENIN, VLADIMIR ILYICH, Michael Bryant

GORKY, ALEXEY MAXIMOVICH, Brian Blessed

KOLLONTAI, ALEXANDRA MIHAILOVNA, Sara Kestelman

MINISTER, Trevor Martin

STALIN, JOSEF VISSARIONOVICH, Terence Rigby

MARTOV/COUNT CZERNIN/DR GEUTIER, Anthony Douse

SPIRIDONOVNA, Catherine Harding

AN ANARCHIST, Michael Stroud

RUSSIAN GENERAL/MDVANI, Godfrey James

ZHELNIK, a sailor, John Labanowski

OLD SOLDIER, Louis Haslar

OFFICIALS, Antony Higginson and John Pollendine

SOVIET SOLDIER/PRAKTOV, James Leith

KRUPSKAYA, NADEZHDA, June Watson

CAPTAIN DRAGANOV, Michael Stroud

POLICEMAN, Peter Tilbury

TROTSKY, LEON DAVIDOVICH, Michael Kitchen

VON KUHLMANN, Peter Gordon

GENERAL HOFFMAN, Edwin Brown

FANYA KAPLAN, Sarah Simmons

SAILORS, SOLDIERS, CHEKISTS, REVOLUTIONARIES, Etc., Julian Battersby, Roger Gartland, Julia Pascal, Diana Payan, Robert Ralph, Andrew Tourell, Drew Wood

Director, Christopher Morahan
Designer, Ralph Koltai

The action of the play takes place on Capri and in Russia from, 1910–1920.

ACT ONE

A white spot comes up. LUNACHARSKY enters. Applause is heard on speakers.

LUNACHARSKY: Thank you – thank you. Thank you. It is always a pleasure to address the Young Communists. You know, these anniversaries of Comrade Lenin's death are not for those of us who knew him altogether sad occasions. Rather are they happy-sad. I make no apology for the personal note. The personal of course is marginal, the historically determined movement of the masses is alone decisive, as you know from your studies of Karl Marx and as our great revolutionary leader J V Stalin is –

(Applause on speakers, prolonged. He joins in.)

– is always at such pains to emphasise. But even Comrade Stalin would himself agree I think that on these occasions a personal note is unavoidable and even in its way illuminating. So then, I will introduce you to Vladimir Ilyich some years before the Revolution, in the home of Alexey Maximovich Gorky, on the island of Capri. Capri, as some of you may know, is a playground of the international bourgeoisie in its more light-hearted, less obviously offensive aspects. But you may be sure that V I Lenin was not there to play. Nor for the matter of that was I. We were getting ready there a school for advanced Party activists. I had prepared a paper for this school. And on the very day when Vladya came to us from Switzerland, I was submitting it to the approval of the other teachers. Including Comrade Lenin. I remember to my shame that as I came to my conclusion, I felt rather pleased with it –

(The lights change to reveal Capri, 1910. A hot day. KOLLONTAI is seated on the ground, GORKY and DZERZHINSKY at a table with a chess game. LENIN sits apart.)

– because this conclusion is a dialectical conclusion.

It does not challenge the reality of matter, but allows its interpenetration by what may loosely be termed spirit. It does not challenge our revolutionary ethic but allows its interpenetration by the best of the Christian liberal ethic; the ethic if you will of love. Thus synthesising for the first time in our history an unconditionally human ethic. And in my submission this is perfectly compatible with both the tone and teaching of Karl Marx. That's it.

(*GORKY applauds.*)

DZERZHINSKY: It's brilliant!

LENIN: It's what?

GORKY: Brilliant.

LENIN: I'm glad that Capri has been good for your lungs, Alexey Maximovich. Your mind seems to have collapsed. His thesis is shit.

KOLLONTAI: A really excellent thesis Anatole Vassilyevich. I think we should open the school with that.

LENIN: Now...

KOLLONTAI: Don't bully me, Vladya, I won't have it. If you have objections to the thesis, please let us have an orderly discussion.

DZERZHINSKY: And let us if we can confine ourselves to decent language.

LENIN: I withdraw the word 'shit'. Substitute 'excrement'.

KOLLONTAI: You consider that appropriate?

LENIN: Highly appropriate – it's a nicer word for the same nasty substance. And Lunacharsky's thesis is Marxist in its terminology and in its substance unashamed idealism! (*Overlapping protest.*)

DZERZHINSKY: Not at all, not at all...

KOLLONTAI: It was nothing of the kind...

GORKY: You haven't listened, Vladya...

KOLLONTAI: He's missed the point, 'Tolly...

LUNACHARSKY: Look, may I speak?

KOLLONTAI: Yes, go on, 'Tolly. He's completely missed the point.

LUNACHARSKY: There is a negated idealism in the dialectic naturally...

LENIN: Your silly sing-song has as much to do with dialectic as the Holy Roman liturgy.

GORKY: Oh come on, Vladya. This is not discussion, this is mere abuse.

LENIN: It merits abuse. Why do you want to discuss it?

DZERZHINSKY: Why?

LENIN: Yes. Why?

DZERZHINSKY: Because we are not your creatures, Comrade Lenin, but revolutionary comrades with opinions of our own.

KOLLONTAI: And happen to be the majority.

LENIN: Oh! Oh I *see*, the majority. It's not a school for revolutionary activists you're getting ready here – it's a school in parliamentary procedure. Well I would say that you are very well equipped.

DZERZHINSKY: This is intolerable.

LENIN: It's what?

DZERZHINSKY: Intolerable!

LENIN: That's the first revolutionary utterance I've heard from you all day.

DZERZHINSKY: My revolutionary record – and that of everybody here is at least as honourable as your own.

LENIN: True – here are ten lire. Towards a glass case for your record. You can run a revolutionary museum too. (*He starts to go, then pauses. To LUNACHARSKY.*) We need a school for activists because we are living through a period of dreadful inactivity. Is that not so?

LUNACHARSKY: Well yes, of course…

LENIN: In such a period the only thing that can see us through is unconditional class hatred. And unconditional human love is nothing but a dirty dream. Why are you still in the Party?

LUNACHARSKY: What?

GORKY: Vladya!

KOLLONTAI: How dare you, Vladya – shame.

LENIN: Well. Why?

GORKY: Stop it, Vladya.

LENIN: What's the matter, 'Tolly? Can't you tell me? Don't you know?

199

LUNACHARSKY: Vladya, please...

LENIN: What?

LUNACHARSKY: I am very much distressed...! You know how greatly I admire you.

LENIN: I have no use for your admiration. I spit in your distress. (*He goes.*)

LUNACHARSKY: Excuse me. (*He goes.*)

(*KOLLONTAI follows.*)

GORKY: Hey-ho.

DZERZHINSKY: Of all the vices gratuitous cruelty is the least sympathetic.

GORKY: He doesn't think it is gratuitous; he thinks it's necessary.

DZERZHINSKY: Mm. Necessary to his purpose or necessary to his nature?

GORKY: He isn't cruel by nature.

DZERZHINSKY: How else? From what I've seen today, Alexey, Trotsky is the greater man, both personally and politically.

GORKY: Mm. Well I shouldn't say so.

DZERZHINSKY: I shall certainly say so.

(*The lights change to moonlight. Piano music is heard. KOLLONTAI enters with a lamp.*)

KOLLONTAI: If Vladya is not careful he will find himself quite isolated.

GORKY: Where's 'Tolly?

KOLLONTAI: He's in the music room. He's horribly upset.

DZERZHINSKY: Finish the game? Now, let me see... Ah yes.

(*LENIN enters.*)

KOLLONTAI: (*Coldly.*) Good evening, Vladya.

(*LENIN raises his hat and goes to the chess game.*)

LENIN: (*To GORKY.*) Is he good?

GORKY: Mm. (*He indicates his vulnerable position in the game.*)

LENIN: Your move?

GORKY: Yes. (*He begins to make a move.*)

LENIN: (*Sucking in his breath.*) Tt-t-t-t.

GORKY: What?

LENIN: The bishop.

(*The piano music stops.*)

GORKY: Oh yes. (*He moves the bishop.*)

(*DZERZHINSKY takes a piece impassively.*)

DZERZHINSKY: *Garde.*

GORKY: (*To LENIN.*) Thank you.

LENIN: Wait a bit, wait a bit... Yes, well, I would never have got myself in that position in the first place.

(*LUNACHARSKY enters.*)

Bravo, bravo. You're a dangerous man 'Tolly. Music like that it's almost better than living.

LUNACHARSKY: I see. Life is discordant and I have chosen harmonious death. Well, allow me to observe that if I did not think that life could be harmonious – and beautiful – yes and spiritual – I would not be, as I am, a revolutionary.

LENIN: No, nor would I.

KOLLONTAI: Oh Vladya, no more.

LENIN: All right. There's an amazing steam yacht in the harbour, flying the Russian flag.

GORKY: Belongs to Feodor Lipkin. He comes here every year.

LENIN: Sensible fellow. Have you seen it?

LUNACHARSKY: Yes, it is beautiful.

LENIN: Mm. Are Lipkin's cotton-mills beautiful too?

LUNACHARSKY: Lipkin's mills are circles of hell.

LENIN: Then what shall we do with his yacht? Because it is by any standards beautiful; it's very nearly spiritual; I daresay there's a piano on it; and thin-skinned ladies who can play the piano. It's a vessel of culture is Lipkin's yacht. But because of Lipkin's mills, it must go down. Now that's the contradiction. And no thesis can resolve it because it is an actual contradiction which only action can resolve.

LUNACHARSKY: Well of course it is! But...

DZERZHINSKY: Nobody here is afraid of action.

(*LENIN looks at him with interest, then back at LUNACHARSKY.*)

LENIN: But?

LUNACHARSKY: It is a very *painful* contradiction!

LENIN: And?

LUNACHARSKY: And I suggest that you remember that.

LENIN: And Anatole Vassilyevich, my dear, kind-hearted friend I suggest that you forget it.

LUNACHARSKY: You never in your life 'suggested' anything.

LENIN: Well I like that...!

KOLLONTAI: It's perfectly true. Talking to you is like standing in front of a firing-squad.

LENIN: What a stupid image... I'm pleased to meet you Felix Edmundovich.

(*DZERZHINSKY inclines stiffly, but makes no other response.*)

Where did you learn to play chess?

DZERZHINSKY: I learned in prison. (*He adds very distinctly.*) In Nineteen Five.

LENIN: Ah... You had a good teacher.

DZERZHINSKY: Brilliant.

LENIN: He's a brilliant man.

DZERZHINSKY: A magnificent man.

LENIN: Yes he is a bit that way inclined.

DZERZHINSKY: In Nineteen Five he was magnificently right.

LENIN: I said so at the time.

DZERZHINSKY: You haven't said so recently.

LENIN: He hasn't been right recently. Or do you think he has?

DZERZHINSKY: I think he has deserved more generosity than you have shown him recently.

LENIN: Mm. Yes I see how Trotsky might attract you. Magnificence and generosity. You ought to be on Lipkin's yacht. They've got all the moral amenities there.

LUNACHARSKY: And must the moral amenities go down too?

LENIN: I don't know, perhaps they float – they don't appear to weigh too heavily on Lipkin do they? But if they don't – then 'Tolly we must let them sink. And let the new society give rise to virtues of its own new forms of love and unimaginable music. There is no peace, no comfort for the human spirit yet. It is fighting to be born...

LUNACHARSKY: That's very fine.

LENIN: It is?

LUNACHARSKY: Oh yes. It's terrible, but it's very fine.

LENIN: (*Briskly.*) Well there we are then. (*He takes the papers from him and tears them across, smiling cheerfully.*)

LUNACHARSKY: No! No, Vladya. (*He takes them back.*)

LENIN: If you are going to disseminate this enervating rubbish among active Party workers, I will have you expelled from the Party.

KOLLONTAI: Try it!

LENIN: Are you?

LUNACHARSKY: I don't agree with your assessment, Vladya, I...

LENIN: Alexey Maximovich, I'm going home tomorrow. Can you arrange it?

GORKY: Tomorrow...! Yes, I can arrange it...

KOLLONTAI: (*Stiffly.*) Goodnight, Vladya.

LUNACHARSKY: Vladya...

(*No response. KOLLONTAI sweeps out, LUNACHARSKY follows.*)

DZERZHINSKY: Good night, Comrade Lenin.
(*DZERZHINSKY gives a stiff bow and goes.
LENIN turns his head to watch him.*)

GORKY: What do you make of him?

LENIN: All right. Bit pure.

GORKY: Are you really going to expel 'Tolly?

LENIN: If I can.

GORKY: You used to be very fond of him.

LENIN: Still am very fond of him. What's that got to do with it?

GORKY: I think it ought to have something to do with it.

LENIN: Well. For a writer of fiction, a suitable thought.

GORKY: Vladya, are you fond of Stalin too?

LENIN: The Caucasian? I hardly know him. I like what I hear.

ROBERT BOLT

GORKY: I hear he's a stupid brute, what do you hear?

LENIN: That he does what needs doing, and doesn't make a
hobby of his soul. Oh you don't make a hobby of it,
you're a writer, you make money at it.

GORKY: Are you going to ask for money?

LENIN: We're desperately short, Alexey.

(*GORKY takes a fat packet from his pocket and gives it to
LENIN.*
LENIN opens it, and sees how much there is.)

Oh, thank you.

GORKY: You frighten me.

LENIN: Not really.

GORKY: Oh yes, really; I know what you think is wrong
with the world, but what world do you want?

(*LENIN grumbles and glowers.*)

LENIN: All right, I suppose you've paid for it. I want a
world where men like you will not have to torment
themselves and men like me... You really love this kind
of conversation, don't you?

GORKY: Go on.

LENIN: Men like me will not be needed. If you ever repeat
that I'll deny it. Now let's go in.

GORKY: And men like Stalin?

LENIN: You know you'd save yourself some torment now,
if you'd read a little Marx.

GORKY: Oh yes?

LENIN: Big events aren't formed by people, people are
formed by big events.

GORKY: Mm.

(*GORKY coughs violently, LENIN is concerned.*)

LENIN: It's getting damp, let's go in.

GORKY: Yes. (*He begins to clear up the chess things.*)

LENIN: Are you all right?

GORKY: Yes.

LENIN: Mother Nature isn't markedly maternal is she?

GORKY: Off and on.

LENIN: Alexey.

GORKY: Mm?

LENIN: I couldn't expel 'Tolly even if I wanted to. Too popular.

GORKY: Good.

(*LENIN draws near, mischievous and gossipy.*)

LENIN: Would I – er – would I have to expel Alexandra Mihailovna too?

GORKY: Yes.

LENIN: My word she doesn't change.

GORKY: No.

LENIN: Free-love and vegetables.

GORKY: Oh Vladya!

LENIN: Oh there's more to her than that. Course there is. Fine, Comrade. So's he really. Oh yes, they'll be all right when things burn up again.

GORKY: Are things going to?

LENIN: Burn up? Yes I think they are. I think there's going to be a war, Alexey. A big one. (*He sounds excited, almost pleased.*)

GORKY: And would you welcome that?

LENIN: What? Good heavens – can't you get it through your head? If there's going to be a war, Alexey, it won't wait for my welcome!

(*GORKY and LENIN go.*

The lights change. There is a distant rumble of gunfire.

LUNACHARSKY enters.)

LUNACHARSKY: It was a war which turned the world into a stockyard. With the workers of the world for stock… Comrades, we have recently encountered among broad sections of the peasant masses a wrong-headed resistance to the vital project of collective farming. We are overcoming this resistance by patient education. And where needs be by revolutionary direct action. Some of you I fear have been led by this necessity to adopt a hostile and superior attitude towards the peasants as a whole. Comrades that is very wrong. It was the peasant armies of the Tsar who made the Revolution. And this so suddenly that all of us were taken by surprise. Except for Comrade Lenin. His arrival at the Finland Station is of course a twice-told tale though I for one can never weary of it. But what you have to understand are the extraordinary contradictions in the situation which confronted him. The seemingly irreconcilable contradictions, the rapid shifts of mood from intoxicating uplift to desperation and despair. The confusion – the excitement – the...

(*LUNACHARSKY's words are drowned by the eruption on stage of the MINISTER, the GENERAL, OFFICIALS, MARTOV, STALIN, an ANARCHIST, SPIRIDINOVNA, sailor ZHELNIK and the CROWD, all arguing vehemently. A table and chairs are set.*)

MINISTER: Order...Order...Order!

(*His words are drowned. A rifle shot from ZHELNIK. Silence.*)

ZHELNIK: Order.

MINISTER: Thank you. My friends, the Provisional Government accepts and ratifies the abdication of the Tsar!

(*Applause.*)

We decree the election of a Constitutional Assembly! By universal franchise!

(*Applause.*)

We decree the immediate release of all political prisoners and – the immediate dissolution of the Secret Police!

(*Cheers.*)

My friends, Russia takes her place at last among the great democracies!

(*Applause.*)

And pledges to her democratic allies, France and Britain, an all-out prosecution of the patriotic war against the German enemy!

(*No applause.*)

(*Anxiously.*) My friends, the Provisional Government – your Government – demands this of the Russian People.

SPIRIDINOVNA: The Provisional Government is a bourgeois Government! The Russian people demand the land!

(*Applause, into which:*)

GENERAL: While you are demanding it, the Germans are taking it! I tell you plainly, lads – at the rate they're going, pretty soon there'll be no land left!

SPIRIDINOVNA: Don't listen to him, Comrades!

GENERAL: What...? Oh Madam, these brave fellows aren't your Comrades; they are mine – we've been through a good deal together – isn't that so, lads?

SOLDIER: I was with you at Tannenburg, sir.

GENERAL: Were you? Good for you. All right my boys, the Tsar has gone. If you would rather take your orders from committees of commercial travellers and money-lending yids – all right! Your privilege. You've fought for it, you've earned it. But any man who'll stand aside and see his country overrun – is a yellow-bellied bastard! And that's what's happening... Tell them, Minister!

MINISTER: Men, the German Third and Seventh Armies are advancing – unopposed!

(*Rumble from the CROWD.*)

OFFICIAL: Committing unheard-of and bestial atrocities!

(*Rumble grows.*)

SECOND OFFICIAL: The Front is open!

(*Rumble grows to a roar.*)

GENERAL: Well, lads – what about it?

(*Enthusiastic uproar: but ZHELNIK fires his rifle again. Silence.*)

ZHELNIK: Wait. We haven't heard the others yet. Of course he wants us to fight... He's a general isn't he?

(*Uneasy murmur from the CROWD 'That's right enough', 'He is by God', 'Well said, Brother', ad lib. ZHELNIK nods.*)

Right. (*To the GENERAL.*) You've had your turn, you sit down.

(*Amazed silence: the GENERAL is incredulous.*)

GENERAL: What?

(*Two beats of silence, then, not hectoring but implacably serious.*)

ZHELNIK: Sit down.

MINISTER: (*Quickly.*) General...

(*The GENERAL swallows his indignation and sits.*)

ZHELNIK: Right. Next speaker.

MINISTER: Er – if I may?

ZHELNIK: Go on then.

MINISTER: (*Carefully, reasonably.*) Maria Spiridinovna, if the Assembly should decide upon redistribution of the land, redistribution will ensue. (*A note of exasperation.*) But surely you can see that for that to be done in an orderly way will take...

SPIRIDINOVNA: It will never be done in an orderly way...!

ANARCHIST: Then let it be done! Long live disorder! Long live chaos! Long live anarchy!
(*Applause, half-mocking, with jeers and laughter. The MINISTER sits.*)

MINISTER: It's a mad-house.
(*MARTOV rises.*)
Yes, yes, Mr Martov.

MARTOV: Thank you. As you know, Mr Minister, we Mensheviks are Marxists.
(*STALIN guffaws. MARTOV is unruffled.*)
Now, Comrades, we have undergone a bourgeois revolution. In Marxist terms we have ended the epoch of feudal tyranny and entered the epoch of bourgeois democracy. And that is a substantial gain. And for the moment I must tell you that the bourgeoisie and proletariat are not class enemies but allies. Minister, the Mensheviks demand a vigorous but limited and strictly defensive war.
(*MARTOV sits, well pleased, to a flutter of uncertain applause, but STALIN is on his feet.*)

STALIN: Comrades! A defensive war is like Menshevik Marxism – piss and wind!

MINISTER: Er...?

STALIN: J V Stalin for the Bolshevik Party. There is no defence without attack, and war is total.

GENERAL: Right by God, right.

STALIN: We do not call upon you, Comrades, to defend the bourgeois revolution as allies of the bourgeoisie – we call upon you to *compel* them to defend it. For if they could they would betray it! We call upon you, through the regimental and battalion committees to insist upon an *all-out* prosecution of the war! The Prussian Army is the champion of international reaction. The Kaiser of the Germans is the cousin of the Tsar. And if his armies conquer Russia he will return it to the Tsar. It is our revolutionary duty therefore to resist his armies. This is obvious. This is inescapable. Comrades, this is the historic task.

MINISTER: (*Agreeably surprised, delicately eager.*) And this is the Bolshevik programme?

STALIN: It is our immediate programme.

MINISTER: Then – Comrades – Brothers – Fellow Russians – Friends! Are we united?

GENERAL: Make up your minds, lads – show the white feather – or come with me!

(*The GENERAL leads the way off, followed by the enthusiastic CROWD. But they are checked by the blast of a locomotive whistle. The stage is cleared.*

LENIN enters, in travelling-clothes and carrying a bunch of red flowers. KRUPSKAYA follows with a Gladstone bag.

During the following a small rostrum and lectern is set up.)

MINISTER: The Provisional Government of National Unity welcomes the return of V I Lenin.

LENIN: Am I not to be arrested?

MINISTER: Good Heavens no, those days are over.

LENIN: That's bad, that's very bad. Who here is from the Soviet?

SOLDIER: The Petrograd Soviet of Worker Soldier Deputies welcomes your return.

LENIN: Where are you going, Comrade?

SOLDIER: Well, to the Front.

LENIN: Has the Soviet ordered you to the Front?

SOLDIER: Well, not to say the Soviet...

LENIN: Then – you have no right to this.

(*LENIN steps forward and rips the red band from his sleeve. A stir and murmur.*)

STALIN: (*To LENIN, indignantly.*) This is the line of the Party. This is the line of the Central Committee.

LENIN: Shit, to the Central Committee.

LUNACHARSKY: (*Alarmed.*) Vladya, it was only after very long and serious debate that we...

LENIN: (*Clearly and distinctly.*) Shut up.

(*LENIN turns on his heel, goes to the lectern, the others flinching away from him. The light has darkened dramatically now, LENIN casting a giant shadow, the others lit fitfully. He becomes the Lenin of the famous photographs. He hammers home his arguments like nails into a plank, staccato.*)

Comrades, what is the purpose of this war? You do not know. And those who made it do not know. Yet those who made this war are dying in it just as you are. And are powerless to stop it. Has it then no purpose? It has no conscious purpose. But it has inexorable causes. It is the last obscene convulsion of a dying system, of a morally exhausted ruling class. The war will stop when the People take power. Unless they take power the war will continue. In Russia the People have taken power and the war has already stopped.

OFFICIAL: Tell that to the Germans!

LENIN: The German people know it. The Russian Revolution will become World Revolution, if the Russian People do not falter. But the Russian People are afraid. (*The giant ZHELNIK wanders towards him, fascinated.*) Afraid of a word. That word is 'Government'. All Government is finally based on force. All force is finally armed force. The armed forces of Russia have declared allegiance to the Soviets. Therefore the Soviets are the Government of Russia. And when the Soviets declare allegiance to the Provisional Government they declare allegiance to an empty word.

MINISTER This is treason!

LENIN: I call for treason.

ANARCHIST: (*Delightedly.*) This is anarchy!

LENIN: It is the very opposite. I demand for the Soviets absolute authority. I demand for the People the means of production. The land to the Peasants, the places of work to the urban workers. Now, I call upon the front-line troops to fraternise with their German comrades. Now! I call upon the garrisons to turn their rifles on their officers. Now! The programme is immediate and bloody civil war! And if that means a German victory – I call for Russian defeat!

(*A frozen silence.*)

GENERAL: That man is a German agent.

(*Uproar. LENIN stands stock still, a pariah.*

Everyone exits.

The lights change to a warm interior, with LENIN and KRUPSKAYA. She takes his coat and goes. He thrusts his hands into his pockets and whistles softly 'Für Elise'. KRUPSKAYA returns without her hat and coat, but with a vase. She glances at him, and begins to put the red flowers in it. He stops whistling.)

LENIN: Well? What do you think?

KRUPSKAYA: (*Distantly.*) I think you are out of your mind.

LENIN: Oh.

KRUPSKAYA: (*Distantly.*) Also, I think you are uncertain.

LENIN: Oh? Why do you think that?

KRUPSKAYA: (*Distantly.*) When you are certain you don't ask what I think.

LENIN: Hm. Nadya, don't desert me, now.

KRUPSKAYA: Oh, you *are* uncertain…

LENIN: Support me.

KRUPSKAYA: Support you in Committee?

LENIN: Yes.

KRUPSKAYA: No. How can I, Vladya? That speech was crazy. The Party is in a classically defensive situation and you are calling for red revolution! No-one will support you.

LENIN: No-one?

KRUPSKAYA: Who? Dzerzhinsky – no. Lunacharsky? No.

LENIN: No. Lunacharsky doesn't *want* red revolution. He wants to address the Duma! In a silk hat, and a frock-coat – with a white carnation in his button-hole!

KRUPSKAYA: Always you defend yourself by attacking someone else, He is a loyal Comrade; and utterly sincere.

LENIN: Well perhaps it'll be a red carnation... Zinoviev might agree with me.

KRUPSKAYA: Not this time; much as he likes agreeing with you.

LENIN: What about Kollontai?

KRUPSKAYA: (*Sitting.*) She of course will agree with her lover.

LENIN: Yes? Who's that?

KRUPSKAYA: How should I know? I haven't seen her for six months.

LENIN: Nadya, you're a prude.

(*She looks hurt. He goes to her hastily.*)

So am I, so am I... (*He kisses her forehead.*) Support me...!

KRUPSKAYA: I *can't*, Vladya...!

(*She looks at him distressed as he leaves her and stands apart, back turned.*)

LENIN: Stalin?

KRUPSKAYA: (*After a beat, curtly.*) Yes, perhaps.

LENIN: You don't like Stalin, do you?

KRUPSKAYA: Do you?

LENIN: If I had to rely on the people I like, I'd go back home tomorrow.

KRUPSKAYA: Does that include me?

LENIN: Apparently. (*He sits.*)

KRUPSKAYA: Vladya, that's inhuman – I simply don't agree with you. You are stupid about men like Stalin, Vladya.

LENIN: No. You are stupid about men like Stalin. You chose to be a revolutionary from the goodness of your bourgeois heart. A man like Stalin is a revolutionary from the circumstances of his birth. And for that there is no substitute.

(*Knocking is heard off. Both rise, alert.*)

KRUPSKAYA: Go on.

(*LENIN and KRUPSKAYA go: he to hide, she to the door. It is routine.*

Voices are heard off.

KOLLONTAI enters, rapidly.)

KOLLONTAI: Vladya...!

    (*LENIN comes back.*)

    Oh Vladya, Vladya, what a speech! What a... Oh! (*She embraces him.*)

LENIN: You agree with me?

KOLLONTAI: Does anyone disagree?

    (*KRUPSKAYA enters.*)

LENIN: Oh yes.

    (*KRUPSKAYA looks at Lenin drily, looks off.*)

KRUPSKAYA: Come in, Comrade.

    (*The giant sailor ZHELNIK enters, still carrying his rifle. KOLLONTAI goes to him, brings him to LENIN, shyly.*)

KOLLONTAI: Vladya, this is Comrade Zhelnik.

LENIN: Ah.

    (*They shake hands.*)

KOLLONTAI: He is a sailor.

LENIN: Yes. Does he agree too?

ZHELNIK: That speech was a bull's eye.

KOLLONTAI: A bull's eye. The arrow to its mark. Yes. He wants to join the Party.

KRUPSKAYA: To join? Alexandraya, are you mad? This is a terrible breach of security! How long have you known this, Comrade?

KOLLONTAI: Oh, I think he can be trusted, Nadezhda. He is a member of the Kronstadt Sailors' Soviet.

LENIN: Oh. Is he?

KOLLONTAI: His shipmates elected him.

LENIN: Do your shipmates agree with my programme too?

ZHELNIK: We can't shoot our officers.

LENIN: Why?

ZHELNIK: We drowned the captain. And the rest have gone.

LENIN: Oh.

KOLLONTAI: The captain was an awful creature – awful!

LENIN: What kind of ship is it?

ZHELNIK: Heavy cruiser. The *Aurora.*

LENIN: You have expropriated a heavy cruiser?

ZHELNIK: Right.

213

LENIN: Can you go through with it?

ZHELNIK: Got no option, now.

LENIN: Oh see how clearly they see it...! Have you got guns?

ZHELNIK: Six-inch and eight-inch.

LENIN: No – rifles.

ZHELNIK: A few. The rest are in the armoury – armoury's locked.

LENIN: But, can't you break in?

ZHELNIK: We've broken nothing yet. Ship's as smart as she ever was. Admiral's inspection if you like.

LENIN: Strict, revolutionary discipline.

ZHELNIK: Strict. Right.

LENIN: Oh what a Comrade. Still, break into the armoury.

ZHELNIK: Right.

> (*Knocking is heard again. LENIN curses softly and, going, says to ZHELNIK.*)

LENIN: Stay.

> (*LENIN and KRUPSKAYA go as before.*)

KOLLONTAI: You've made a good impression on him.

ZHELNIK: That's nice. He's made a good impression on me. You can tell him if you like.

KOLLONTAI: Fedor Gavrilovich – don't be so *proud...*

> (*They look at each other. This unlikely couple is in love.*
> *Voices off; STALIN enters.*)

KOLLONTAI: Yosef.

STALIN: (*Grunting.*) What's he doing here?

KOLLONTAI: Vladya wants him.

> (*STALIN grunts again.*
> *KRUPSKAYA comes back, her arm linked in GORKY's, followed by LUNACHARSKY and DZERZHINSKY.*
> *GORKY is coughing.*)

KRUPSKAYA: Are you all right?

GORKY: Yes, yes. (*He coughs again.*)

KRUPSKAYA: You'd better keep your coat on.

GORKY: I will. Stop fussing. Hello, Alexia.

KOLLONTAI: (*Distantly.*) Hello.

GORKY: Oh. (*He smiles at KRUPSKAYA.*)

KRUPSKAYA: Vlady's very angry with you.

GORKY: Not as angry as he's going to be.

> (*LENIN enters.*
> *The others watch as LENIN marches up to GORKY, plants*
> *himself.*)

LENIN: Did you know – that the reactionary Press is printing pieces from your magazine – exactly as they stand – as anti-Party propaganda?

GORKY: Yes.

LENIN: And doesn't that bother you – just a bit?

GORKY: It bothers me quite a lot. But as you know I'm easily bothered.

LENIN: Well don't bother me! (*He moves away, then turns.*) What are you doing here anyway? This is a Committee Meeting.

GORKY: You haven't got a quorum yet. And, Vladya, if you carry the Committee, I am going to leave the Party. (*A stir.*)

KOLLONTAI: Alexey, you can't!

LENIN: If I don't carry the Committee, I may leave the Party.

> (*Consternation.*)

KRUPSKAYA: Vladya, you're possessed.

LENIN: Yes!

KRUPSKAYA: A month ago you said that revolution was not to be looked for!

LENIN: A month ago we were in Switzerland! I didn't look for it – I found it!

GORKY: Where did you find it?

LENIN: On the streets! (*Roaring.*) Where would you expect to find it? (*He glares round, twitching with suppressed anxiety. He forces himself back to his papers, hunched and dangerous.*)

GORKY: You are possessed by vanity and crude excitement. What you have found is nothing better than desperation.

LENIN: What better could there be?

LUNACHARSKY: Vladya, couldn't we talk about this calmly?

LENIN: (*Bitterly.*) That I dare say we could manage.
(*LUNACHARSKY looks round. KRUPSKAYA nods
encouragement, urging him on.*)

LUNACHARSKY: What revolution are we talking about,
Vladya?

LENIN: Oh go to b – (*He rubs his hand hard down his face,
fighting for control.*) I beg your pardon. (*His face is white,
his voice unnaturally flat.*) I am talking about socialist
revolution.

GORKY: And what you will get is a peasant rising!
Mindless, bloody, barbaric! Reaction may come of it.
Chaos may come of it. But socialism cannot.

LENIN: Why?

KRUPSKAYA: (*Despairingly.*) Because that can only come
from proletarian revolution, Vladya!

LUNACHARSKY: And we have no proletariat! Surely, this
is elementary…?

LENIN: It is a simplified abstraction. I am looking at what
I can see. You are remembering what you have read.
I see no peasants on the street. I see soldiers and sailors.

GORKY: They are peasants all the same. And, Vladya,
when the peasant talks of revolution, he is thinking of a
meadow. And when he understands the difference
between socialism and a meadow he will hate your
revolution from the bottom of his soul.

LUNACHARSKY: Correct.

LENIN: Incorrect.

GORKY: Goddammit – I was born a peasant!

LENIN: But now, you're a middle-class literateur. (*He goes to
ZHELNIK.*) He was born a peasant too. But now he's a
conscripted sailor. And a man in uniform who mutinies
is revolution incarnated. And all that's needed is for us
to articulate his demands!

GORKY: What are your demands, Brother?

ZHELNIK: Stop the war. Take the land.

LENIN: Correct.

GORKY: But who will the land belong to then?

ZHELNIK: Us.

LENIN: Correct.

GORKY: To you – individually? Or everyone collectively? (*ZHELNIK looks at him, narrowly.*)

LUNACHARSKY: What Comrade Gorky means is...

ZHELNIK: I know what he means. (*To GORKY.*) Big question.

GORKY: You're right. What's the answer?

ZHELNIK: We'll cross that bridge when we come to it.

LENIN: (*Quietly.*) Correct. By God correct. I do not say the revolution is certain of success. I say we have the means to attempt it. Here. (*He puts his hands on ZHELNIK's shoulders.*) And now. The choice is therefore either to attempt it now, or admit that we don't want it. And never really did.

LUNACHARSKY: That's not a choice, that's moral blackmail.

LENIN: If it feels like blackmail you're feeling guilty. Yosef, what do you think?

STALIN: I am waiting for the other Comrades.

LENIN: Clearly. While you're waiting what do you think?

STALIN: I think your line is theoretically correct. I doubt if it is practical.

LENIN: If it isn't both it's neither. You're talking like a fool.

KRUPSKAYA: He's talking sense.

LENIN: Why is my line not practical?

STALIN: In my opinion to organise the masses we need time to build a massive Party. This...

LENIN: If we take the line the masses want, we will be massive overnight! Felix Edmundovich – what do you think?

DZERZHINSKY: I think your line is Trotsky's line. What do you think about that?

LENIN: If you will not follow me, I will follow Trotsky. (*Consternation. Exclamations.*)

KOLLONTAI: Vladya, I agree with every word you've said. But you cannot split the Party – now.

LENIN: There are rotten elements inside the Party that the Party can't afford just now. (*He is looking at GORKY.*)

(*Knocking is heard off.*)
Let our Comrades in as you go out. (*He turns away.*)
(*GORKY goes.*)

KRUPSKAYA: (*To ZHELNIK.*) You must go now too,
Comrade.

LENIN: He can wait a minute.
(*A noise off. A burst of voices and a slamming door.*
GORKY comes flying back.)

GORKY: Police!

LUNACHARSKY: What...?

GORKY: Police!
(*All but KRUPSKAYA rush off.*
A uniformed POLICEMAN rushes on, and off after them.
With him, walking, DRAGANOV, an anonymous official.
He holds out his hand to KRUPSKAYA.)

DRAGANOV: (*Politely.*) Papers? (*She gets them from her bag*
and gives them to him.)
(*The POLICEMAN comes back.*)

POLICEMAN: I think they've given us the slip, sir!

DRAGANOV: Oh. Well, do what you can.
(*The POLICEMAN rushes off again.*
DRAGANOV returns the papers.)

DRAGANOV: Thank you.

KRUPSKAYA: May I go?

DRAGANOV: Yes.

KRUPSKAYA: I thought the Secret Police had been
disbanded, Captain Draganov?

DRAGANOV: Ah. It's not the kind of thing you can do
overnight you see. At your service... At anybody's
service, actually. A technician you know, just a
technician.
(*The POLICEMAN rushes on, breathless.*)

POLICEMAN: They have – they've given us the slip!

DRAGANOV: Oh dear, what a pity.

POLICEMAN: You don't seem very concerned!

DRAGANOV: Oh I am – oh yes – after them!
(*The POLICEMAN rushes off again.*)
An enthusiast. These are difficult times for a man like
that. (*He smiles at her.*) Thank you.

(*KRUPSKAYA goes.*)

(*To himself.*) A certain flexibility seems indicated.

(*The lights go out with an electric hiss.*)

(*Looks up.*) That for instance. Is it, I ask myself, a show of revolutionary strength by the comrades at the generating station? Or an authorised power-cut? (*He strikes a match.*) It's important to know these things. And daily more difficult.

(*The lights come up on a bare stage. A chandelier has been lowered.*

The MINISTER enters.)

MINISTER: The vital thing is a sense of proportion. One must not see catastrophe where perhaps there is no more than a healthy show of popular initiative.

DRAGANOV: No, Minister.

MINISTER: On the other hand, Draganov, we cannot assume that the times in which we live are not catastrophic, merely because it is we who live in them. After all, someone has to live in catastrophic times.

DRAGANOV: Yes, Minister.

MINISTER: Mm. You're an intelligent fellow Draganov, how would you describe the situation?

DRAGANOV: ...Fluid.

MINISTER: You don't exactly rush to commit yourself do you Draganov?

DRAGANOV: I am as you say an intelligent fellow.

MINISTER: I tried to get a table at the *Belle Etoile* last night.

DRAGANOV: Yes?

MINISTER: Couldn't. The most expensive restaurant in Petrograd – bursting at the seams. Does that look like revolution?

DRAGANOV: Er...

MINISTER: You're absolutely right, it does. The workers at the Putilov have occupied the factory, and the Seminovsky guards decline to move them out. The Bolsheviks have occupied the Smolny Institute. And nobody would even dream of trying to move them out. Nobody indeed would dream of going near the place. In my opinion, Draganov, these people of the *Belle Etoile* are spitting in the wind. Where do they obtain their pâté and cigars? I will tell you. They obtain them at the frontier with the assistance of the frontier guard. The patriotic officers deploy the secret funds with which you so lavishly provided them, in night clubs. In my opinion, Draganov, the Russian upper, middle, middle-upper and blue-blooded classes merit overwhelmingly whatever happens to them.

DRAGANOV: It's, er...

MINISTER: Yes?

DRAGANOV: It's a little late in the day, Minister, but I'm beginning to respect you.

MINISTER: Oh, thank you, Draganov. I hardly know how to respond. I have always entertained for you the most lively sentiments of loathing and contempt. Ah, General...

(*The GENERAL enters.*)

You know our good Draganov?

GENERAL: Yes.

MINISTER: Captain?

DRAGANOV: The practical plans for insurrection have been put in charge of the man Bronstein, Trotsky. Ulyanov, Lenin, is still in hiding but I'm pretty sure he's here. The date of insurrection depends upon the Minister. The signal will be gunfire from the battleship *Aurora*.

MINISTER: In what sense does the date depend upon myself?

DRAGANOV: The date for the Constituent Assembly will be the date of insurrection – or perhaps a couple of days before.

(*The MINISTER nods, looks away.*)

MINISTER: (*To no-one.*) Why?

DRAGANOV: They are determined at all costs to anticipate the Assembly.

MINISTER: But why? This man Ulyanov – this latest document of his, this – (*Producing a pamphlet.*) – 'State and Revolution' – it does not seem unsympathetic? It is if anything dottily idealistic. He seemingly expects the

Brotherhood of Man within a generation. Why then will he not allow the people to declare themselves?

DRAGANOV: He is quite certain that they will.

MINISTER: It's a very strong position... Well, General?

GENERAL: The Second Don and Kuban Cossacks are ready to move at twelve hours' notice. With artillery.

MINISTER: I have told you repeatedly; I will not use Cossacks!

(*The GENERAL shrugs.*)

MINISTER: (*Quietly.*) Will you or will you not accept the High Command?

GENERAL: I cannot deal with Bolshevism if my officers must deal with Bolshevik Committees. And if I cannot shoot deserters I cannot keep an army in the line against the Germans.

MINISTER: To dissolve the Committees is politically impossible. And I regard the shooting of deserters as an atavistic horror.

GENERAL: (*Contemptuously.*) Your day is done, sir.

(*The GENERAL goes.*

The lights start to fade. There is the noise of a distant mob.)

MINISTER: Oh what a pity, Draganov, what a pity.

(*A cannon shot is fired. DRAGANOV and the MINISTER freeze. At the moment of impact the lights black-out. Silence. The MINISTER and DRAGANOV exit in the darkness. The lights come up. The chandelier has been flown. The stage is red. On a table, which is covered with a red cloth, stands a telephone. TROTSKY has the receiver to his ear. He is watched by STALIN, DZERZHINSKY, KOLLONTAI, KRUPSKAYA and LUNACHARSKY. All have rifles. LENIN is seated, his face in his hands, exhausted.*)

TROTSKY: Very well... Good (*He puts down the receiver. To LENIN.*) It's done.

(*LENIN takes his face from his hands, rubs it.*)

LENIN: Tell them.

(*TROTSKY advances on the audience.*)

TROTSKY: Comrades! Last night Red Guard Detachments, together with detachments from revolutionary Kronstadt, took command of Petrograd.

(*Applause on speakers.*)

The central telephone exchange, banks, bridges, post and telegraph bureaux, police stations and railway termini are ours. Warrants have been issued for the arrest of the bourgeois Government and the Winter Palace is surrounded.

(*Applause.*)

Comrades, they will say that we are men of violence; they will say we are adventurers. I, Leon Davidovich Trotsky, reply in your name – yes – we are embarked upon that violent adventure which goes by the name of Human History! Comrades, they will say we have created chaos, that we have turned society upside down. I reply – no – we have turned society right way up. It is right that the people should take command – and right that you should obey!

(*Applause.*)

Comrades, the left wing liberals and right wing socialists, the moderates, the Mensheviks, will demand a part in our Government. I reply to these gentlemen – no – it is a revolutionary Government and you took no part in the revolution. Away with you – to the dustbin of History!

(*Applause.*)

Our Party, Comrades, is not a machine for gathering votes, it is the weapon of the working class! Comrades, here is the sword-smith who hammered that weapon: Vladimir Ilyich Lenin...

(*LENIN stands. Applause from speakers; tumultuous, hoarse, punctuated by individual ecstatic cries. He stands unmoved as it billows about him; at last holds up his hand; it ceases.*)

LENIN: We will now proceed to the construction of the socialist order.

(*Applause.*)

The People's Commissar for Welfare.

KOLLONTAI: Effective from today, all ranks, degrees and titles are abolished. All who work are free and equal!

(*Applause.*)

LENIN: For Nationalities.

STALIN: All Peoples of the Russian Empire being free and equal peoples have the right to self-determination!
(*Applause.*)

LENIN: For Security.

DZERZHINSKY: The Office of Magistrate is abolished. Police interrogation is abolished. Trial and investigation are the office of the open People's Courts!
(*Applause.*)

LENIN: For Foreign Affairs.

TROTSKY: The People's Commissariat proposes to the Allied and the Central Powers an immediate, democratic and honourable Peace, without loss or detriment to any nation!
(*Applause.*)

LENIN: For Education.

LUNACHARSKY: All children of the Russian People have an equal right to an enlightened education!
(*There is the distant fire of heavy guns. All but LUNACHARSKY hear it and react.*
All exit except ZHELNIK and LUNACHARSKY.
Throughout, LUNACHARSKY continues, absorbed.)
– To this end, Comrades, the People's Commisariat decrees throughout all Russia, polytechnical, co-educational and self-administrating schools!

ZHELNIK: Comrade…

LUNACHARSKY: What…? (*He is impatient of the interruption, but looking round he sees the empty stage and registers the booming guns.*) Oh. What…?

ZHELNIK: The Cossacks, Comrade. Are you coming?
(*LUNACHARSKY is torn between his revolutionary duty and his cultural enthusiasm.*)

LUNACHARSKY: Yes. Yes of course. Each school council will comprise teachers, senior pupils and representatives of the local working population!
(*Rattle of machine-gun fire, close.*)
Teachers to be subject to election!

ZHELNIK: Comrade!

(*LUNACHARSKY waves him to be silent, breathless, wanting to get it all in before he goes.*)

LUNACHARSKY: All schools will provide free hot breakfasts! Homework, punishments and compulsory examinations are abolished!

(*Small-arms fire is heard, closer.*

ZHELNIK goes.

LUNACHARSKY goes after him, dropping his papers, retrieving them, dropping his rifle, sorting himself out.

The machine-gun fire is prolonged and vicious. The light grows cold. Two banners are lowered, the Imperial Eagles of Germany and Russia. A table, with a green cloth, and chairs are set.

TROTSKY enters with a briefcase. He takes papers from it, then clasps his hands behind his back and muses. KUHLMANN, CZERNIN and HOFFMAN enter, also with briefcases.)

KUHLMANN: Good morning! Good morning! (*He glances at his watch.*)

What admirable promptitude. Er, von Kuhlmann.

(*KUHLMANN extends his hand. TROTSKY hesitates, takes it, wipes his hand on the seat of his trousers. Unperturbed, KUHLMANN rattles on.*)

For Austria, Count Czernin. And General Hoffman for the High Command.

TROTSKY: Gentlemen.

(*All but KUHLMANN sit, arranging their papers during the following.*)

KUHLMANN I should like some coffee. Coffee, gentlemen? Coffee, Mr Trotsky?

TROTSKY: Thank you, no.

KUHLMANN: Well perhaps not; I drink too much coffee, far too much. (*Sitting.*) Are your quarters satisfactory? Please don't hesitate, if there is anything that you would like…

TROTSKY: I would like to get on.

KUHLMANN: Admirable. (*Consulting his papers.*) And the terms of your proposal are admirable too. Germany for

the Germans, Russia for the Russians – Austria of course
for the Austrians – and no hard feelings. Admirable. But
I feel you should address these terms to the aggressor
nations, France and Britain.

TROTSKY: We have done so.

KUHLMANN: May I know with what result?

TROTSKY: With no result.

KUHLMANN: Well there it is you see. I fear that Germany
and Austria can only stop the war by winning.

TROTSKY: Or by losing.

(*HOFFMANN puts his booted foot on the table.*)

KUHLMANN: Or, as you say, by losing. Here on the
Russian Front however – I don't know how to put it with
sufficient delicacy – but here we do seem to have won.
Wouldn't you say?

TROTSKY: I don't deny that German Generals – almost it
would seem by nature – have very superior boots.

HOFFMANN: We could be in Petrograd by April.

TROTSKY: No.

HOFFMANN: Without the slightest difficulty.

TROTSKY: No.

HOFFMANN: Your defences are deserted, your armies are
in rags.

TROTSKY: The armies of Bonaparte fought in rags.

KUHLMANN: You have a Bonaparte?

TROTSKY: We have a revolution. There is still one
excellent army between you and Petrograd.

KUHLMANN: Oh?

TROTSKY: Your own.

KUHLMANN: You think our soldiers would refuse to
march?

TROTSKY: You would be ill-advised to let them march to
Petrograd.

KUHLMANN: Why, what would they see there that is so
appealing?

TROTSKY: Their comrades in command.

CZERNIN: Your comrades in command.

KUHLMANN: And that you see is less appealing.

HOFFMANN: Is this a military conference or a philosophical debate?

TROTSKY: The two are not distinct. Believe me, Herr von Kuhlmann, bring your troops to Petrograd and you bring dry straw to a naked flame.

HOFFMANN: Not straw, Trotsky, steel.

KUHLMANN: In matters of philosophy the General, like Marx, believed in a material reality.

TROTSKY: Flame is a reality.

KUHLMANN: But steel is the material in question. Now the terms you have proposed are –

TROTSKY: – admirable.

KUHLMANN: Please...? Ah... (*With an appreciative little laugh.*) Admirable, yes. But not acceptable.

TROTSKY: No? (*It has a note of appeal.*)

KUHLMANN: No.

TROTSKY: Then if you can't accept the admirable, what would be sufficiently contemptible?

KUHLMANN: (*Apologetically.*) Reality.

TROTSKY: We couldn't just this once, attempt to make reality admirable?

KUHLMANN: Oh, that I must leave to you, Mr Trotsky, I really don't feel up to it.

HOFFMANN: You take our terms. Or fight.

TROTSKY: (*To KUHLMANN.*) According to your terms you take two-thirds of our coal and iron, one third of our factories, a million miles of territory and sixty millions of our people.

KUHLMANN: Approximately.

TROTSKY: How can we take such terms?

HOFFMANN: I don't think you can fight.

TROTSKY: Count Czernin, I am dealing here with Prussian Policemen – you embody in your own esteem six centuries of Christian culture. If you take the Ukraine, this winter we shall starve. Is that what you desire?

CZERNIN: The question is unfairly phrased. There is no question of our 'taking the Ukraine'. The People's Government of the Ukraine has signed a separate peace.

TROTSKY: And thereby showed that it was not a People's Government.

CZERNIN: The People voted for it.

TROTSKY: That means nothing.

CZERNIN: Oh... (*To KUHLMANN.*) Do you understand?

KUHLMANN: I think so, yes. If the Ukrainians had a proper People's Government in Mr Trotsky's view, they would have the right to self-determination, provided that they did not exercise it, and the right to vote, for Mr Trotsky. It's really very similar to any other Government.

TROTSKY: Very. All Government is similar, and similarly vile. Our aim is to dispense with it. Meanwhile, you use troops to shoot down men, we use troops to shoot down masters; the only difference being that a different man gets shot; which hardly matters.

CZERNIN: Well. Candid anyway.

TROTSKY: Yes that's another difference. When we take power we take responsibility; we know that we must do vile things. You do vile things and use the democratic vote to spread responsibility so thin that no-one feels responsible. And that is why while you are drifting from disaster to disaster, we shall drive on to success.

KUHLMANN: Time is on your side in fact?

TROTSKY: Oh yes indeed.

KUHLMANN: Then clearly we must cut time short. One week, Mr Trotsky. Then we march.

(*All get up and go.*

The lights change to the grey of Moscow. More chairs are set at the table. The banners of Austria and Germany are flown, and replaced by the Red Flag.

LENIN, STALIN, LUNACHARSKY, KOLLONTAI and DZERZHINSKY enter and sit. All have papers.)

LENIN: Well?

TROTSKY: We take their terms or fight.

DZERZHINSKY: We fight then.

LENIN: With what?

DZERZHINSKY: Bare handed if we must.

227

(*LENIN is impatient.*)

I'm serious Vladya. It would be better for the Revolution to go down with honour than survive on terms like these.

LENIN: The honour of the Revolution consists in surviving. On any terms it can.

DZERZHINSKY: We must defend it then.

KOLLONTAI: We must fraternise too.

DZERZHINSKY: And fraternise of course.

LENIN: I see. Shoot with one hand and wave with the other.

LUNACHARSKY: But Vladya, I find this most extraordinary. The rank and file of the German Army are the German proletariat. And when they understand that we are fighting for the proletarian revolution...

LENIN: Anatole Vassilyevich; if you're in a trench and someone's shooting at you from another trench, it must be difficult to understand that his intentions are progressive. And I doubt if we could get an army to go back into the trenches anyway. (*To TROTSKY.*) Could we?

TROTSKY: I doubt it. Why do you ask me?

LENIN: If you can't do it, I don't see which of us can.

(*STALIN glowers and shifts in his seat.*)

TROTSKY: I couldn't do it in a week.

STALIN: (*Growling.*) Well, of course you couldn't.

LENIN: Then in view of the fact that we have no army I suggest that we don't fight. And in view of the fact that these are the terms I suggest that we accept them.

DZERZHINSKY: Never.

KOLLONTAI: No.

LUNACHARSKY: We *can't* accept these terms, we *can't*!

TROTSKY: If we accept these terms I think the country may reject the terms and us, together.

LENIN: The country will do no such thing; you are thinking – all of you are thinking – of your own good names! I am going to put it to the vote again; and if you vote like that again I will offer you my resignation.

DZERZHINSKY: I will accept your resignation before I will accept these terms.

LENIN: In favour?

LUNACHARSKY: Wait – Vladya, I think they will take the Ukraine.

LENIN: Well of course they will take the Ukraine...!

LUNACHARSKY: Have you thought what that will mean?

LENIN: Yes, I have thought what that will mean... In favour?

STALIN: Yes.

KOLLONTAI: Yes.

DZERZHINSKY: No.

LUNACHARSKY: Yes – Good God.

LENIN: Comrade Trotsky?

TROTSKY: Abstain.

LENIN: Carried. (*He signs the document.*)

LUNACHARSKY: Good God...

LENIN: How long *would* it take to raise an army?

TROTSKY: We could raise a voluntary army in a month.

LENIN: Would it be any good?

TROTSKY: It would be very good but very small.

LENIN: How small?

TROTSKY: Too small.

LENIN: Conscription?

TROTSKY: Yes.

KOLLONTAI: What?

TROTSKY: And death for desertion.

LUNACHARSKY: *What?* –

LENIN: Be quiet, Anatole; you know nothing about it. (*To TROTSKY.*) Suppose that you could raise an army – could you lead it in the field?

TROTSKY: ...Yes.

LENIN: Sure?

TROTSKY: Yes.

STALIN: We seem to have found our Bonaparte.
(*A stillness.*)

TROTSKY: (*Quietly.*) ...That remark is very nearly, though not quite, as stupid as it is insulting.

LENIN: Er, Comrade Stalin means no insult, Leon...

TROTSKY: Then Comrade Stalin exhibits an alarming ignorance not only of the counter-revolutionary role which history bestowed on Bonaparte, but also of the

Marxist view of history. Perhaps we ought to club together for the purchase of some not too difficult Marxist primer for the use of Comrade Stalin?

LENIN: Leon, enough.

TROTSKY: Very well, enough.

LENIN: Thank you. Now I propose...

TROTSKY: The 'Man of the Moment' is not a 'great man', he is merely the man that the moment needs. And it is not my fault if the revolutionary moment of October did not appear to be in any very urgent need of Comrade Stalin.

LENIN: Enough! You both did your revolutionary duty in October; as you both invariably do. Now let us have no more of this. Please.

STALIN: Storm in a teacup.

LENIN: Good. Now I propose that Comrade Trotsky should give up his present duties and take on the Commissariat for War.

TROTSKY: No. In view of the comparison which has just been made it is an honour which I can't accept.

LENIN: You will accept; try not to think of the honour. Oh. (*Passing the treaty document.*) Your final diplomatic duty. Put your name on that.
(*TROTSKY looks down at the document thoughtfully and does not move.*
LENIN watches him.)
Your name does seem to mean a lot to you.
(*STALIN gives a short laugh and signs the document. LENIN takes it.*)

LENIN: Thank you, Comrade.

STALIN: Oh, I haven't got a name.

LENIN: Felix Edmundovich...

DZERZHINSKY: I still regard this document as absolutely fatal. If you want me to resign I will.

LENIN: In what way is it fatal?

DZERZHINSKY: It is fatal to our honour. And our honour is essential.

LENIN: I don't want you to resign. I want you to accept the most important task of all.

DZERZHINSKY: Oh?

LENIN: The Cheka.

(*The others go still. STALIN softly takes his feet down.*
LUNACHARSKY is incredulous.)

LUNACHARSKY: *Felix?*

LENIN: Yes.

DZERZHINSKY: (*Calmly, almost amused.*) I couldn't do it.

LENIN: Why?

DZERZHINSKY: Vladya, I have spent three-quarters of
my adult life in prisons... You understand? I'm not
talking about exile – I'm talking about prisons, I'm
talking about prison cells, I'm talking about torture. The
very presence of a policeman makes me physically sick!
Now I know it must be done and I thank you for your
confidence. But you might as well ask me to clean the
streets by eating garbage.

LENIN: Do you think it should be done by someone with
an appetite for garbage?

DZERZHINSKY: You are perfectly merciless – you should
do it.

LENIN: I haven't the time.

DZERZHINSKY: (*To LUNACHARSKY.*) What shall I do?

LUNACHARSKY: Vladya is right, Felix.

DZERZHINSKY: Would you do it?

LUNACHARSKY: No.

STALIN: We're talking like a lot of liberals. It doesn't
matter who does what. What matters is what's done.

LENIN: Correct. May I put it to the vote?

DZERZHINSKY: Very well.

LENIN: In favour...?

(*They show.*)

Carried.

(*DZERZHINSKY gets up and goes.*
They look after him. Then LENIN speaks on a note of finality,
cheerfully routine.)

Thank you, Comrades.

(*All but LENIN and STALIN gather up their papers and*
go. LUNACHARSKY lingering, says something, sadly, shaking
his head.)

LUNACHARSKY: Poor Felix…

LENIN: What?

LUNACHARSKY: Poor Felix.

LENIN: Oh go away.

LUNACHARSKY: (*Going, turns.*) I…

LENIN: Go away!

    (*LUNACHARSKY goes.*)

    Idiot…

STALIN: You're fond of him all the same.

LENIN: Yes I am. And you had better be fond of him,
    Yosef. He's the future.

STALIN: Bit soft for me.

LENIN: Well, I wouldn't want you in charge of children.

STALIN: You don't seem to want me in charge of anything,
    much.

LENIN: Are you very keen to be in charge of something?

STALIN: I'd like to be useful.

LENIN: You are, without exception, the most useful
    Comrade on the whole Committee.

End of Act One.

ACT TWO

LUNACHARSKY is revealed in a spot as for the start of Act One.

LUNACHARSKY: The common canteen in the Party
Headquarters was operated round the clock. It was
continuously crowded and the din was always deafening.
One day when I was eating there a perfect silence fell.
And looking up I saw an elderly woman, oddly dressed,
very tall and very thin, and with her: five emaciated
wolfhounds. 'Give me some food you swine,' she said.
Nobody moved. She stamped her foot. 'Food!' Well
somebody gave her a dish of potatoes. She looked at it
and then in a high, imperious voice like the shriek of an
eagle: 'Not enough!' Everybody laughed at that. But
suddenly she stooped, and when she rose we understood
that she had set her food before the dogs. At that there
was a roar of anger – there were plenty of children who
needed food – and she and her dogs were bundled out
without much ceremony. Her name was Countess
Kretilinsky and later that same day she drowned herself.
I half expected Comrade Lenin to dismiss the tale as
unimportant. But I remember that it made him silent.
And after a little, 'Hmp' he said. 'Those people are
having a very bad time.' And after a little again 'Hmp'
he said. 'History is hard.' History was mercilessly hard
on Russia in those post-war years. With the end of war
came civil war, and with the civil war came famine. By
the spring of 1920, Russia was living hand to mouth. (*He
goes.*)
(*The lights come up on an interior – a round table and
chairs.*
*ZHELNIK enters unsteadily. KOLLONTAI comes after him,
agitated.*)
KOLLONTAI: Fedor, come away.
ZHELNIK: Shurrup. (*He roars.*) Where is he?
(*KRUPSKAYA enters with a cloth-covered tray.*)
KRUPSKAYA: Comrade Zhelnik…?

KOLLONTAI: Oh Nadezhda…

KRUPSKAYA: What's the matter? Comrade? Are you drunk?

ZHELNIK: Drunk enough.

KRUPSKAYA: Alexandra Mihailovna. How dare you bring him here? This evening Vladya has a public meeting, two Committees and…

ZHELNIK: Never stops, does he?

KRUPSKAYA: No he doesn't…!

(*LENIN enters, briskly, unbuttoning his overcoat, but checks.*)

KOLLONTAI: I'm sorry Vladya, Fedor's drunk.

ZHELNIK: 'S righ'.

LENIN: Comrade, you're a fool…

ZHELNIK: Never said I wasn't.

LENIN: You used to he a revolutionary.

ZHELNIK: Right. Kronstadt Sailor. Don't you forget it.

KOLLONTAI: He doesn't know what he's saying, Vladya.

ZHELNIK: Shrrup! Bourgeois bitch…

(*He looks round at her and she goes to him and puts her hand on his shoulder.*)

LENIN: You've been working too hard, Fedor. You'd better take a rest.

ZHELNIK: Work?

LENIN: Vital work.

ZHELNIK: You don't know anything, do you? Look… Oh what's the good…

LENIN: Go on.

ZHELNIK: We come to this village. We say 'Comrades, we hear that you have grain'. They say 'No, we haven't'. Usual. So we find the grain; there's half a barn full. We say 'Comrades, we must take this grain for the starving workers'. They say 'Let 'em starve'. Usual. So we start to load the grain. And somebody sets fire to it. Gone in five minutes, barn and all. And so, we shoot them. Men, women, kids… We shoot them.

(*LENIN takes out a notebook and pencil.*)

LENIN: Who was in charge of the detachment?

ZHELNIK: I was.

LENIN: You were?

ZHELNIK: Ah – but we have this Chekist with us. And the Cheka's always in charge, isn't it?

LENIN: The Cheka takes precedence, yes.

ZHELNIK: Oh he took that all right. He says 'Comrades we're going to make an example here.' He says 'It's a nest of counter-revolution. We're going to show them what Red Terror means!'

LENIN: Well?

ZHELNIK: They were peasants!

LENIN: A peasant can be counter-revolutionary. Many of them are.

ZHELNIK: Vladimir Ilyich – I'm a peasant! My brothers are peasants! We're all – *peasants*!

LENIN: Look. They burned the grain.

ZHELNIK: They burned it, yes –

LENIN: – and the Revolution needs it?

ZHELNIK: Yes but…

LENIN: Then what they did was counter-revolutionary.

ZHELNIK: They weren't thinking about *that*!

LENIN: No. No I don't suppose they were. But if you *act* against the Revolution, then – no matter what you *think* – you are in fact a counter-revolutionary.

ZHELNIK: Children?

(*LENIN's face goes drab for a beat.*)

LENIN: We shot the children of the Tsar; did you object to that?

ZHELNIK: That was different.

LENIN: Why was it different?

ZHELNIK: Well perhaps it wasn't so bloody different!

LENIN: Are you a Tsarist?

ZHELNIK: I'd have shot the Tsar myself!

LENIN: The moment that the Tsar was dead, the little Tsaravich became the Tsar. It's not a matter of guilt; it's a matter of necessity.

(*ZHELNIK growls, the women look unhappy.*)

What was the name of this Chekist?

ZHELNIK: Shatki; he's a Lithuanian Jew.

LENIN: What's that got to do with it?
ZHELNIK: Nothing.
LENIN: Do you want to be put on different work?
ZHELNIK: I want to go back to Kronstadt.
LENIN: Very well. (*He puts away the notebook.*)
 (*ZHELNIK gets up unsteadily, LENIN watching him.*)
 I'm disappointed in you, Comrade.
ZHELNIK: Well – I'm sorry.
 (*ZHELNIK goes. KOLLONTAI follows.*
 LENIN broods. KRUPSKAYA takes the cloth from the tray;
 a glass of milk, sandwiches.)
KRUPSKAYA: Vladya...
LENIN: Not hungry.
KRUPSKAYA: Eat, man.
 (*Abstractedly he obeys. She watches him.*)
 He was drunk, Vladya.
LENIN: He wasn't so drunk... (*He swallows, agreeably*
 surprised.) What's this?
KRUPSKAYA: Goose.
LENIN: Goose?
KRUPSKAYA: Some peasants came and left it for you. Eat.
LENIN: Get me some cheese.
KRUPSKAYA: Oh for goodness sake – they left a whole
 barrow load. Everyone got one.
LENIN: What?
KRUPSKAYA: People are concerned about you Vladya; me
 among them. Eat.
LENIN: Are you – (*His voice is thick.*) – are you telling me
 that Leading Comrades – here in this building – are
 getting more than the ration?
KRUPSKAYA: Occasionally.
 (*LENIN whips out the notebook again and scribbles.*)
 I gave one to the janitor.
LENIN: Oh you gave one to the janitor. What noble
 condescension. Nadya, did none of them refuse?
KRUPSKAYA: Dzerzhinsky sent his to the common
 canteen.
LENIN: The rest of them should be cleaning gutters. (*He*
 rises, buttoning his coat.)

KRUPSKAYA: Well I shall eat it.

LENIN: I hope it chokes you.

KRUPSKAYA: Oh Vladya, what petty-bourgeois scrupulosity – it's a gift!

LENIN: It's tribute!

(*The lights fade to a black-out. A white spot falls vertically. In it stands Fanya KAPLAN, white-faced, carrying a heavy handbag.*)

KAPLAN: (*Calling.*) Comrade Lenin!

(*LENIN joins her.*)

LENIN: Comrade?

KAPLAN: My name is Fanya Kaplan. I am a member of the Peasant Revolutionary Party.

LENIN: Oh yes?

KAPLAN: We have been excluded from the Soviets.

LENIN: Yes, very properly.

KAPLAN: All parties but yours are excluded from the Soviets.

LENIN: Have you specific business, Comrade?

KAPLAN: I have a petition.

LENIN: Very well.

(*He holds out his hand while she unclasps her handbag but, pausing.*)

KAPLAN: The Tsar used to accept petitions.

LENIN: Yes.

KAPLAN: How does it feel?

LENIN: Depends on the petition.

KAPLAN: This is my petition. (*She pulls a pistol from her bag and fires.*)

(*LENIN cries out and reels away into the dark.*

KAPLAN steps after him and gets off one more shot, before two CHEKISTS rush on and seize her.

The lights come up. DZERZHKINSKY is seated at a small table with papers in front of him. He wears a black leather coat. The CHEKISTS bring KAPLAN before him, and he speaks, without passion.)

DZERZHINSKY: Fanya Kaplan, you are charged with wounding and attempting to assassinate V I Lenin,

Chairman of the Council of People's Commissars. Do you admit this action?

KAPLAN: I do.

DZERZHINSKY: Do you regret this action?

KAPLAN: I bitterly regret that it was not successful.

DZERZHINSKY: The sentence is death.

KAPLAN: Long live the Revolution!

(*The CHEKISTS take KAPLAN out.*
DZERZHINSKY takes his glasses off; presses his fingertips
to his eyes, puts back his glasses and reads from a paper.)

DZERZHINSKY: Comrades of the Cheka. I have just received by wireless telegraph a message from the Volga Front where L D Trotsky, Commissar for War, has taken personal command. The so-called Czeck Brigade and other White Guard forces have arrested Soviet officials and commenced a counter-revolutionary insurrection. English, French and American armies occupy Archangel, Vladivostock and Murmansk. White Guard bands command the Urals, and the Don. Savinkov's Officer Brigade is ninety miles from Moscow. Thus, the attempt upon the life of V I Lenin is revealed as part of a co-ordinated effort to destroy the Revolution. An essential element of Revolution is Revolutionary Terror. And just as the Red Army in its battles cannot pause to see that no-one who is individually innocent is harmed, neither can the Cheka pause to establish individual guilt. Class guilt is sufficient guilt. From the officer caste and from the bourgeoisie take hostages, representative and in large numbers. The slightest sign of opposition must be crushed by merciless mass execution. Hooligans, looters, drunkards and curfew-breakers in particular are likewise to be executed, on the spot. Chekists strike. He who flinches, he who wavers, he who pauses to indulge in legalistic scruples is himself an agent of the enemy and should be so regarded. Long live the Revolution. Long live the Revolutionary Terror! (*He stares at nothing, lifeless.*)

(*LUNACHARSKY enters and approaches. Quietly, as to an invalid.*)

LUNACHARSKY: Vladya asked me to come and see you.

DZERZHINSKY: Oh yes... (*He finds some papers.*)

LUNACHARSKY: (*Sits.*) How terrible everything is, Felix.

DZERZHINSKY: We shall win in the end.

LUNACHARSKY: Yes... Felix, did you think that it would be so terrible? In Capri did you think so?

(*DZERZHINSKY looks at him.*)

DZERZHINSKY: (*Very deliberately.*) I was never in Capri.

LUNACHARSKY: I envy you...

(*DZERZHINSKY looks at him again and finds it necessary to stand up and move away, with the papers.*)

DZERZHINSKY: Comrade Lunacharsky, certain serious shortcomings in your work have been drawn to the attention of the Cheka.

LUNACHARSKY: What?

DZERZHINSKY: For example: in the year commencing January 1920...

LUNACHARSKY: One moment! (*The gentleman is dreadfully angry. He collects himself.*) One moment... My work, of all work has nothing to do with the Cheka.

DZERZHINSKY: Is it not Party work?

LUNACHARSKY: I am a Party Member and therefore all my work is Party work.

DZERZHINSKY: The Cheka's only work is to enforce the Party's will. It was you more than anybody who persuaded me to undertake it. (*He returns to the paper.*) In January 1920 your Commissariat indented for nine million pairs of children's shoes. This figure was unrealistic but...

LUNACHARSKY: It was not unrealistic. It was minimal.

DZERZHINSKY: It was judged to be unrealistic by the Politburo of the Party. Which did however authorise you to obtain five hundred and fifty thousand pairs. But by January 1921 you had secured no more than half that number. Why?

LUNACHARSKY: What?

DZERZHINSKY: You failed in your assignment, Comrade. Why?

LUNACHARSKY: I failed, my dear Edmundovich, because those few remaining factories which are producing shoes are not producing children's shoes – but boots for the Red Army! You have a nice pair of boots yourself I notice.

DZERZHINSKY: I need them. Someone in your Commissariat appears to have his feet up.

LUNACHARSKY: Do you mean myself?

DZERZHINSKY: I don't yet know the culprit.

LUNACHARSKY: 'Culprit?'

DZERZHINSKY: When there is a failure there is either negligence or sabotage.

LUNACHARSKY: What utter and disgusting rubbish. When that idiotic woman came so close to killing Vladya, there was failure in the Cheka.

DZERZHINSKY: And the culprits have been punished.

LUNACHARSKY: Well, there are no culprits in my Commissariat and no-one will be punished.

DZERZHINSKY: You are satisfied by failure?

LUNACHARSKY: I am satisfied by effort.

DZERZHINSKY: By insufficient effort.

LUNACHARSKY: My maximum effort!

DZERZHINSKY: If your people are making a maximum effort your people are incompetent. And you are the culprit.

LUNACHARSKY: They are people most of whom it is a privilege to work with; most of whom are working fourteen hours a day – in conditions which defy description!

DZERZHINSKY: And yet they failed.

LUNACHARSKY: And yet they failed. Precisely.

DZERZHINSKY: The failure should have been reported.

LUNACHARSKY: It was repeatedly reported. And now if we have come to the limits of your sudden interest in education… (*He makes to go.*)

DZERZHINSKY: We have not. (*He seems almost nervous. A beat.*) Last year, at your request, sixteen hundred children were evacuated from the famine districts of the Volga. (*LUNACHARSKY goes still.*)

LUNACHARSKY: (*Quietly.*) Yes?

DZERZHINSKY: How many of those children have you under care?

LUNACHARSKY: It's hard to say. They run away.

DZERZHINSKY: And then?

LUNACHARSKY: You know as well as I what then. They run about like starving dogs.

DZERZHINSKY: And starving dogs are dangerous; there have been incidents – which…

LUNACHARSKY: I don't need to be told about the incidents!

DZERZHINSKY: I have been instructed to gather up these children and return them to the Volga.

LUNACHARSKY: I warn you, Comrade, this I shall protest.

(*DZERZHINSKY smiles a little.*)

DZERZHINSKY: There is no need to warn me Anatole Vassilyevich. In fact, speaking personally…

LUNACHARSKY: D'you remember how to speak, personally?

(*DZERZHINSKY's face goes stiff again.*)

DZERZHINSKY: A timely caution. Thank you. That is all.

(*LUNACHARSKY rises, going.*)

DZERZHINSKY: (*Collecting up his papers, to his receding back.*) You will use the proper channels for your protest, Comrade.

LUNACHARSKY: I will protest this from the housetops!

DZERZHINSKY: Be careful, Comrade.

(*It is a warning, a friendly threat. But LUNACHARSKY goes back to him, stands threateningly close and, warningly:*)

LUNACHARSKY: No, Felix Edmundovich. You be careful!

(*LUNACHARSKY and DZERZHINSKY go in opposite directions.*

The lights change. The stage is cleared and a wooden box is set. SAILORS, SOLDIERS, WORKERS and one CLERK enter, with ZHELNIK, who sits on the box. One carries a banner. ZHELNIK is a bit embarrassed, but very earnest.)

ZHELNIK: The Temporary Revolutionary Council of Sailors, Soldiers and Workers of Kronstadt is in session. Very well Brothers.

A SAILOR: Cheka.

(*Angry and instant agreement.*)

SECOND SAILOR: Peasants.

(*Agreement the same.*)

FIRST WORKER: – Unions.

CLERK: Rations.

SOLDIER: – Elections.

SAILOR: – The Party!

(*Angry agreement.*

TROTSKY enters, opposite.

The chorus dies. TROTSKY wears a uniform and boots. He regards the crowd coldly. The crowd looks to ZHELNIK, who rises – a bit awed, but stubbornly and with menace.)

ZHELNIK: These are the demands of the Kronstadt Council: One: Free canvassing for all genuinely revolutionary Parties.

TROTSKY: No Party is so genuinely revolutionary as the Bolshevik Party. Therefore canvassing for other Parties is counter-revolutionary. Demand rejected.

ZHELNIK: Two: Control of the factories by worker committees.

TROTSKY: The factories now belong to the workers and committee control is unproductive. Demand rejected.

ZHELNIK: Three: An end to methods of grain procurement which terrorise the peasantry. And freedom for the peasant to use his land as he thinks fit.

TROTSKY: The land and its produce belong to the People. Demand rejected.

ZHELNIK: Finally: The immediate release of all persons placed in prison by the Cheka, or the immediate review of all such cases by an elected, independent, non-Party commission.

TROTSKY: As the Party to the People so the Cheka to the Party. Demand rejected.

ZHELNIK: Right.

(*ZHELNIK folds up the paper, looking firmly at TROTSKY, who, dropping his official manner steps towards them with a warm and confident smile.*)

TROTSKY: Now, Comrades, listen…
  (*They explode into an uproar of angry shouts, jeers and whistles. His face goes severe again. Suddenly the uproar dies and he looks round to see the cause of it.*
  KOLLONTAI has entered behind him.
  The CROWD falls back a bit from ZHELNIK, embarrassed by the situation.)
KOLLONTAI: Oh Fedor… Oh my dear… Don't you see…?
ZHELNIK: (*Growling.*) See what?
TROTSKY: (*Gently, sadly.*) Come away, Alexia.
  (*But she motions him back.*)
KOLLONTAI: Comrades, do you think the Party does not understand? Do you think we do not know the Revolution has been stern, and dreadful…? (*Her voice breaks; she wipes her eyes impatiently.*) But, Comrades, did we ever think it would be easy? Peaceful? Fair? Like a duel at dawn between two officers, with an umpire and a doctor standing by – and all sit down together afterwards for breakfast? No no. Revolution is a *real* fight. Naked as nature. And cruel as nature. And will you join the enemy? Fedor? Will you fight with the White Guard? Comrades, you have been duped…!
ZHELNIK: We've been duped all right.
  (*The light begins to fail and distant guns are heard like soft drums. TROTSKY reads a proclamation.*)
TROTSKY: To the Kronstadt rebels from the Worker Peasant Government. Lay down your arms immediately. Release at once the Commissars you have illegally arrested and submit yourselves to Revolutionary Justice. Simultaneous with this I have ordered General Tukachevsky –
  (*A stir among the CROWD.*)
  – to advance against you the Red Army. Only those who submit unconditionally can expect the mercy of the Soviet Republic. This warning is the last.
  (*The guns grow louder, the light darker; the CLERK steps forward.*)
CLERK: Against you and General Tukachevsky we advance the blood-stained banner of the labouring people!

SAILOR: We stand or fall – at Kronstadt!

(The guns roar, blackness falls.)

KOLLONTAI: Fedor!

(There is a flash, and the lights change to green dappled sunlight. The bellowing guns recede. Birdsong is heard. The stage is set with a table and several chairs.

LENIN, TROTSKY, STALIN, KRUPSKAYA and LUNACHARSKY enter from one side, KOLLONTAI from the opposite. She wears black.

LENIN glances at KOLLONTAI under his brows as she sits, white-faced, at the table. All sit. They have folders, TROTSKY a pile of them. LENIN speaks: his personality has darkened; he looks older.)

LENIN: The subject is Kronstadt. This is a report from Comrade General Tukachevsky. It is of course completely confidential. Will someone read it – ?

I would like to save my voice.

KOLLONTAI: I will read it.

(LENIN is momentarily startled.)

LENIN: Very well.

(KOLLONTAI speaks with an effort, but clearly.)

KOLLONTAI: He says: 'In five continuous years of war I cannot remember such a slaughter. Our heavy artillery began on March the seventh and was so heavy that windows were shattered as far away as Orenbaum. The sailors fought like wild beasts. I cannot understand where they found such fury. Each house where they were located had to be taken by storm. An entire company fought for an hour to occupy one house and suffered heavy losses. It had been held against them by three sailors armed with hand-grenades and one machine-gun. It was not until the evening of the seventeenth that all resistance was overcome. Long live the Revolution.'

(They stir.)

LENIN: The subject is Kronstadt. Propose, Comrade...

(GORKY enters. A confrontation.)

Who let you in?

KRUPSKAYA: I did, Vladya.

LENIN: What d'you want?

GORKY: I want to go back to Capri.

LENIN: Sit down.

GORKY: Vladya, I don't...

LENIN: Sit down...! And listen.

> (*GORKY sits apart.*)
>
> Propose Comrade Trotsky to lead the discussion.
>
> (*TROTSKY leans forward, eager to begin.*)

KOLLONTAI: Propose Comrade Lenin to lead the discussion.

STALIN: Agree.

TROTSKY: Very well.

LENIN: Get on. What does it matter who leads...? (*He squints painfully and pinches the bridge of his nose.*) Get on. (*GORKY looks at him.*)

TROTSKY: The Kronstadt rising forces us to face a seemingly impossible event. The Revolutionary vanguard turns upon the Revolution. Why?

KOLLONTAI: Because the Revolution turned on them.

STALIN: In my analysis the Kronstadt mutiny resulted from the discontent; aroused in petty-bourgeois elements; by White Guard agitation. (*The platitudes come from him woodenly.*)

TROTSKY: (*Condescendingly.*) Successful agitation presupposes discontent. No, I think we have to penetrate a little deeper than the agitated surface.

DZERZHINSKY: There was agitation.

TROTSKY: No doubt there was...

STALIN: Well then?

TROTSKY: Look. May I get on?

STALIN: Oh. Sorry.

> (*TROTSKY sits back.*)

TROTSKY: Comrade Stalin will lead the discussion.

> (*LENIN hits the table with the flat of his hand.*)

KRUPSKAYA: Lead, Vladya.

LUNACHARSKY: Yes.

LENIN: Right. They did not turn upon the Revolution. They turned upon the Party. And they turned upon the

State. Because the Party and the State are rotten with bureaucracy and we are rotten with conceit. We are moreover criminally ignorant. We know the Proletariat, perhaps. Inside the Commissariats we know every corridor and cupboard. Of the peasant we know nothing. And all he knows of us is this: that we expropriate. What more could he know? The average peasant cannot read. And we pay him with a pamphlet when we drive away his pig. We tell him we must have his harvest for the workers of the world. To him, the world outside his parish is a dubious abstraction. Our motives are incomprehensible, our actions – only too familiar. Kronstadt rose against us as it rose against the landlords, and we like any landlord have the impudence to be surprised.

(*GORKY looks at LENIN with amazement.*)

I thought you might be interested. Therefore, we propose the immediate dissolution of the grain procurement squads.

KOLLONTAI: Hallelulia...

LUNACHARSKY: Well...

LENIN: Mp?

LUNACHARSKY: Well – Hallelulia yes – I hate the grain procurement squads, but – how *shall* we procure it...?

LENIN: (*To TROTSKY.*) Go on.

TROTSKY: Each peasant will continue to deliver to the State a small percentage of his annual harvest. The rest he will be free to sell.

LUNACHARSKY: Free?

TROTSKY: Yes.

LUNACHARSKY: But, do you mean that he will sell to anybody who can buy?

TROTSKY: Yes.

LUNACHARSKY: Sell at a profit? And – the weak to the wall?

TROTSKY: A market economy, yes.

DZERZHINSKY: But – forgive me Leon Davidovich – but it seems to me that what you are proposing is capitalist enterprise.

TROTSKY: Yes.

STALIN: Then what you are proposing is counter-revolution.

(*TROTSKY's head whips round. He controls himself and then, patiently.*)

TROTSKY: What we are proposing is a limited admission of capitalist enterprise contained within the context of the Socialist State.

STALIN: A capitalist economy necessitates a bourgeois State.

TROTSKY: You've been studying your Marxist primer. Advance now if you will to the study of the dialectic.

LENIN: Stop it! The dialectic is a two-edged weapon, Leon. It is possible to cut yourself.

TROTSKY: What's that supposed to mean?

STALIN: Comrade Stalin's point is very well taken. Of course there will be every kind of vile attack upon the Party and the State from the racketeers and speculators who will now come out of hiding. But it does not follow that the Party and the State must weaken. It follows that the Party must tighten its grip on the State. And the Party must be purged.

LUNACHARSKY: Purged?

LENIN: Mp? Yes. Now Leon.

LUNACHARSKY: Just a minute. In what sense 'purged'?

TROTSKY: It is a medical expression, Anatole Vassilyevich, signifying the excretion by an organism of whatever is corrupt.

DZERZHINSKY: Corrupt!

TROTSKY: I don't of course mean personal corruption, corruption in the bourgeois sense of taking bribes and things like that. I mean institutional corruption.

LUNACHARSKY: Institutions are composed of persons; I don't like the distinction.

TROTSKY: Then let me make it clear. Your Commissariat is institutionally corrupt precisely because you are personally, and if I may say so, excessively innocent.

LUNACHARSKY: Then you'd better get rid of me.

TROTSKY: Quite possibly. Now the Party is an institution too...

STALIN: The Party is an 'institution'?

TROTSKY: Comrade Stalin, Marx – as I am sure you know – believed in a material reality. And the Party exists in reality. It is not an idea in somebody's head, but a material institution. That is, of course, if Marx was right. (*He turns to the others.*) It is not of course an institution just like any other. In the year before the Revolution when there was nothing much to gain by membership and everything to lose, we had at most ten thousand members. We have a hundred thousand paid officials now, and three quarters of a million members. Half of whom are not much more than middle-class careerists. There are actually paid officials who were members of the old bureaucracy. The Party has been interpenetrated by reactionary elements. I am not saying, Anatole, that all these people know themselves to be reactionary. Some of them in all sincerity believe themselves to be converted. But they are helplessly imbued with a bureaucratic and reactionary turn of mind, and the Party must expel them – yes – even though they may not know themselves for what, objectively, they are.

LENIN: Correct.

LUNACHARSKY: But if they do not know themselves, how the devil can we know them?

GORKY: Good.

LENIN: You were told that you could listen, not that you could speak. The local secretaries know them.

LUNACHARSKY: But if we're looking for careerists it's just the local secretaries that we're likely to be looking for.

TROTSKY: We will begin with the local secretaries.

LUNACHARSKY: 'We will'? Who will?

TROTSKY: The Central Secretariat.

LUNACHARSKY: And who will purge the central secretariat? The Cheka?

TROTSKY: Yes.

LUNACHARSKY: And who purge the Cheka? Leon, it's an endless regress!

LENIN: (*Suddenly, loudly, angrily.*) Why endless?

GORKY: Why? Good heavens, can't you see? It's as ancient as the hills! Who will guard the guardians? It's Plato's problem! Do you think you're going to solve it with a Party Directive?

LENIN: Yes. Plato was a slave-owning idealist. His Republic needed perfect men. Our Republic needs Party men.

GORKY: You said the Party was corrupt.

LENIN: Honest Party men.

GORKY: Diogenes looked for an honest man – with a lighted lamp at noon.

LENIN: And he probably passed a dozen men more honest than himself. He wasn't looking, he was making a point. A man who insists on impossible standards isn't an ethical paragon – he's an ethical clown – like you…

GORKY: B –

LENIN: Be quiet! (*He squints, gapes, looks bewildered.*)

KRUPSKAYA: (*Softly.*) Vladya?

LENIN: All right… Now – to identify a Party man we do not need a lamp at noon. We need the following material facts: When did he become a member, what has he been doing since, from what class background did he come? We need these facts in a written record, accurate and up-to-date. It's going to be a colossal job. Mechanical and never-ending, unrewarding and unsung.

STALIN: Which being so, we'll offer it to Comrade Stalin, unless I miss my guess.

LENIN: We know that he's a Party man already; from his record.

STALIN: I think you mean a Party functionary.

KOLLONTAI: We're all party functionaries, Yosef.

STALIN: Oh no, oh no. Some of us are Party Leaders.

LENIN: Do you accept or not?

STALIN: You say you know my record. When did I refuse? I've been a bandit for the Party. I've been a soldier for

the Party. I've washed dishes for the Party. If the Party
wants a clerk, all right I'll be a Party clerk.

LENIN: Thank you.

STALIN: But it is absolutely obvious – that you and
Comrade Trotsky met before this meeting and decided
what it should decide. Thus violating the collective
leadership. Thus demonstrating your contempt for the
collective leadership. This cult of individual leaders, this
reliance upon individual ability, is basically incorrect. I
condemn this practice. I censure this practice. I demand
that it cease.

LENIN: I accept your censure. I second your demand.

STALIN: In the period confronting us – it seems to me –
that Party unity must be maintained, at any cost
whatever.

LENIN: Now that's the most important thing that has been
said by anyone today. I'd like to end this session there.

LUNACHARSKY: Well, I...

KRUPSKAYA: Vladya's tired.

LUNACHARSKY: Are you?

LENIN: A little.

LUNACHARSKY: Very well.

(*They rise, gathering up their things.*)

DZERZHINSKY: Can we meet tomorrow?

LENIN: What? This evening if you like.

KRUPSKAYA: Tomorrow.

(*They are going. However, KOLLONTAI crosses to GORKY.
She kisses him on the forehead.*)

KOLLONTAI: Don't leave us Alexey.

(*KOLLONTAI and LUNACHARSKY go with
DZERZHINSKY.*)

LENIN: Yosef. It really is a most important job.

STALIN: I'm not blind, Vladya. It's a job for a mediocrity.

(*STALIN goes.*)

TROTSKY: Then we've got the right man for it.

GORKY: Have you?

TROTSKY: Oh come, be fair. Comrade Stalin's mediocrity
is really quite exceptional.

LENIN: Bonaparte was witty too.

TROTSKY: What?

LENIN: I say...

TROTSKY: I heard what you said, Vladya. What did you mean?

LENIN: Have you a minute?

TROTSKY: I have indeed. (*He sits, quietly.*)

LENIN: You are by head and shoulders the most able person in the Party.

TROTSKY: I'm terribly sorry; what ought I to do about it?

LENIN: You could be less aware of it. It doesn't put you above the Party.

TROTSKY: I'm getting a bit sick of this.

LENIN: You've heard it before then?

TROTSKY: Well of course I have... Do you believe it?

LENIN: What?

TROTSKY: That I put myself above the Party; that I am the potential Bonaparte.

LENIN: I don't know a more likely candidate.

TROTSKY: Have you thought of yourself?

LENIN: I've been too busy.

TROTSKY: You have done no more than me.

LENIN: I haven't done as much as you. But it's taken all of me to do it. There's a bit of you to spare. Hand it over. Eh?
(*TROTSKY takes off his spectacles and smiles at him from tired eyes.*)

TROTSKY: You have a very seductive way of saying unforgivable things.

LENIN: Unforgivable?

TROTSKY: It would be unforgivable... (*He looks away, then back. Quietly.*) Vladya, if you believe that I may use the Army to commandeer the Party and arrest the Revolution, you ought to have me shot.

LENIN: Well I'm sure that's very handsome. But if I found myself believing that any individual could change the course of History, I wouldn't have him shot. I'd go and study my Marxist primer.
(*TROTSKY does not smile.*)

TROTSKY: I'll do that. (*He rises, pauses.*) Thank you. (*Goes.*)

LENIN: (*Calling after TROTSKY.*) Now don't go and shoot yourself, there's a good chap...

GORKY: Why did you do that?

LENIN: What?

GORKY: You've castrated him.

(*LENIN gives it a moment's thought.*)

LENIN: Rubbish. (*But he looks after TROTSKY.*) Needed trimming anyway. Too well equipped by half. Well; it's been a long time.

GORKY: Yes.

LENIN: Are you well?

GORKY: All right. Are you?

LENIN: No I'm not. I've still got one of that bloody woman's bullets in me. (*He works his shoulder irritably.*) Did you know her?

GORKY: No.

LENIN: Well. A brawl. People do what they must.

GORKY: Do they?

(*LENIN looks at him, alert.*)

LENIN: Yes.

GORKY: Vladya, if she'd been a better shot, who would be sitting where you're sitting now?

LENIN: This foolish friend of mine believes, in spite of all he's seen, that history goes the way it does because some hero's what he is. You haven't budged an inch, have you?

GORKY: You're a modest megalomaniac. (*He rises.*) And I want to go back to Capri.

LENIN: You want to go a good deal further back than that, Alexey, don't you?

(*GORKY pulls three sealed envelopes out of his pocket.*)

GORKY: This is a list of innocent and useful people imprisoned without trial. They include the Menshevik Tseretelli. This is a list of people who may or may not have been innocent. They were executed by the Cheka. And this is a list of personal friends who have simply disappeared. (*He is too moved to speak for a moment, shifts aimlessly, and then, rounding on LENIN.*) You promised us new life, release, refinements, unimaginable forms. And all you have released is atavistic envy. There is no novelty whatever in your revolution, Vladya; no love, nor life, nor hope, nor even curiosity. It is merely ferocious.

LENIN: 'Merely' ferocious?

GORKY: You're proud of that?

LENIN: Yes.

GORKY: Complacently ferocious. This country always was barbaric but by God before the Revolution, at least it was ashamed!

LENIN: You were ashamed – your sort was ashamed. Look at him! The celebrated good, well-paid bad conscience – (*He sweeps the papers to the floor.*) – of the shits – that made us shameful! *That's* why you've turned against the Revolution, Alexey Maximovich – it's done you out of a job!
(*GORKY is going, furious. And this time he will go.*)
Alexey.
(*GORKY stops, hesitates, turns square. LENIN retrieves one of the papers.*)

LENIN: Would you stay if we let you publish?

GORKY: You wouldn't. Not what I want to print.
(*LENIN retrieves a second paper.*)

LENIN: How far would you want to go?

GORKY: Oh well beyond your tolerance; I'd want to print the truth.

LENIN: Mp... No I couldn't let you publish that. (*He stoops and retrieves the last of the papers.*) You're right. There's a lot of envy – and precious little love... But you seem to think that it's somebody's fault!

GORKY: I think it's your fault, Vladya.

LENIN: Yes I know you do. (*He sits with the papers.*) And I'm damned if I see how a sensible man can think anything so silly! (*He takes one of the lists in his hands, preparing to unfold it, and delivers his credo.*) It is the passion of the masses which dictates the nature of the day. Sometimes the masses have no passion, and then the days are dead. But when it takes the form of envy, then envy is the form of life. We have no right to embrace our enemies, today, Alexey.

GORKY: I am not asking you to embrace enemies...

LENIN: Aren't you?

GORKY: No. I'm asking for a bit of necessary tolerance – for people like Tseretelli. He's not a White Guard Officer. He's a Left of Centre Socialist.

LENIN: But if I am allowed to tolerate him he has a right to be tolerant too. And he's admirably tolerant – like every Left of Centre Socialist. He'd embrace a White Guard Officer and think himself benevolent... Oh yes he would! – Catch him after a good dinner, with a tolerant White Guard Officer. And who wouldn't *he* embrace? (*He sighs, but continues firmly, as a challenge.*) One step leads to another. And any step now is forward or back.

GORKY: And this is the way forward?

LENIN: Yes.

GORKY: I want to go back.

LENIN: Go then.

GORKY: May I take Ekaterina?

LENIN: What? Yes.

GORKY: Who shall I see?

LENIN: See anyone!

(*GORKY goes.*
LENIN looks after him, rubs his forehead, squinting painfully, pulls a type-written list from its envelope.
LUNACHARSKY enters.
LENIN squints at the paper, holds it away from him, looks up at the light, puzzled.)
Can you read this?

LUNACHARSKY: Yes.

LENIN: I can't. (*He looks round, puzzled.*) I can't see anything clearly... (*He rises unsteadily.*) Wah...!

LUNACHARSKY: (*Quietly.*) What?

LENIN: I've got the most amazing headache – I hope I'm not going to be ill. (*He goes.*)

LUNACHARSKY: Comrade Lenin's amazing headache was the onset of the cerebral atrophy which first incapacitated him and two years later, took him from us. (*He clears his throat.*) The political loss was of course incalculable. But the personal loss was more immediate. (*KRUPSKAYA enters, forcedly calm.*)

KRUPSKAYA: 'Tolly will you come? Vladya appears to be quite unwell.

LUNACHARSKY: Wha…?

KRUPSKAYA: 'Tolly – he can't speak.

(LUNACHARSKY and KRUPSKAYA go.
The lights change to hot sunlight. The stage is cleared, a table and three chairs set.
CHEKISTS enter with MDVANI and thrust him into a chair.
MDVANI attempts to get up but is thrust down again.
STALIN enters; he is carrying a folder and smoking the famous pipe. He takes this from his mouth and stops short, surprised.)

STALIN: What's this?

(The CHEKISTS are bewildered. Stalin gives an indulgent laugh and then, amicably.)

Get out, you fools.

(The CHEKISTS go.)

(As though apologising for a ludicrous faux pas.) Sorry, Victor.

MDVANI: Drop it, Yosef. I remember you.

STALIN: Victor, I am not here to settle old accounts.

MDVANI: You're here to clean up the Georgian Party. It's a joke.

STALIN: Why do you say that?

MDVANI: I wouldn't use you to pull through a sewer.

STALIN: Very well. What is this? (*He shows him some small sheets of closely written paper.*)

MDVANI: That's a personal letter from me to my wife.

STALIN: Yes. Do you remember what's in it?

MDVANI: Comradely criticism is perfectly legitimate.

STALIN: Comradely… V I Lenin is – (*He reads.*) 'a paralytic theologian who ought to be retired', Comrade Zinoviev 'a Jewish cretin, Lenin's bootlicker', Comrade Lunacharsky is 'a neurasthenic nanny', I am described as 'a back-street lout' and Comrade Kollontai is 'a randy old librarian with her brains between her legs'.

MDVANI: Look. It's a private letter. Matter of fact I was pissed when I wrote it.

STALIN: Humorous exaggeration.

MDVANI: Yes!

STALIN: Mm. Well none of this much matters because this is pettily personal. But do you remember what you said about the whole collective leadership?

MDVANI: No.

STALIN: No?

MDVANI: Not exactly.

STALIN: 'A gang of greater Russian military chauvinists, no better than the Tsar'. (*He underlines the last five words so that they hang heavily in the silence.*)

MDVANI: Did you get that letter from Natasha?

STALIN: No. Pratkov got it. From Natasha.

MDVANI: Pratkov! You have used the Georgian Cheka to spy on the Georgian Central Committee? You bloody clumsy fool. D'you think you'll get away with that?

STALIN: I don't see that it's anything to get away with, Victor.

MDVANI: We'll see what the Party Conference thinks.

STALIN: You won't be at the Party Conference.

MDVANI: Delegations aren't appointed from the Centre, Yosef, they're elected by the Party here.

STALIN: But I am here, to purge your Party.

(*MDVANI stares appalled, beginning to understand, beginning perhaps to guess the future.*

DZERZHINSKY enters, also with a file; he is poker-faced and quietly certain of his purpose. He sits by STALIN.)

MDVANI: Felix Edmundovich – I wish to make a formal protest…

DZERZHINSKY: Please sit down. (*To STALIN.*) How far have you got?

(*STALIN passes him the letter.*)

MDVANI: That document was stolen.

DZERZHINSKY: It is a criminal document, Comrade Mdvani. (*He places it neatly in the file, pedantic and calm as a clerk.*) I have some questions for you, Comrade.

MDVANI: Where is my wife?

(*DZERZHINSKY hesitates.*)

DZERZHINSKY: Your wife is at home.

(*MDVANI rubs his hand over his face. DZERZHINSKY is irritated by his own weak-mindedness.*)

Now I have some questions for you.

(*MDVANI sits back and signifies his readiness.*)

DZERZHINSKY: In the matter of the integration of the Transcaucasian Republics...

MDVANI: Yes?

DZERZHINSKY: What have you done?

MDVANI: We have discussed it with the Party of Armenia. Several times.

DZERZHINSKY: And what emerged from these discussions?

MDVANI: That neither Party wanted it.

DZERZHINSKY: You know of course that it is Politburo Policy that you should integrate?

(*This is the sticking-point. MDVANI looks at him and takes a breath.*)

MDVANI: We appeal from the Politburo to the Soviet Constitution.

(*STALIN looks up.*)

DZERZHINSKY: (*Cautiously.*) To which part of the Constitution?

MDVANI: The part which guarantees the national integrity of the National Republics.

DZERZHINSKY: It does not guarantee reaction in the guise of national integrity.

MDVANI: Reaction!

DZERZHINSKY: Three years ago you had in Georgia three collective farms. How many have you now?

MDVANI: (*On a note of patient reiteration.*) Felix Edmundovich, our peasants do not like collective farms. And our peasants here are not potato-eating Russians, they are Georgian mountaineers.

DZERZHINSKY: Do you wish me to record the phrase 'potato-eating Russians'?

MDVANI: No. Thanks.

ROBERT BOLT

DZERZHINSKY: What do your peasants like?

MDVANI: Five acres and a fence.

DZERZHINSKY: And you are satisfied to let them have
five acres and a fence.

MDVANI: 'Let' them... Listen, Felix, my father was a
peasant...

DZERZHINSKY: Was he a wealthy peasant?

MDVANI: Your father was a Polish noble, don't talk to me
about wealth. He had one little field; it wasn't much of a
field; it was a stony-hearted bitch of afield. But by God it
had a good fence. He was half-insane about the field; he
used to talk to it. He would have fucked it if he could...
(*He is lost – but now looks at DZERZHINSKY.*) And he
would certainly have killed you if you'd laid a finger on
the fence.

DZERZHINSKY: So collectivisation here is impossible.

MDVANI: Unless you want an all-out war between the
Party and the peasants, yes.
(*DZERZHINSKY thinks a second, then speaks gently and
seriously, like a doctor who begins to suspect his patient has
cancer.*)

DZERZHINSKY: In the event of such a war, on which side
would we find you fighting, Victor?
(*MDVANI looks at him, startled.*)

MDVANI: I hope that's a hypothetical question.

DZERZHINSKY: It's your hypothesis.

MDVANI: I would be on the side of the masses.

DZERZHINSKY: The Party would be on the side of the
masses.

MDVANI: In a war against the masses?

DZERZHINSKY: In any war.

MDVANI: Felix, is this contemplated?

DZERZHINSKY: Who knows what History contemplates?
(*He looks sad and dreamy, like a martyr envisaging his
inevitable end. Then continues briskly.*) It is not
contemplated policy. Current policy is to collectivise the
peasants by persuasion and example.

MDVANI: Felix, I've been doing that!

DZERZHINSKY: No. I think perhaps you think you have. But I do not think you can. You do not speak of peasant farming as the beastly backward thing it is; you speak of it with sympathy and fellow-feeling; I think you speak of it with pride. You are drifting towards a separated Georgia based on petty private ownership and national intransigence. And that would be a rotten apple in the basket of the Soviet State.

(*This is political, perhaps actual death. He looks down unhappily.*)

You joined the Party in the spring of 1917.

MDVANI: Yes.

(*DZERZHINSKY makes a tick.*)

DZERZHINSKY: Until that date you were a member of the Mensheviks.

MDVANI: Correct.

(*DZERZHINSKY makes another tick.*)

DZERZHINSKY: Thank you.

STALIN: I have a question, Felix. May I have that letter? (*He glances at it, drawing at his pipe.*) This isn't a question I want to ask. But we were told to work without fear or favour. And what we have uncovered here, objectively considered, is conspiratorial, petty-bourgeois, counter-revolutionary chauvinism. Now, the only member of the leadership who does not come in for your 'comradely criticism' appears to be Comrade Trotsky. Is he aware of your conspiracy?

(*DZERZHINSKY is startled. MDVANI chuckles grimly.*)

MDVANI: That question is 'conspiratorial' – (*Bitterly sarcastic.*) – Comrade.

DZERZHINSKY: (*Uneasily.*) I'm bound to say, Yosef…

STALIN: Without fear or favour.

DZERZHINSKY: Answer the question.

MDVANI: All right. No, Comrade Trotsky is not aware of our petty-bourgeois, counter-revolutionary chauvinist conspiracy –

DZERZHINSKY: Thank you.

MDVANI: – he is aware of our legitimate aspirations.

STALIN: And what does he say about them?

MDVANI: He says that they are chauvinistic, petty-bourgeois and counter-revolutionary.

STALIN: I expected no less of Comrade Trotsky.

MDVANI: By God, you haven't changed.

(*DZERZHINSKY rises.*)

DZERZHINSKY: (*Formally.*) Thank you, Comrade.

(*MDVANI rises.*)

The honesty with which you have responded to my questions will be counted in your favour.

MDVANI: Dzerzhinsky – you're mad. (*He looks at STALIN.*) God knows what you are. (*He starts to go.*)

(*DRAGANOV enters.*

MDVANI crosses DRAGANOV. Both stop.)

You bastard – you pig-shit.

(*MDVANI goes.*)

DZERZHINSKY: Comrade Pratkov?

DRAGANOV: Comrade.

DZERZHINSKY: One moment. (*He consults papers with STALIN.*) Draganov...

DRAGANOV: (*Turning.*) Com... (*He realises his mistake too late.*) Oh Christ...

DZERZHINSKY: Captain Draganov; you are an agent.

DRAGANOV: No.

DZERZHINSKY: Yes!

DRAGANOV: For whom am I working?

DZERZHINSKY: You are working for the class to which you helplessly belong.

DRAGANOV: It no longer exists.

DZERZHINSKY: You exist. You joined the Party under an assumed identity.

DRAGANOV: Yes.

DZERZHINSKY: If you are not an agent, why?

DRAGANOV: I wanted a Party Ration Card.

DZERZHINSKY: You are being very frank.

DRAGANOV: Why not?

DZERZHINSKY: You also had the blasphemous temerity to join the Cheka.

DRAGANOV: Yes.

DZERZHINSKY: Why did you do that? (*He looks straight at him.*)

DRAGANOV: (*Half claim, half apology.*) It's my job. (*DZERZHINSKY flushes.*)

DZERZHINSKY: Give me your card; your papers. (*DRAGANOV hands them over. DZERZHINSKY tears them across.*)
Outside.

STALIN: Disgusting bourgeois cynicism. Shoot him.

DZERZHINSKY: Yes. (*To a CHEKIST.*) See to that.

CHEKIST: Right.
(*DZERZHINSKY goes. STALIN gathering his things together, the CHEKIST watching him alertly.*)

STALIN: Does Comrade Mdvani know that his telephone was monitored?

CHEKIST: No.

STALIN: Are you certain?

CHEKIST: Yes. I was in charge of the case.

STALIN: Did you get this letter?

CHEKIST: Yes.

STALIN: How?

CHEKIST: Does it matter?

STALIN: Perhaps not. (*He knocks out his pipe.*) You seem to know your business, Comrade – er…

CHEKIST: Kuskow.

STALIN: Kuskow. Yes. Well it's as good a name as any.
How long would you say you have been a policeman?

CHEKIST: I joined the Cheka in the year of its inception, Comrade.

STALIN: No previous experience?

CHEKIST: No, Comrade.

STALIN: You must have natural aptitude. It's time you were promoted, Comrade. (*He goes.*)
(*The lights change from Georgia to dappled sunlight, and the previous furniture is replaced by a table and two wicker chairs. The CHEKIST stands at ease, but snaps to attention as he sees LENIN.*)

LENIN enters, walking with a stick, dragging his paralysed right arm and leg. He glowers at the CHEKIST and speaks, thickly and with arbitrary jerks where his tongue refuses service.)

LENIN: Who-o are y-ou?

CHEKIST: Yakolyev, Igor Borisovich.

LENIN: Where is F-ustnits-ky?

CHEKIST: Ordered on to other duties I believe, Comrade Lenin.

LENIN: By whom?

CHEKIST: By Comrade Stalin, Comrade Lenin.

(*LENIN grunts.*)

LENIN: Are you fer-om G-eorgia?

(*The CHEKIST stares then laughs admiringly.*)

CHEKIST: Yes. But I'm not a Georgian. How did you know?

LENIN: I am cer-lairv-oyant.

(*GEUTIER, KOLLONTAI, KRUPSKAYA enter.*
LENIN throws his good arm out and sideways.
KOLLONTAI goes to him, stoops; they embrace.)

(*To GEUTIER, over KOLLONTAI's back.*) Y-ou go a-way.

(*GEUTIER smiles, goes on taking things from his doctor's bag.*)
G-o – away!

(*This is more serious.*)

KRUPSKAYA: (*Pleadingly.*) Vladya...

LENIN: What?

KRUPSKAYA: Don't be troublesome.

LENIN: Not in a pos-ition to be ter- ter – (*He pauses, glaring into space.*) ter – (*He pauses again: raises his clenched fist and smashes it on to the table. Still nothing comes.*) – troublesome!

(*The rage and resentment in it are frightening. KOLLONTAI bites her lip. LENIN is fighting for breath. GEUTIER comes with a spoonful of medicine.*)

GEUTIER: Ilyich.

LENIN: N – o.

KRUPSKAYA: Vladya.

GEUTIER: Come along please. (*Smiling bleakly, he approaches with the spoon again.*)

LENIN: N – o!

KRUPSKAYA: (*Flaring.*) You are worse than a child! I would rather nurse a monkey!

LENIN: You would drive a monkey mad!

(*KRUPSKAYA goes.*)

GEUTIER: It isn't her fault Vladimir Ilyich. It is a Politburo ruling, as you perfectly well know.

LENIN: She put them up to it.

GEUTIER: It is largely owing to your wife that you're allowed to work at all. Did you know that?

LENIN: No.

GEUTIER: Well, it is so. Comrade Stalin in particular would have you kept from work completely...

LENIN: Would he now?

GEUTIER: (*Taking LENIN's pulse.*) He would. And so would I. (*Referring to the pulse.*) Oh look now, this is very bad. What have you been doing?

LENIN: Nothing.

GEUTIER: Then what are you thinking of doing?

LENIN: Nothing.

GEUTIER: Esteemed and indispensable Vladimir Ilyich, If you excite yourself beyond a certain point you will probably suffer another stroke. And if you suffer another stroke it will either reduce you to the status of a vegetable or if you are fortunate, kill you on the spot. So, whatever Madame Kollontai has come to talk to you about I trust you will use a little of your legendary determination to behave a little less like a retarded child, and a little more like a responsible adult. Good day to you both. (*He goes.*)

LENIN: (*To KOLLONTAI, eagerly.*) Now... (*He sees the CHEKIST.*) Go away.

CHEKIST: Comrade Lenin, my instructions were...

LENIN: Go!

(*The CHEKIST goes.*)

Now, what has Stalin been doing in Georgia?

KOLLONTAI: You heard what Doctor Geutier said.

LENIN: F – fuck Doctor Geutier!

KOLLONTAI: He's been doing the job you gave him
 Vladya. He has purged the Georgian Party.

LENIN: He is per-uking on the Party. Isn't he?

KOLLONTAI: Yes. The Georgian Central Committee have
 torn up their Party cards. And...

LENIN: Hmp?

KOLLONTAI: Several of the Georgian Comrades have –
 disappeared.

LENIN: Get rid of him.

KOLLONTAI: What?

LENIN: No no. Attack him at C-ongress. Vote him out.
 Send him to M-M-ongolia.

KOLLONTAI: Me?

LENIN: Who else have you g-ot?

KOLLONTAI: Rykov, Tomsky – No-one who could tackle
 Stalin.

LENIN: Trotsky could.

KOLLONTAI: Yes, Trotsky could. Trotsky would love it.

LENIN: N, n-o- *Ser-talin* is the Bonaparte, Alexia! It's
 him... It's him... Get rid of him! You must...! What's the
 matter?

KOLLONTAI: Vladya, two-thirds of the Delegates to
 Congress will be Stalin's nominees.

LENIN: I have written a s-peech for Ter-otsky to deliver to
 them, in my name. (*He lugs a fat envelope from his pocket,
 conspiratorially.*) It will blow Ser-talin through the roof, in
 fragments. Now what's the matter?

KOLLONTAI: If he delivers it in your name, aren't you
 afraid he will step into your shoes?

LENIN: Would they fit him?

KOLLONTAI: No.

LENIN: Then he won't be able to will he? Get it to him
 somehow. Tell him what I've said. You'd better go now.

KOLLONTAI: Good-bye my dear. (*She starts to go.*)

LENIN: History is devilishly hard you know.

KOLLONTAI: What?

LENIN: Don't hold Ker-onstadt against Leon Dav-idovich.
 (*KOLLONTAI goes.*)

(*The lights fade to moonlight. LENIN sleeps.*)
(*Waking abruptly.*) It, had to be done... Nadya! Nadya!
(*The CHEKIST enters.*)
CHEKIST: Comrade?
LENIN: If I see you again I will report you to your sup-
sup-periors!
(*The CHEKIST goes. KRUPSKAYA enters with a lamp and
some papers.*)
KRUPSKAYA: I don't like that man.
LENIN: Ser-talin's man. Is that document still in the safe?
KRUPSKAYA: Yes.
LENIN: Mm. Sure?
KRUPSKAYA: Yes.
LENIN: Mm.
KRUPSKAYA: Vladya, what am I to do with it?
LENIN: O-pen it when I am d-ead. What's the time?
KRUPSKAYA: Ten past. Vladya, are you expecting to hear
from Congress?
LENIN: Ter-otsky will ser-laughter him.
KRUPSKAYA: Vladya, Doctor Geutier said that if
Congress proceedings were likely to excite you, you
ought not to have them.
LENIN: Oh yes?
KRUPSKAYA: So we shall not be hearing.
LENIN: Shall.
KRUPSKAYA: Vladya, no arrangements have been made
for you to hear.
LENIN: Made my own arrangements.
(*She sits, silent and angry.*)
KRUPSKAYA: Do you think that you are made of iron?
LENIN: No.
KRUPSKAYA: Perhaps you think I am?
LENIN: Yes.
KRUPSKAYA: Well I'm not!
(*She weeps. He thrusts a handkerchief at her, clumsily. She
almost snatches it.*)
LENIN: We had a good time in Si-beria. Didn't we?
KRUPSKAYA: You only married me for company.

LENIN: Not true. N-eeded a secretary.
(*She laughs at him and he at her. He looks away.*)
Had Martov for company.
KRUPSKAYA: Yes.
(*He hears the hesitation: looks at her.*)
LENIN: They say that he is dying too.
KRUPSKAYA: Vladya. He's dead.
LENIN: Martov?
KRUPSKAYA: Yes.
(*He looks away again. She looks at him.*)
D'you remember Pyotr?
LENIN: Mm? No.
KRUPSKAYA: You do. He bit the policeman.
LENIN: Oh! The dog. Yes, I remember Pyotr. He was a bit
petty-bourgeois.
KRUPSKAYA: He bit the policeman.
LENIN: Yes. But he felt awful about it afterwards...
KRUPSKAYA: Did he?
LENIN: Yes... (*He registers her attention. Then, crisply and
firmly.*) Petty-bourgeois.
(*A DRIVER comes in with a big brown envelope.*)
KRUPSKAYA: You can give that to me, Victor.
LENIN: Me!
(*The DRIVER gives LENIN the envelope, and goes.
LENIN gets it open but cannot read what is inside. She holds
out her hand for it. Suspiciously he hands it to her. She opens
it, takes out a wad of typescript, hesitates. He points at it.*)
Ter-otsky.
KRUPSKAYA: Vladya...
LENIN: R-ead!
KRUPSKAYA: Vladya, Leon Davidovich isn't there.
LENIN: What?
KRUPSKAYA: He's very ill; he's been sent to the South.
LENIN: Not there?
KRUPSKAYA: No, Vladya.
LENIN: (*Softly.*) Oh, the foo-ool – the *foo-ool...*!
KRUPSKAYA: Vladya, he's *ill.*
LENIN: (*Shaking his head.*) No... No... Oh the fool... (*He
looks at the papers in her hand, desolate. Then his gaze focuses
in sharp alarm.*) Ser-talin!

(*KRUPSKAYA hesitates. He lunges for the papers; she withdraws them from his reach.*)

Nadya, which means more to you – me or the Party?

KRUPSKAYA: Oh what a cruel question. What would you say if I should ask you?

LENIN: The Party!

(*She reads, resignedly.*)

KRUPSKAYA: 'For the Organisational Bureau J V Stalin opened his report by regretting the absence of Comrade Lenin.'

(*A white Spot comes up on one side of the stage.*
STALIN enters.
Applause on speakers.)

STALIN: I doubly regret his absence because it would rejoice his heart to be here. Comrade Lenin regards Party unity as the apple of his eye. Comrades – I have never seen a Conference so united and unanimous.

(*Applause.*)

STALIN: However, there has lately been some talk within the Party of a Democratic Opposition. To what are they opposed? They are not they say opposed to the Party, but to the Party apparatus. Comrades, perhaps we should provide the Democratic Opposition with some elementary Marxist primer!

(*Laughter.*)

I am not myself an intellectual, but I have always understood that Marx believed in a material reality. Perhaps I am in error?

(*Laughter.*)

Or perhaps Marx was in error?

(*Laughter.*)

But if Marx was not in error, then the Party is not an idea existing in somebody's head, but an actual institution existing in reality and in attacking its actual apparatus the Democratic Opposition are attacking the actual Party; for which they wish to substitute a mere idea of the Party – or – perhaps – an actual Party of their own.

LENIN: Sh – Shit!

STALIN: Comrades, the Party will tolerate neither alternative!

(*Applause, with a ground note of threat.*)

The Democratic Opposition are no doubt subjectively sincere. But if there is one thing that I have learned in fifteen years of close association with my teacher, V I Lenin, it is this: that a person can be quite sincerely revolutionary in his own esteem, and yet may play, objectively, a counter-revolutionary role. And Comrade Lenin never shrank from the exposure of such persons – even in the Party – even indeed in the Party leadership.

(*Silence.*)

I will follow that example. Nobody is indispensable. The Party alone is indispensable. I pledge my own unquestioning obedience to the actual existing Party. It is the Party of Marx. It is the Party of Vladimir Ilyich...

(*Thunderous applause. STALIN freezes. LENIN rears out of his chair. The applause continues.*)

LENIN: N-N-N-No! (*He reels away upstage.*)

(*The CHEKIST appears in front of him.*)

Ny-Ny-Nyeh...!

(*LENIN flails at the man with his stick, spins and falls back into his arms.*

Blackout and silence.)

KRUPSKAYA: Vladya!

(*The regular boom of a funeral salute is heard in the distance. The lights come up. The stage is bare except for a row of six chairs.*

TROTSKY, KOLLONTAI, LUNACHARSKY, DZERZHINSKY and STALIN enter, each carrying an identical file. They sit. KRUPSKAYA enters, also with a file.

Led by TROTSKY, they rise respectfully, then sit again, with KRUPSKAYA. A beat.)

KRUPSKAYA: Propose Comrade Trotsky to lead.

TROTSKY: Thank you, no.

KOLLONTAI: (*Sceptically.*) No?

TROTSKY: No.

DZERZHINSKY: (*Nonplussed.*) Shall I?

(*TROTSKY signifies indifference.*)

KOLLONTAI: Yes.

DZERZHINSKY: Then I begin by asking if you all accept this document as Comrade Lenin's Will and Testament?

KOLLONTAI: It is his Will and Testament; he left it in my keeping.

DZERZHINSKY: I will read the relevant passage and ask for...

STALIN: Save your breath. In the light of this document, I offer you my resignation.

KRUPSKAYA: I move that Comrade Stalin's resignation be accepted.

KOLLONTAI: I second.

DZERZHINSKY: (*To TROTSKY.*) Shall I put it to the vote?

TROTSKY: You are leading. Lead.

DZERZHINSKY: (*Hesitantly.*) I think it merits *some* discussion...

KRUPSKAYA: (*Hotly.*) Why? Does this leave any room for doubt?

DZERZHINSKY: It leaves me in some doubt, Nadezhda.

LUNACHARSKY: I must confess, me too.

DZERZHINSKY: (*Reading.*) 'Our enemies desire to see our Party split. Such a split is possible. Half the danger rises from the personalities of Trotsky and Stalin.'

KRUPSKAYA: Well?

DZERZHINSKY: Please Nadezhda. (*Reading.*) 'Trotsky is without a doubt the most able man we have. But he is too self-confident'... Comment?

KOLLONTAI: True on both counts. By far the most able; and dangerously self-confident.
(*TROTSKY shifts and goes still again.*)

DZERZHINSKY: Very well. Now. (*Reading.*) 'Com-' (*He clears his throat.*) Excuse me. (*Reads.*) 'Comrade Stalin is too brutal'... Comment?

STALIN: Yes. (*His voice is heavy, He is looking at the floor.*) Revolution is a brutal business.
(*It makes a silence.*)

DZERZHINSKY: (*Reading.*) 'As Party Secretary, Stalin has enormous power. I doubt if he will use it with sufficient caution.' Here I feel I must comment. Since when were we required to use our power with caution? I thought we were to use it, ruthlessly, and with effect.

STALIN: I never failed to effect any of the jobs he gave me!

DZERZHINSKY: Well – exactly.

KRUPSKAYA: What are you doing?

DZERZHINSKY: I am wondering very much what Vladya would have done.

KRUPSKAYA: Would have…? (*Reading, vehement.*) 'He ought to be removed from office – and replaced – by some more tolerant and loyal person!' That is what he did!

DZERZHINSKY: But – forgive me – but perhaps he was not at his best when he did it?

KRUPSKAYA: What?

DZERZHINSKY: Since when did Vladya desire tolerance in anyone?

KRUPSKAYA: And loyalty?

DZERZHINSKY: (*With a touch of severity in his gentleness.*) Personal, or Party loyalty, Nadezhda?

(*LUNACHARSKY sucks in his breath.*)

LUNACHARSKY: What a cruel question.

(*KRUPSKAYA looks from one to another.*)

KRUPSKAYA: Leon…! Lead!

TROTSKY: (*Ironically.*) Lead?

KOLLONTAI: Leon, you are longing to lead.

(*TROTSKY suppresses a spasm of irritation.*)

TROTSKY: Comrades, if we had – as many of you think we have – a Bonaparte within the Party, now would be his moment. If we had a man so overweening in his self-esteem that he would like to step into the shoes of V I Lenin, now would be his moment. If we had a man so squalidly ambitious that he would sell his revolutionary birthright for a mess of personal pottage, now would be his moment! Such a man could seize this moment I assure you without difficulty! (*He plummets down from his indignation. Dramatically calm.*) Happily there is no such man amongst us. Since you ask for my opinion, Nadya, I think this document invites the very thing it fears; the fragmentation of the leadership, and faction in the Party. And those who wish to see that are – as Vladya says –

our enemies. And though this – (*The document.*) – is the work of the greatest Marxist of our day, it is also the work of an afflicted man.

LUNACHARSKY: (*Softly.*) Correct – (*Apologetically.*) – correct, Nadezhda.

DZERZHINSKY: Comrades, with the greatest diffidence I move: that this document should be suppressed; and Comrade Stalin should remain in office… Seconded?

LUNACHARSKY: Yes.

DZERZHINSKY: I put my motion to the vote.

KOLLONTAI: (*Hotly.*) Why your motion? Why not Nadezhda's?

TROTSKY: (*Mildly.*) Because you asked him to lead, Alexia.

DZERZHINSKY: For?

LUNACHARSKY: Aye.

TROTSKY: Aye.

KOLLONTAI: Abstain.

DZERZHINSKY: Nadezhda?

KRUPSKAYA: Oh God, I wish he were alive…

DZERZHINSKY: We all wish that.

KRUPSKAYA: Aye.

DZERZHINSKY: Carried.

(*Nobody seems quite happy about it. They rise quietly, gathering their things*
KOLLONTAI, DZERZHINSKY and KRUPSKAYA go.
STALIN goes to TROTSKY, thrusting out his hand.
TROTSKY takes it without enthusiasm but firmly, making a commitment.
STALIN goes.)

LUNACHARSKY: That was generous, Leon Davidovich.

TROTSKY: Generous?

LUNACHARSKY: Magnificently generous.

(*LUNACHARSKY's voice is full of serious admiration.*
TROTSKY smiles.)

TROTSKY: What a likeable chap you are, Anatole Vassilyevich. And how I despise you.

(*TROTSKY goes.*
LUNACHARSKY speaks to the audience.)

LUNACHARSKY: I remember wishing at the time that L D Trotsky had taken up the reins. It was only gradually

that the revolutionary vigilance of Comrade Stalin revealed him for what he was: a life-long enemy of the working masses, and objective agent of reaction... (*He breaks from his regretful muse.*) But I should like to end on a more encouraging note. These anniversaries of Comrade Lenin's death ought not to be sad occasions. Comrades, some of you Young Communists no doubt already feel yourselves to be destined for great things. To you I say: there was a time when L D Trotsky seemed to be the man of destiny. Remember that. Some of you, less confident, already feel yourselves to be no more than patient servants of the Party. To you I say that Comrade Stalin is no more than a patient servant of the Party.
(*Applause. LUNACHARSKY smiles approvingly, but gestures for silence.*)
When the history of the Revolution comes to be written, bourgeois historians will present a pageant of Great Men. Great Heroes or Great Villains who imposed themselves upon events by their own divine or devilish abilities. We Marxists know that this is nonsense. No-one can impose himself. Great men are called to leadership not because they are greatly gifted but because their gifts are *needed*, by their time, and their society. Ivan the Terrible was merely the expression of a terrible society. And similarly our collective leadership expresses our collective, democratic, socialist society. Comrade Stalin, we salute you. Comrade Lenin, we remember you, with gratitude and love. Thank you.
(*LUNACHARSKY goes, as the lights fade.*)

The End.